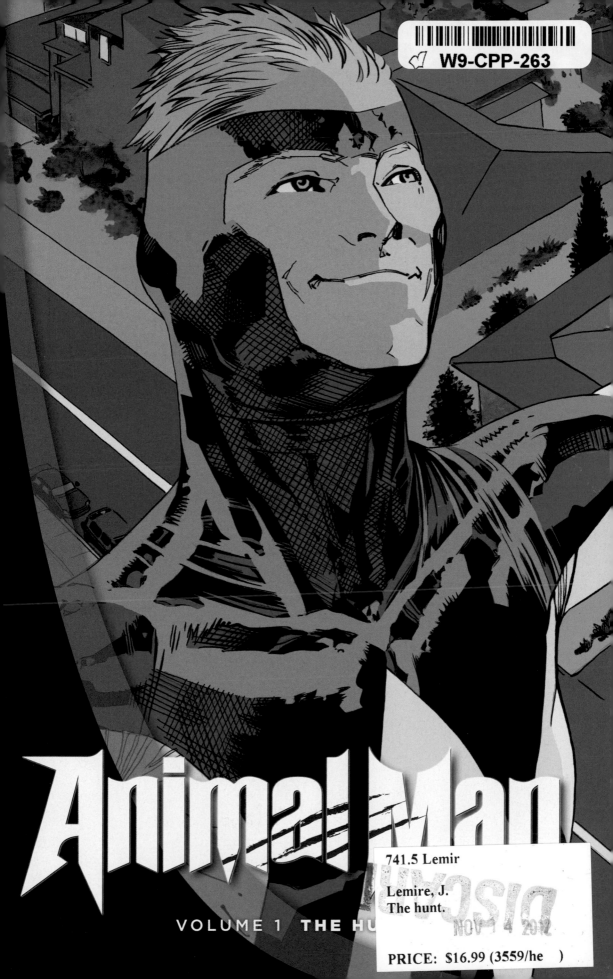

Animal Man

VOLUME 1   THE HUNT

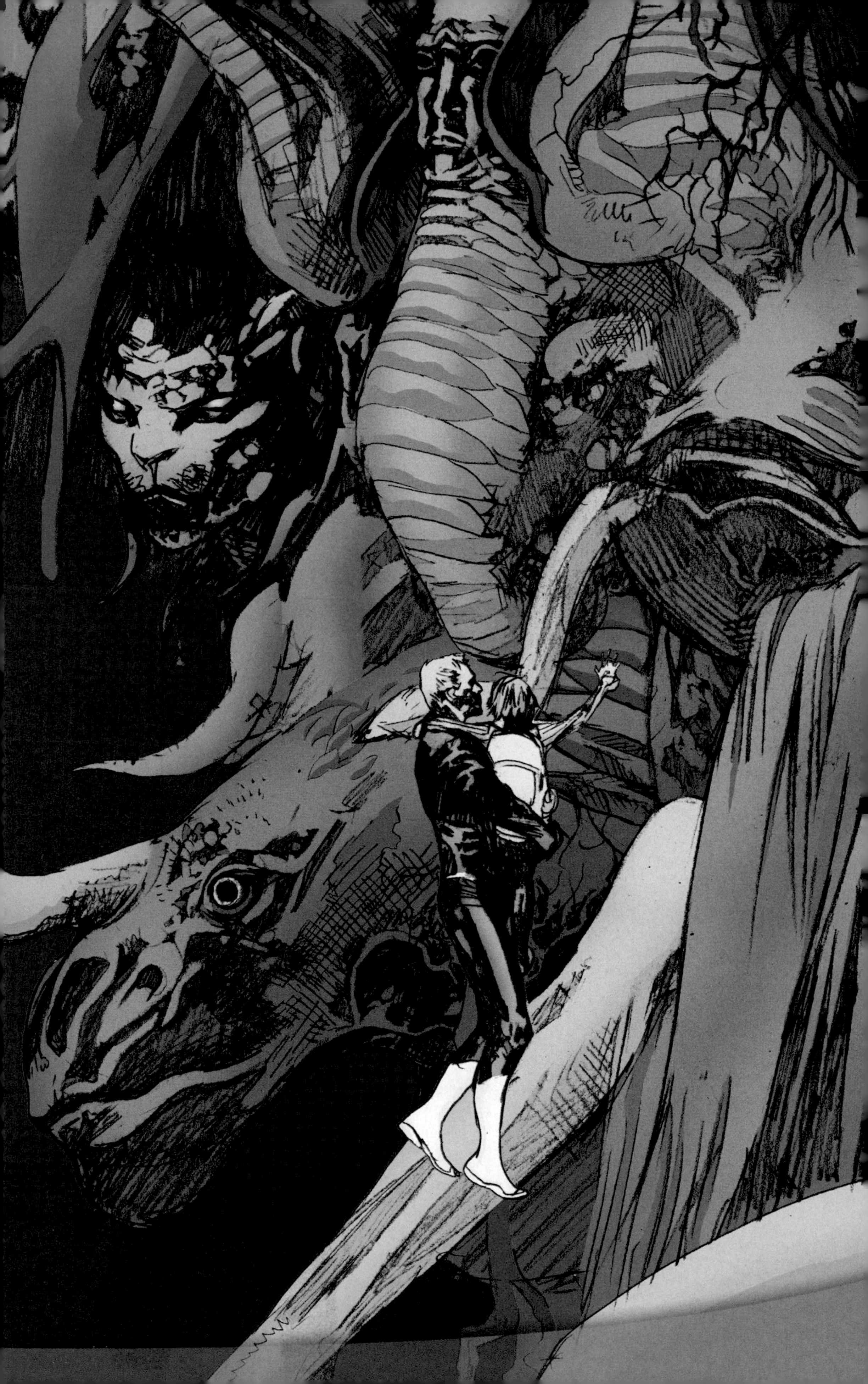

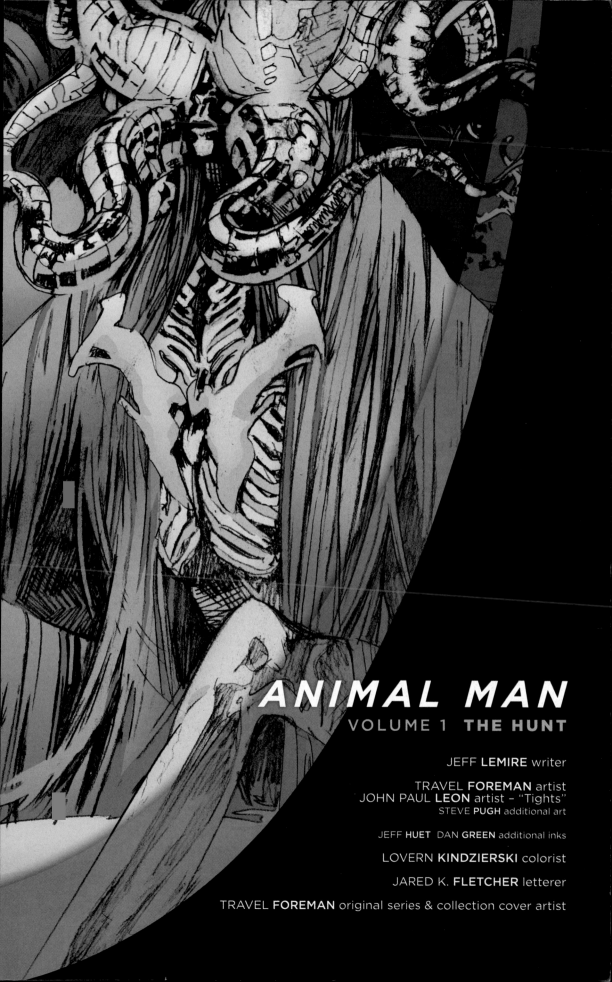

ANIMAL MAN
VOLUME 1 THE HUNT

JEFF **LEMIRE** writer

TRAVEL **FOREMAN** artist
JOHN PAUL **LEON** artist – "Tights"
STEVE **PUGH** additional art

JEFF **HUET** DAN **GREEN** additional inks

LOVERN **KINDZIERSKI** colorist

JARED K. **FLETCHER** letterer

TRAVEL **FOREMAN** original series & collection cover artist

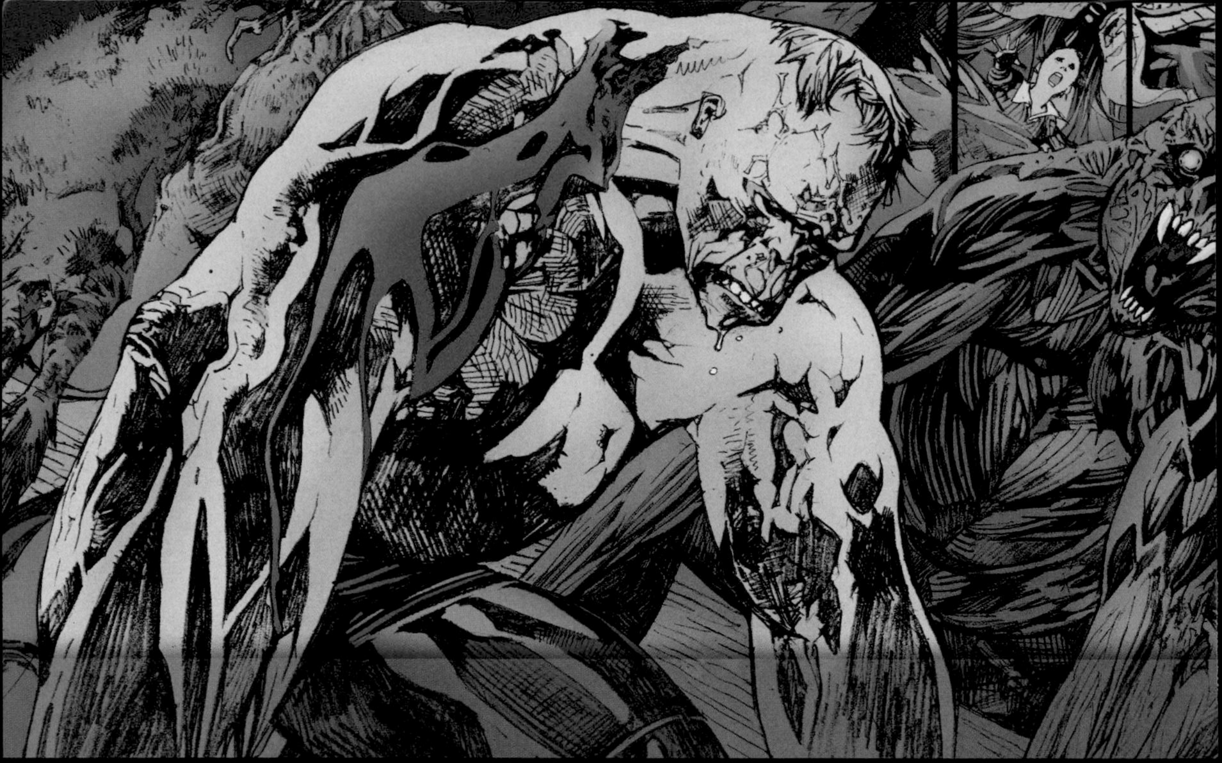

JOEY CAVALIERI Editor - Original Series KATE STEWART Assistant Editor - Original Series
ROBIN WILDMAN Editor ROBBIN BROSTERMAN Design Director - Books ROBBIE BIEDERMAN Publication Design

EDDIE BERGANZA Executive Editor BOB HARRAS VP - Editor-in-Chief

DIANE NELSON President DAN DIDIO and JIM LEE Co-Publishers
GEOFF JOHNS Chief Creative Officer JOHN ROOD Executive VP - Sales, Marketing and Business Development
AMY GENKINS Senior VP - Business and Legal Affairs NAIRI GARDINER Senior VP - Finance
JEFF BOISON VP - Publishing Operations MARK CHIARELLO VP - Art Direction and Design
JOHN CUNNINGHAM VP - Marketing TERRI CUNNINGHAM VP - Talent Relations and Services
ALISON GILL Senior VP - Manufacturing and Operations DAVID HYDE VP - Publicity
HANK KANALZ Senior VP - Digital JAY KOGAN VP - Business and Legal Affairs, Publishing
JACK MAHAN VP - Business Affairs, Talent NICK NAPOLITANO VP - Manufacturing Administration
SUE POHJA VP - Book Sales COURTNEY SIMMONS Senior VP - Publicity BOB WAYNE Senior VP - Sales

ANIMAL MAN VOLUME 1: THE HUNT
Published by DC Comics.

DC Comics, 1700 Broadway, New York, NY 10019
A Warner Bros. Entertainment Company
Printed by RR Donnelley, Salem, VA, USA. 3/30/12. First Printing.
ISBN: 978-1-4012-3507-9

Library of Congress Cataloging-in-Publication Data
Lemire, Jeff.
Animal Man volume 1 : the hunt / Jeff Lemire, Travel Foreman.
p. cm.
"Originally published in single magazine form in ANIMAL MAN 1-6" - T.p. verso.
ISBN 978-1-4012-3507-9
1. Graphic novels. I. Foreman, Travel. II. Title.
PN6728.A58L46 2012
741.5'973 - dc23
2011051856

SUSTAINABLE FORESTRY INITIATIVE
Certified Chain of Custody
At Least 25% Certified Forest Content
www.sfiprogram.org
SFI-01042
APPLIES TO TEXT STOCK ONLY

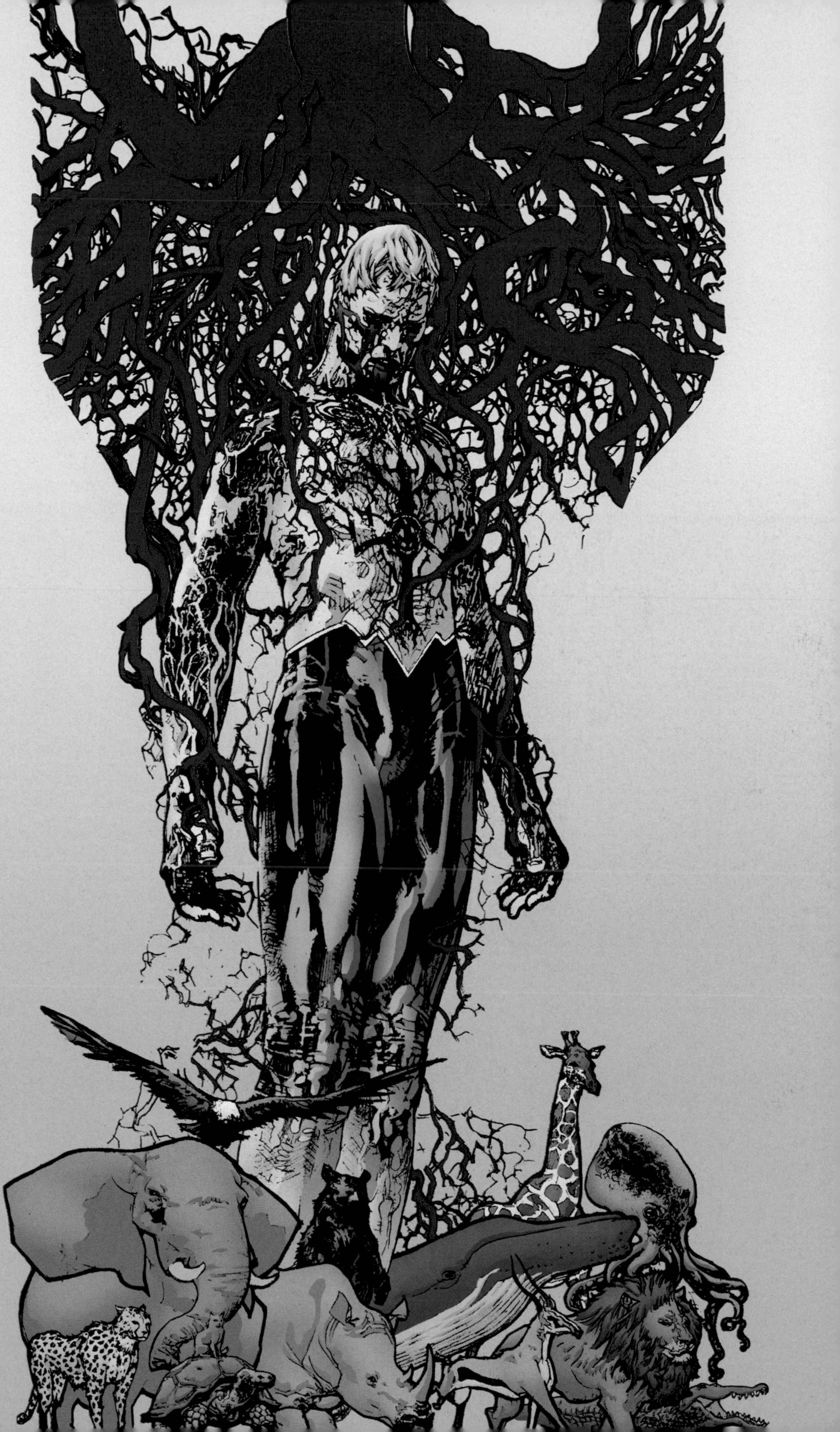

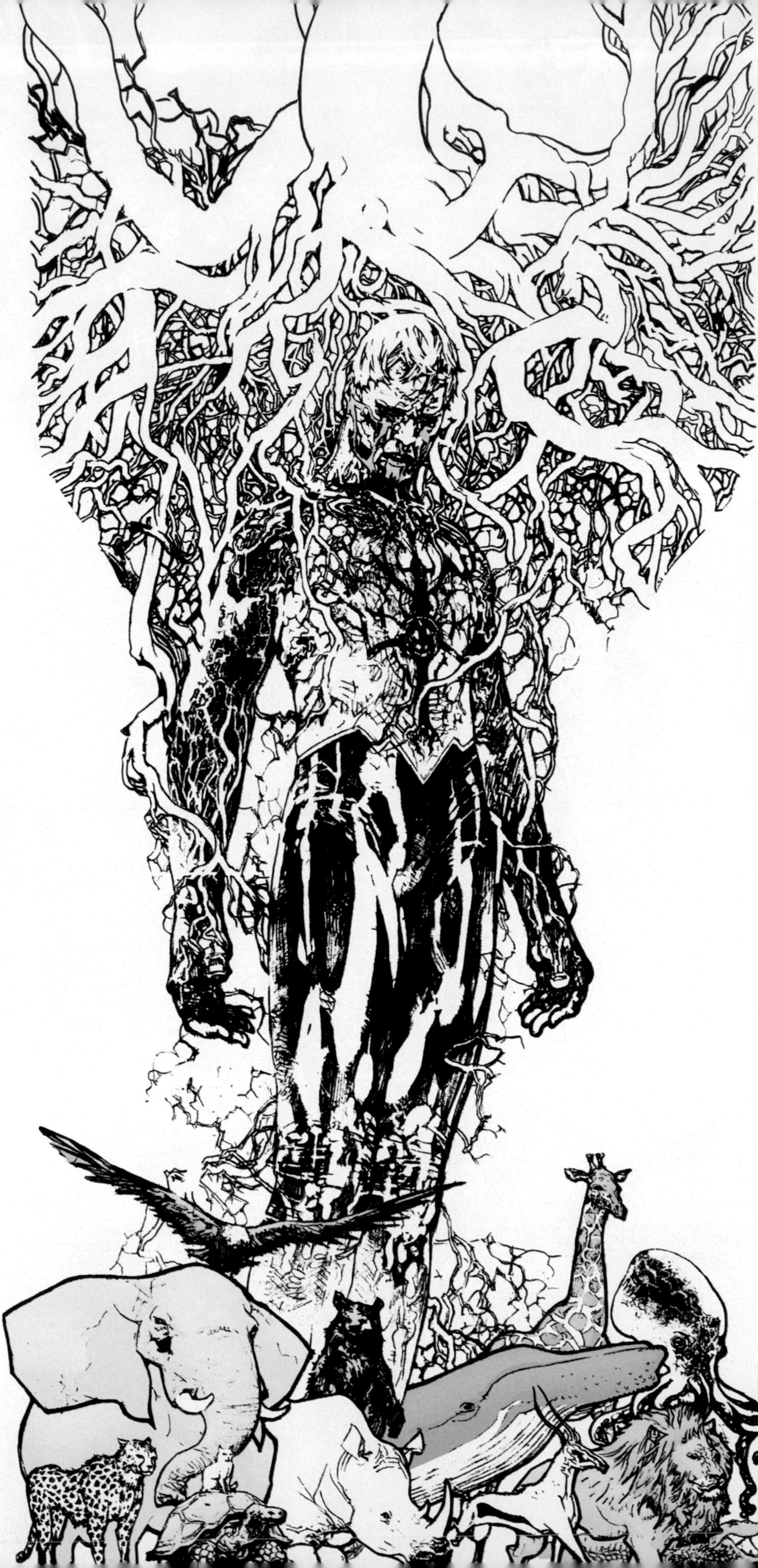

BUDDY BAKER
[SUPERHERO/ACTOR/ACTIVIST]

"I REALIZED I COULD MAKE MORE OF A DIFFERENCE EDUCATING PEOPLE ON ANIMAL RIGHTS THAN I COULD BY PUNCHING OUT A SUPER VILLAIN, YOU KNOW? IT WAS KIND OF A NATURAL PROGRESSION. AN EVOLUTION."

O*ver the last three years, San Diego-based family man Buddy Baker has perhaps been better known as the goggles-wearing superhero "Animal Man." But more recently, Baker's on-again, off-again career as a costumed crimefighter has given way to a new role, that of an animal rights activist and spokesperson. Baker's iconic image has even been adopted by youth culture. His politics and past exploits have made him something of a poster boy for the young left-wing hipster crowd. Perhaps most surprising, though, is Baker's current turn in front of the movie cameras, starring in indie-darling Ryan Daranovsky's edgy drama "Tights," playing, what else, a washed-up superhero determined to go down fighting. The Believer caught up with Buddy in his favorite vegan restaurant in downtown L.A.*
—Jeff Lemire

THE BELIEVER: You seem to be a guy who can't sit still. You started out as a Hollywood stunt man, then you popped up as a superhero, and now you're an actor. Yet you've been happily married for almost a decade. How do you reconcile that inherent restlessness with the stability of your family life?

BUDDY BAKER: Well, I don't know if I'd say I'm restless. I just kind of like to roll with the punches, you know. I take opportunities as they present themselves. When I got my superpowers, becoming a hero just seemed like the thing to do. And that led to all kinds of new experiences, and really opened my eyes to the injustices facing animals in our world. I realized I could make more of a difference educating people on animal rights than I could by punching out a super villain, you know? It was kind of a natural progression. An evolution.

BLVR: Yes, but then, why the decision to return to the film world after so many years away? And why as an actor this time instead of coming back as a stunt man, where you got your start?

BB: Again, the opportunity just sort of presented itself. My superhero "career" hadn't really been going anywhere in the last couple of years. Like I said, I had sort of become more of a spokesman than a superman. Flying around space and catching maniacs in funny costumes was never really my thing, although I did do my fair share of that [laughs]. But

anyway, Ryan [Daranovsky] contacted my agent out of the blue and asked if I'd be interested in reading for the role. Once I heard about the project, and realized how perfect it was for me, I couldn't turn it down. I thought it would be fun.

BLVR: So is this a one-time thing? Or are you going to actively pursue more acting roles? You must be aware that there is already some Oscar buzz surrounding you.

BB: Hell, I really don't know. I've been offered other things, but nothing I really cared for. It was fun, a great experience, but who knows what's next?

BLVR: Let's switch gears for a minute. Your image, specifically your iconic look with the skintight suit with the stylized "A" on the front as Animal Man, has become something of a flag for youth culture of late. How does it feel to have your face plastered on kids' dorm rooms and T-shirts all over the country?

BB: It's weird [laughs]. My wife makes fun of me every time she sees a kid wearing one of those Animal Man "Evolve or Die" T-shirts. But the truth is, I think it's pretty great, you know. If my time as Animal Man has helped open people's eyes to the fact that we share this planet with all other creatures, and that we are all connected…then I'm not complaining.

BLVR: I have to ask, do you get any money for all those T-shirts?

BB: Sigh…no, not a penny [laughs]. I think that's what really ticked Ellen (my wife) off [laughs]. But come on… I was a punk when I was that age. The whole DIY, bootleg thing is a part of who I am. I'm certainly not going to go after anyone to get cash.

BLVR: Finally, you seem to speak about your time as Animal Man as if it were a thing of the past. You've barely been active lately. Is your time as a legitimate superhero over?

BB: No. Not at all. Animal Man will always be a big part of who I am. I may not go out on regular patrols like I used to, but I'll never give it up. As long as the world still needs Animal Man, he'll be around.

Illustration by Travel Foreman

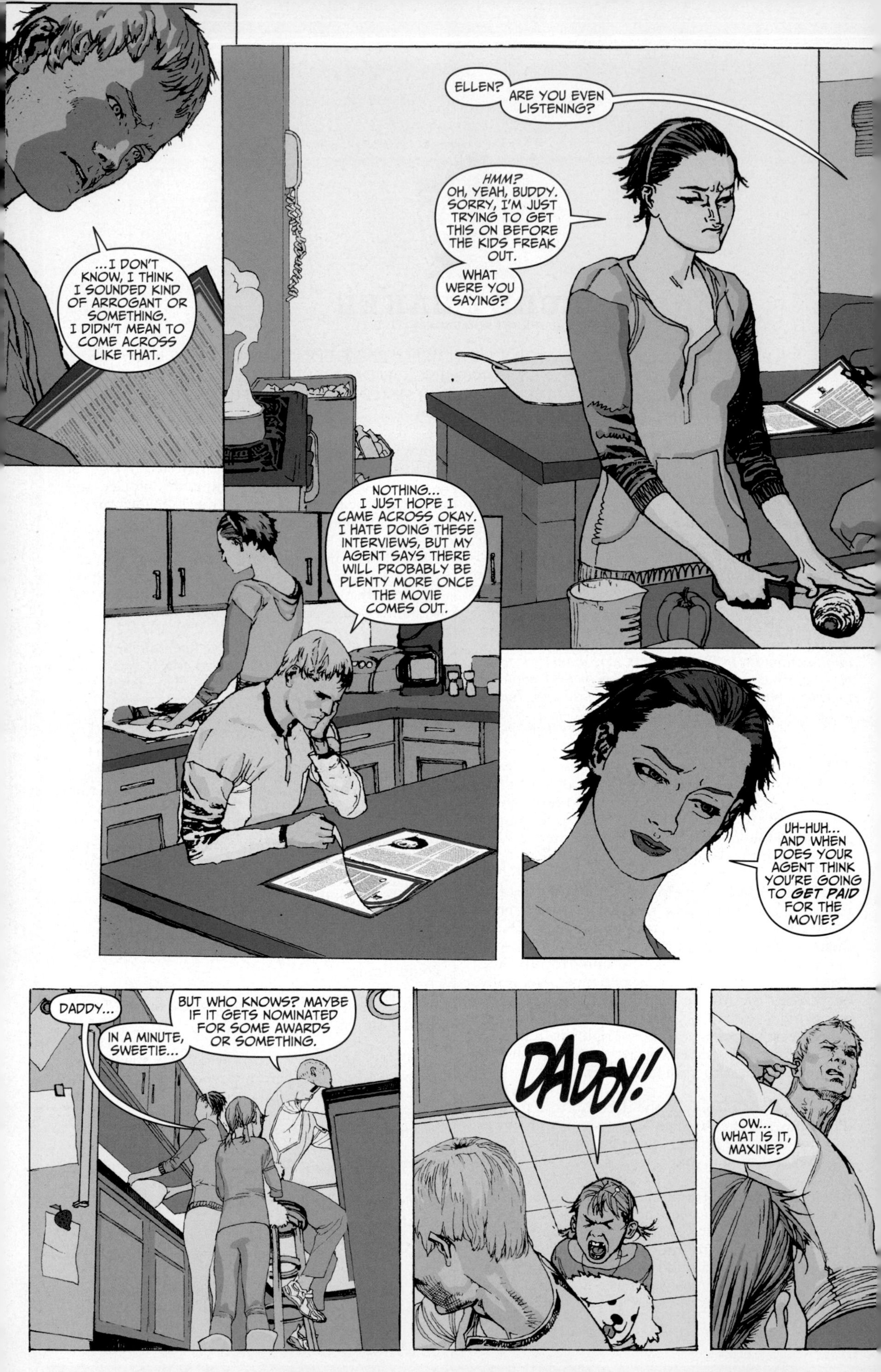
...I DON'T KNOW, I THINK I SOUNDED KIND OF ARROGANT OR SOMETHING. I DIDN'T MEAN TO COME ACROSS LIKE THAT.
ELLEN?
ARE YOU EVEN LISTENING?
HMM? OH, YEAH, BUDDY. SORRY, I'M JUST TRYING TO GET THIS ON BEFORE THE KIDS FREAK OUT.
WHAT WERE YOU SAYING?
NOTHING... I JUST HOPE I CAME ACROSS OKAY. I HATE DOING THESE INTERVIEWS, BUT MY AGENT SAYS THERE WILL PROBABLY BE PLENTY MORE ONCE THE MOVIE COMES OUT.
UH-HUH... AND WHEN DOES YOUR AGENT THINK YOU'RE GOING TO GET PAID FOR THE MOVIE?
BUT WHO KNOWS? MAYBE IF IT GETS NOMINATED FOR SOME AWARDS OR SOMETHING.
DADDY...
IN A MINUTE, SWEETIE...
DADDY!
OW... WHAT IS IT, MAXINE?

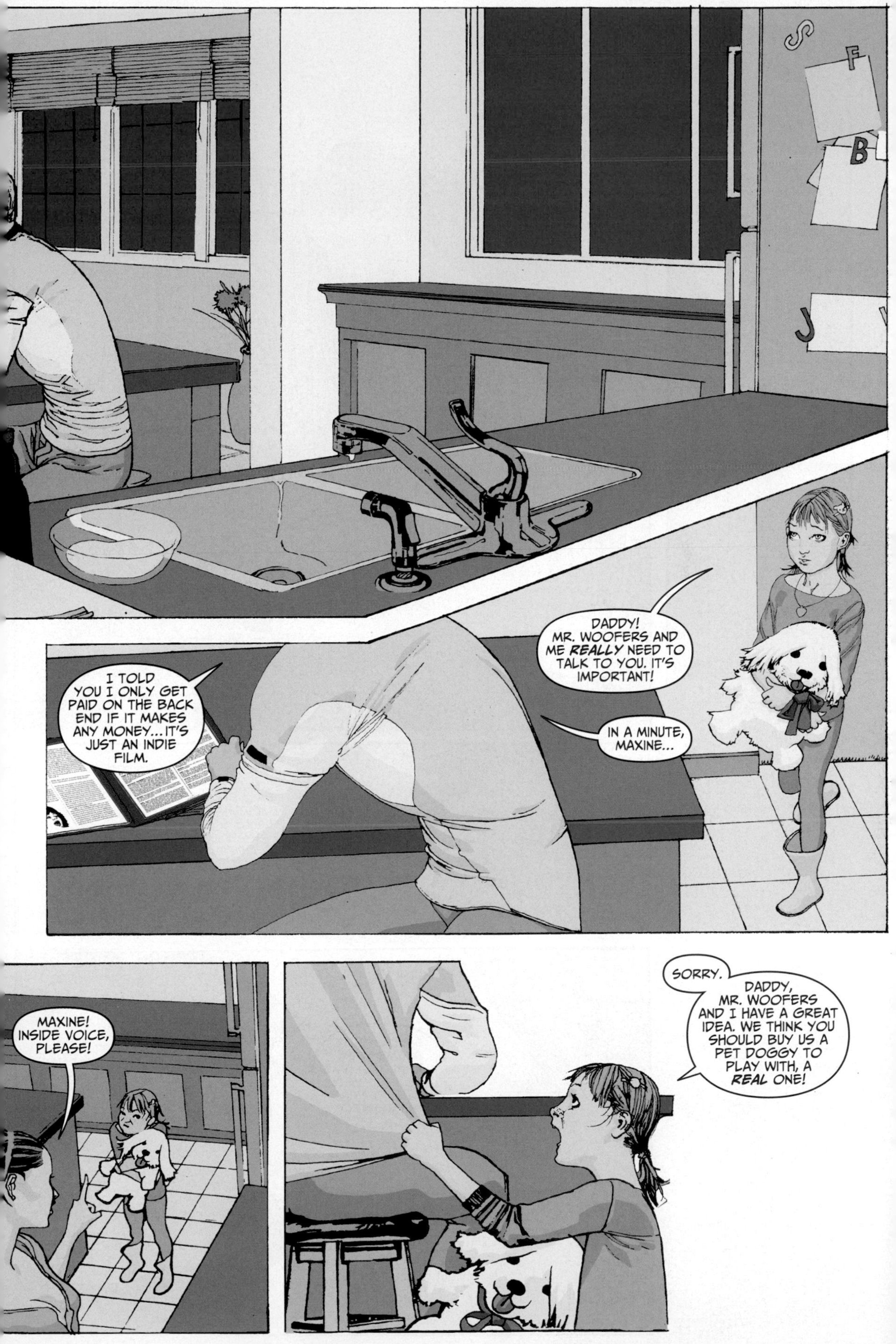
DADDY! MR. WOOFERS AND ME REALLY NEED TO TALK TO YOU. IT'S IMPORTANT!
I TOLD YOU I ONLY GET PAID ON THE BACK END IF IT MAKES ANY MONEY... IT'S JUST AN INDIE FILM.
IN A MINUTE, MAXINE...
MAXINE! INSIDE VOICE, PLEASE!
SORRY.
DADDY, MR. WOOFERS AND I HAVE A GREAT IDEA. WE THINK YOU SHOULD BUY US A PET DOGGY TO PLAY WITH, A REAL ONE!

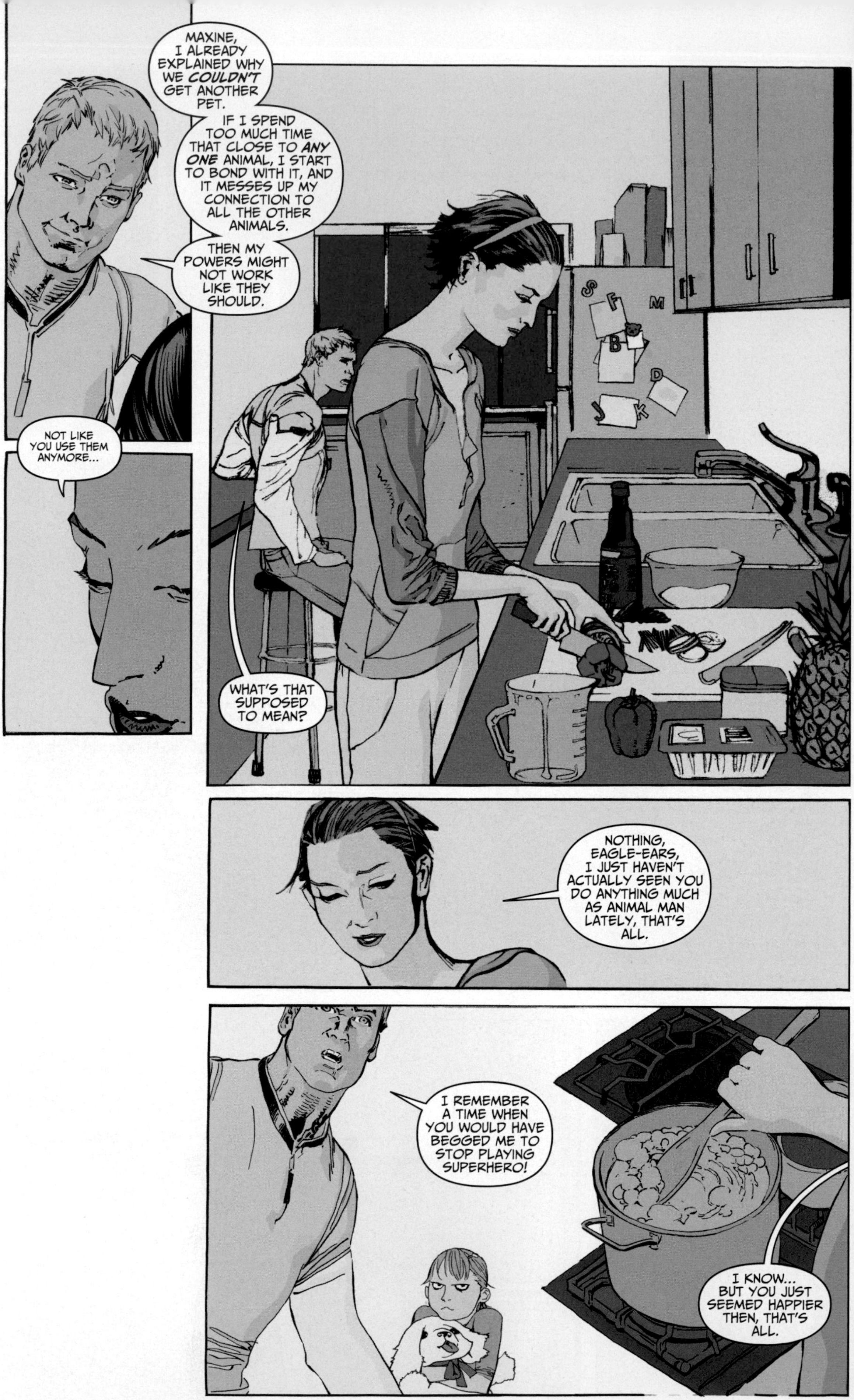
MAXINE, I ALREADY EXPLAINED WHY WE COULDN'T GET ANOTHER PET.
IF I SPEND TOO MUCH TIME THAT CLOSE TO ANY ONE ANIMAL, I START TO BOND WITH IT, AND IT MESSES UP MY CONNECTION TO ALL THE OTHER ANIMALS.
THEN MY POWERS MIGHT NOT WORK LIKE THEY SHOULD.
NOT LIKE YOU USE THEM ANYMORE...
WHAT'S THAT SUPPOSED TO MEAN?
S F M B D J K
NOTHING, EAGLE-EARS, I JUST HAVEN'T ACTUALLY SEEN YOU DO ANYTHING MUCH AS ANIMAL MAN LATELY, THAT'S ALL.
I REMEMBER A TIME WHEN YOU WOULD HAVE BEGGED ME TO STOP PLAYING SUPERHERO!
I KNOW... BUT YOU JUST SEEMED HAPPIER THEN, THAT'S ALL.

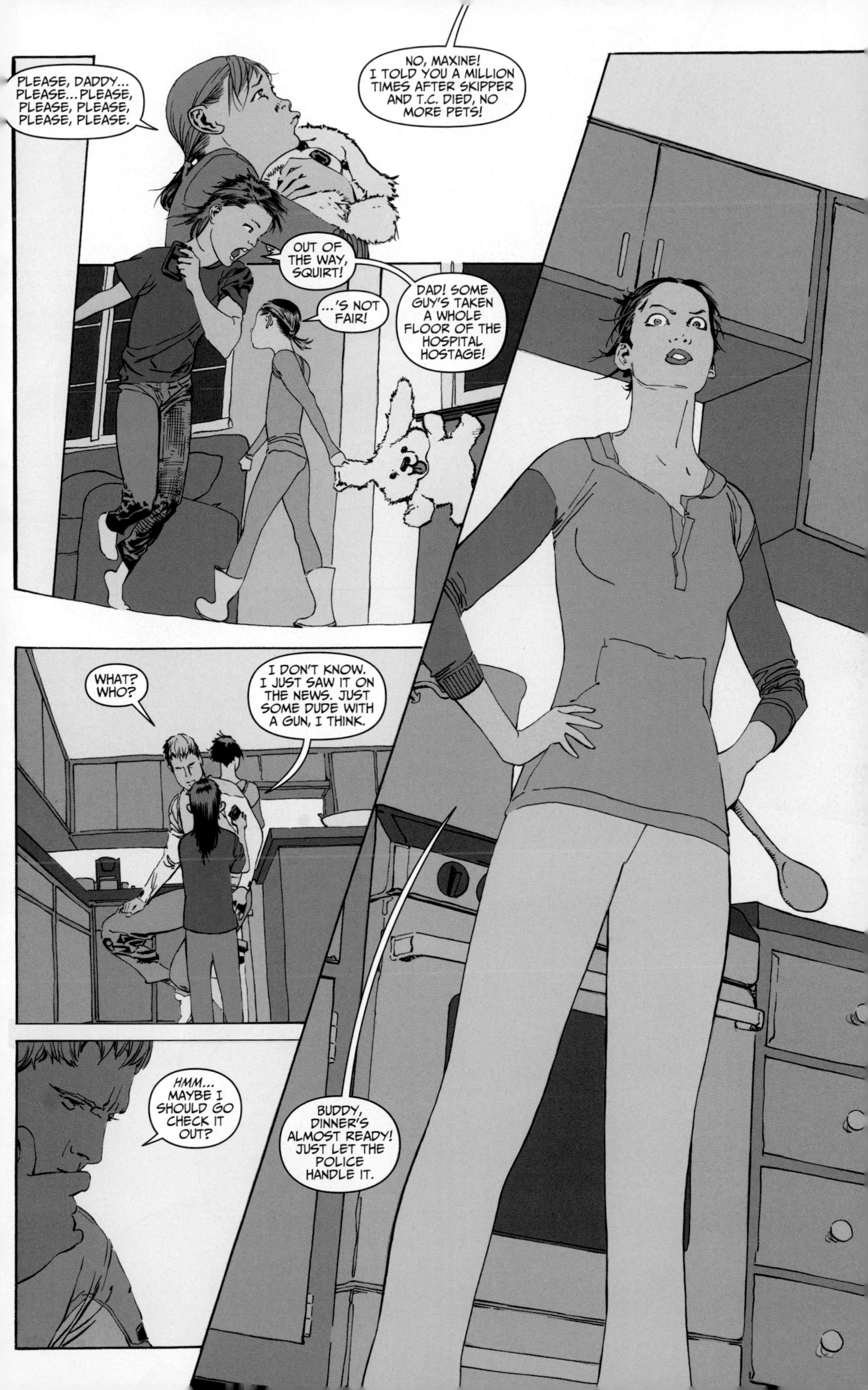
NO, MAXINE! I TOLD YOU A MILLION TIMES AFTER SKIPPER AND T.C. DIED, NO MORE PETS!
PLEASE, DADDY... PLEASE... PLEASE, PLEASE, PLEASE, PLEASE, PLEASE.
OUT OF THE WAY, SQUIRT!
...'S NOT FAIR!
DAD! SOME GUY'S TAKEN A WHOLE FLOOR OF THE HOSPITAL HOSTAGE!
WHAT? WHO?
I DON'T KNOW. I JUST SAW IT ON THE NEWS. JUST SOME DUDE WITH A GUN, I THINK.
HMM... MAYBE I SHOULD GO CHECK IT OUT?
BUDDY, DINNER'S ALMOST READY! JUST LET THE POLICE HANDLE IT.

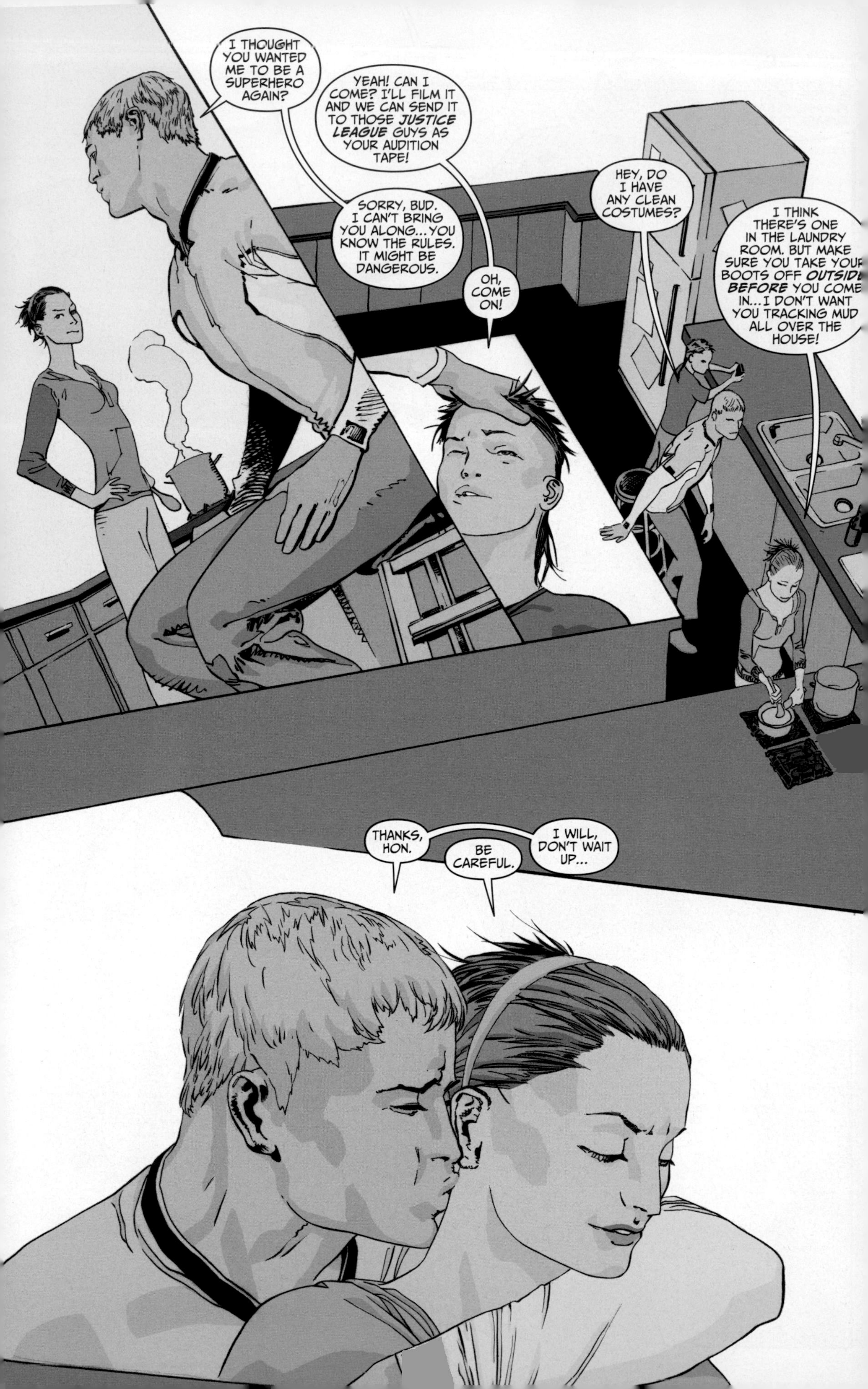
I THOUGHT YOU WANTED ME TO BE A SUPERHERO AGAIN?
YEAH! CAN I COME? I'LL FILM IT AND WE CAN SEND IT TO THOSE *JUSTICE LEAGUE* GUYS AS YOUR AUDITION TAPE!
SORRY, BUD. I CAN'T BRING YOU ALONG...YOU KNOW THE RULES. IT MIGHT BE DANGEROUS.
OH, COME ON!
HEY, DO I HAVE ANY CLEAN COSTUMES?
I THINK THERE'S ONE IN THE LAUNDRY ROOM. BUT MAKE SURE YOU TAKE YOUR BOOTS OFF *OUTSIDE BEFORE* YOU COME IN...I DON'T WANT YOU TRACKING MUD ALL OVER THE HOUSE!
THANKS, HON.
BE CAREFUL.
I WILL, DON'T WAIT UP...

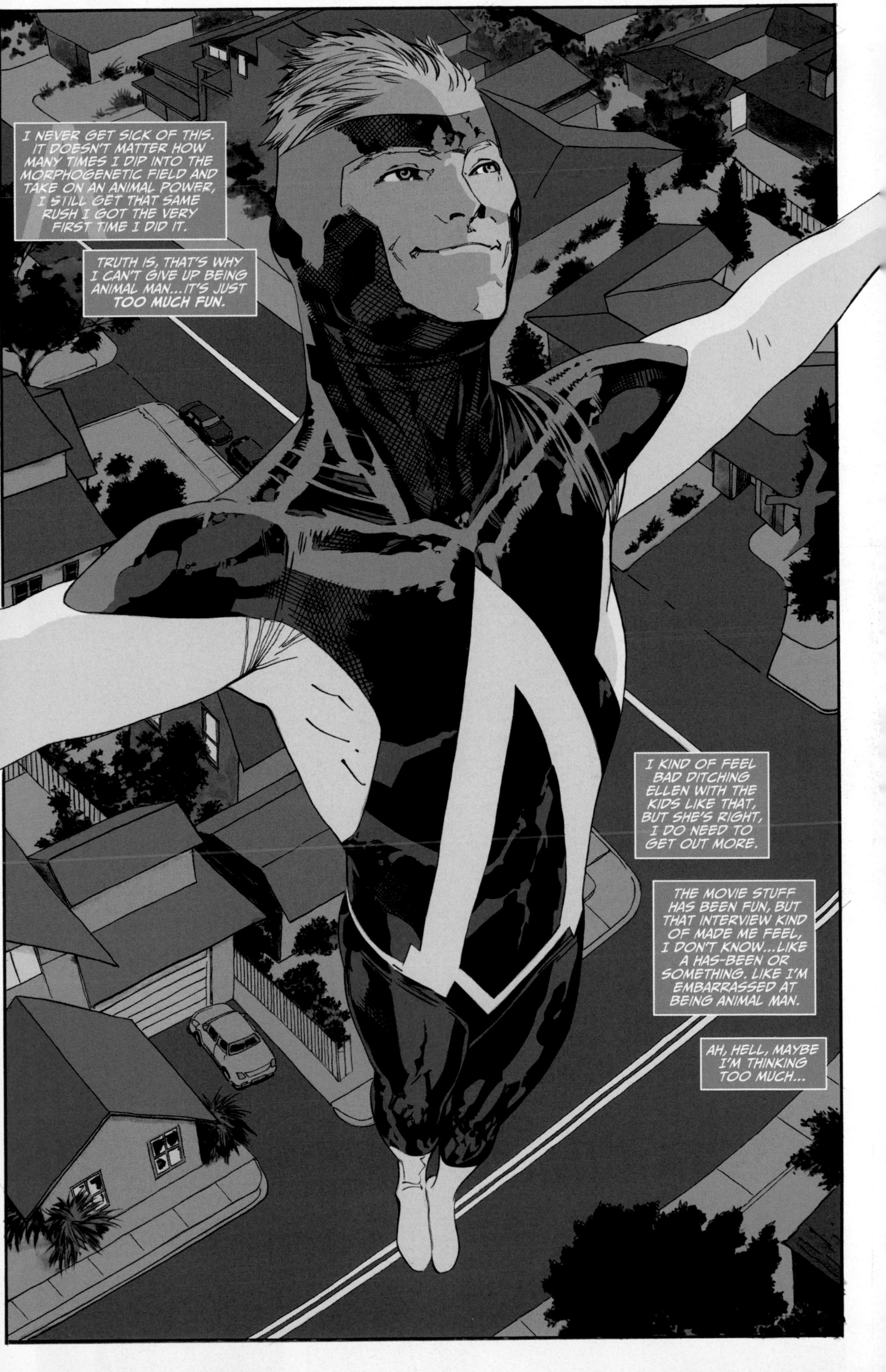
I NEVER GET SICK OF THIS. IT DOESN'T MATTER HOW MANY TIMES I DIP INTO THE MORPHOGENETIC FIELD AND TAKE ON AN ANIMAL POWER, I STILL GET THAT SAME RUSH I GOT THE VERY FIRST TIME I DID IT.
TRUTH IS, THAT'S WHY I CAN'T GIVE UP BEING ANIMAL MAN...IT'S JUST TOO MUCH FUN.
I KIND OF FEEL BAD DITCHING ELLEN WITH THE KIDS LIKE THAT, BUT SHE'S RIGHT, I DO NEED TO GET OUT MORE.
THE MOVIE STUFF HAS BEEN FUN, BUT THAT INTERVIEW KIND OF MADE ME FEEL, I DON'T KNOW...LIKE A HAS-BEEN OR SOMETHING. LIKE I'M EMBARRASSED AT BEING ANIMAL MAN.
AH, HELL, MAYBE I'M THINKING TOO MUCH...

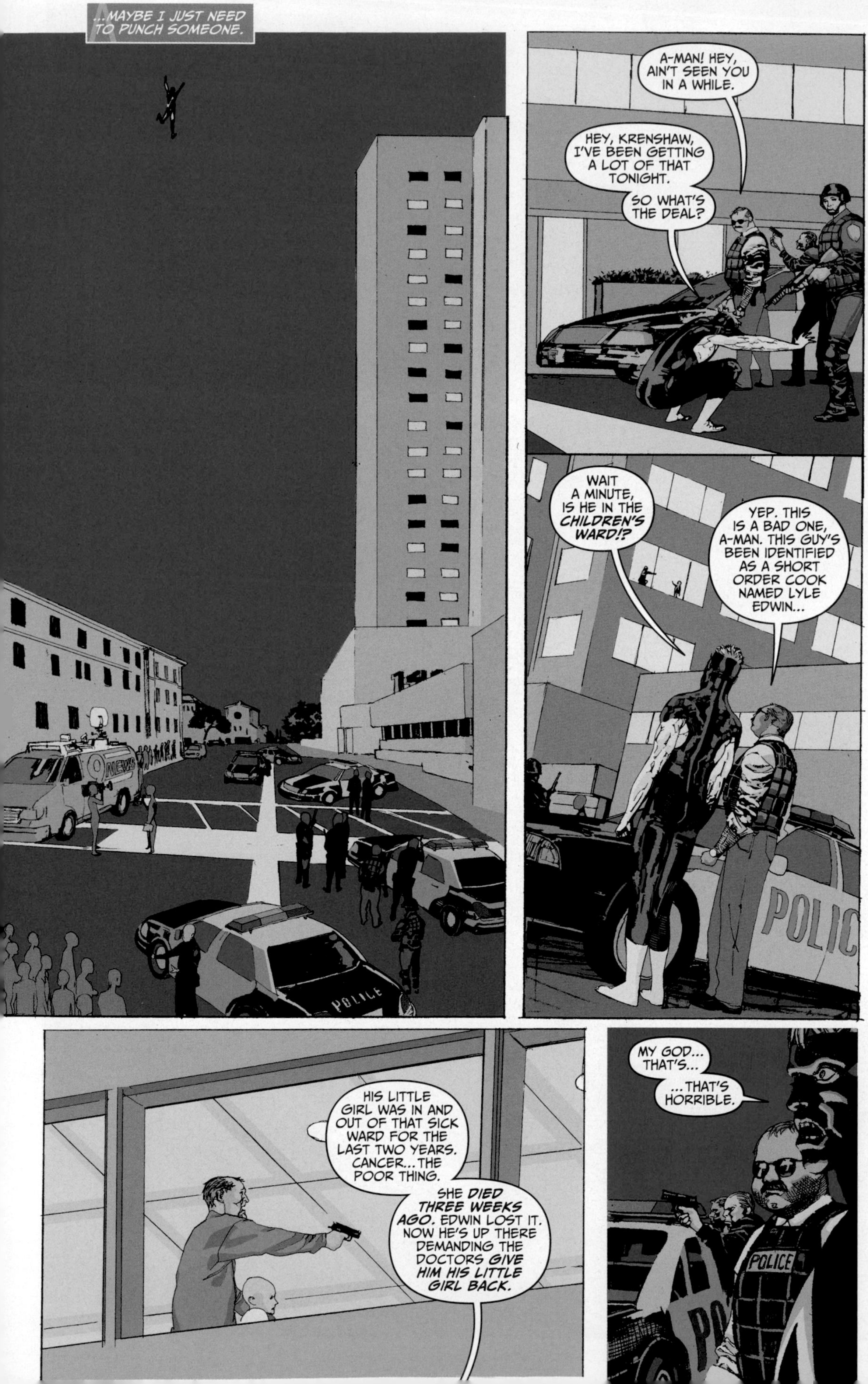
...MAYBE I JUST NEED TO PUNCH SOMEONE.
A-MAN! HEY, AIN'T SEEN YOU IN A WHILE.
HEY, KRENSHAW, I'VE BEEN GETTING A LOT OF THAT TONIGHT.
SO WHAT'S THE DEAL?
WAIT A MINUTE, IS HE IN THE CHILDREN'S WARD!?
YEP. THIS IS A BAD ONE, A-MAN. THIS GUY'S BEEN IDENTIFIED AS A SHORT ORDER COOK NAMED LYLE EDWIN...
POLIC
HIS LITTLE GIRL WAS IN AND OUT OF THAT SICK WARD FOR THE LAST TWO YEARS. CANCER...THE POOR THING.
SHE DIED THREE WEEKS AGO. EDWIN LOST IT. NOW HE'S UP THERE DEMANDING THE DOCTORS GIVE HIM HIS LITTLE GIRL BACK.
MY GOD... THAT'S...
...THAT'S HORRIBLE.
POLICE

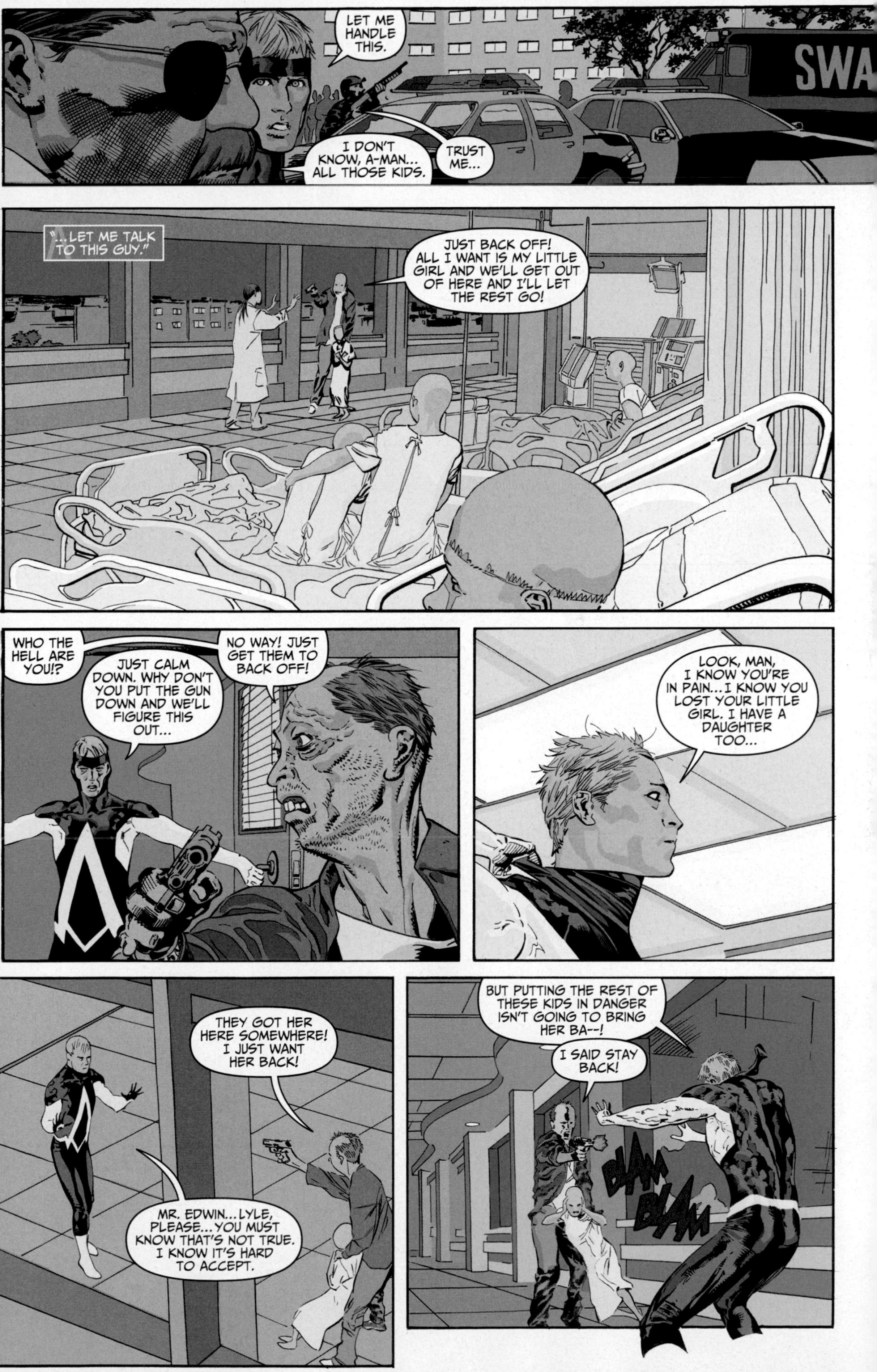
LET ME HANDLE THIS.
I DON'T KNOW, A-MAN... ALL THOSE KIDS.
TRUST ME...
"...LET ME TALK TO THIS GUY."
JUST BACK OFF! ALL I WANT IS MY LITTLE GIRL AND WE'LL GET OUT OF HERE AND I'LL LET THE REST GO!
WHO THE HELL ARE YOU!?
JUST CALM DOWN. WHY DON'T YOU PUT THE GUN DOWN AND WE'LL FIGURE THIS OUT...
NO WAY! JUST GET THEM TO BACK OFF!
LOOK, MAN, I KNOW YOU'RE IN PAIN...I KNOW YOU LOST YOUR LITTLE GIRL. I HAVE A DAUGHTER TOO...
THEY GOT HER HERE SOMEWHERE! I JUST WANT HER BACK!
MR. EDWIN...LYLE, PLEASE...YOU MUST KNOW THAT'S NOT TRUE. I KNOW IT'S HARD TO ACCEPT.
BUT PUTTING THE REST OF THESE KIDS IN DANGER ISN'T GOING TO BRING HER BA--!
I SAID STAY BACK!
BLAM
BLAM

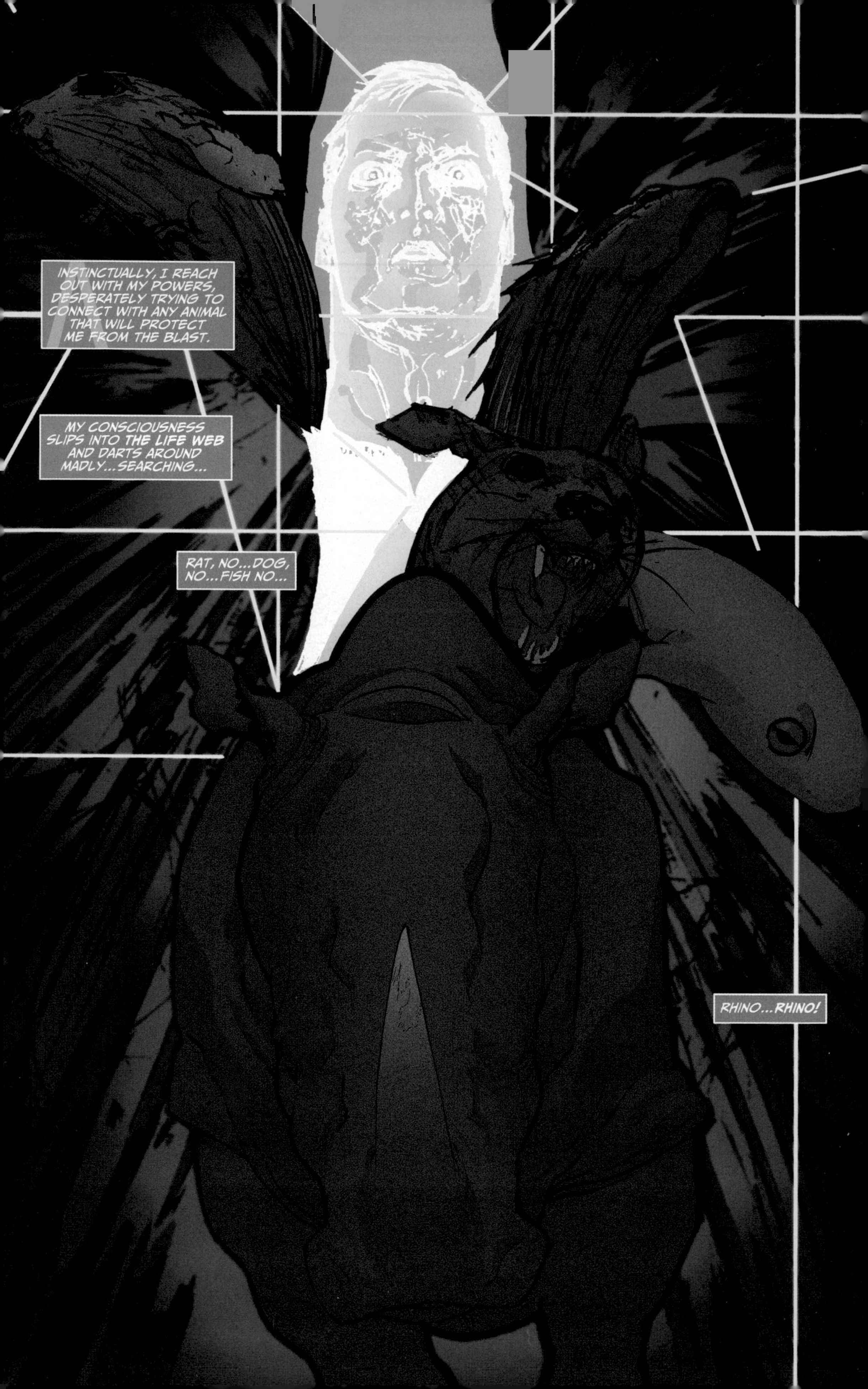
INSTINCTUALLY, I REACH OUT WITH MY POWERS, DESPERATELY TRYING TO CONNECT WITH ANY ANIMAL THAT WILL PROTECT ME FROM THE BLAST.
MY CONSCIOUSNESS SLIPS INTO THE LIFE WEB AND DARTS AROUND MADLY...SEARCHING...
RAT, NO...DOG, NO...FISH NO...
RHINO...RHINO!

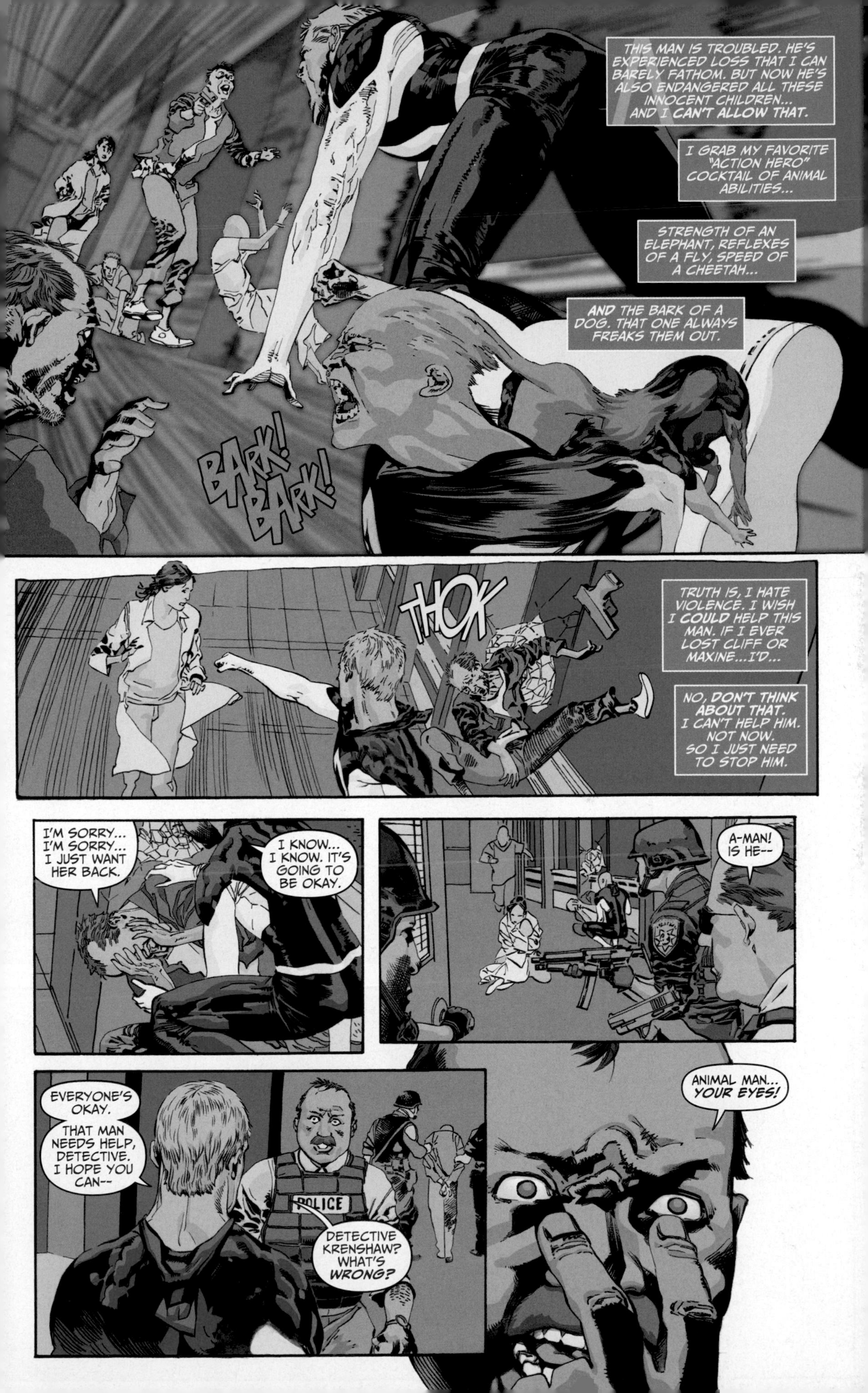
THIS MAN IS TROUBLED. HE'S EXPERIENCED LOSS THAT I CAN BARELY FATHOM. BUT NOW HE'S ALSO ENDANGERED ALL THESE INNOCENT CHILDREN... AND I CAN'T ALLOW THAT.
I GRAB MY FAVORITE "ACTION HERO" COCKTAIL OF ANIMAL ABILITIES...
STRENGTH OF AN ELEPHANT, REFLEXES OF A FLY, SPEED OF A CHEETAH...
AND THE BARK OF A DOG. THAT ONE ALWAYS FREAKS THEM OUT.
BARK! BARK!
THOK
TRUTH IS, I HATE VIOLENCE. I WISH I COULD HELP THIS MAN. IF I EVER LOST CLIFF OR MAXINE...I'D...
NO, DON'T THINK ABOUT THAT. I CAN'T HELP HIM. NOT NOW. SO I JUST NEED TO STOP HIM.
I'M SORRY... I'M SORRY... I JUST WANT HER BACK.
I KNOW... I KNOW. IT'S GOING TO BE OKAY.
A-MAN! IS HE--
EVERYONE'S OKAY.
THAT MAN NEEDS HELP, DETECTIVE. I HOPE YOU CAN--
POLICE
DETECTIVE KRENSHAW? WHAT'S WRONG?
ANIMAL MAN... YOUR EYES!

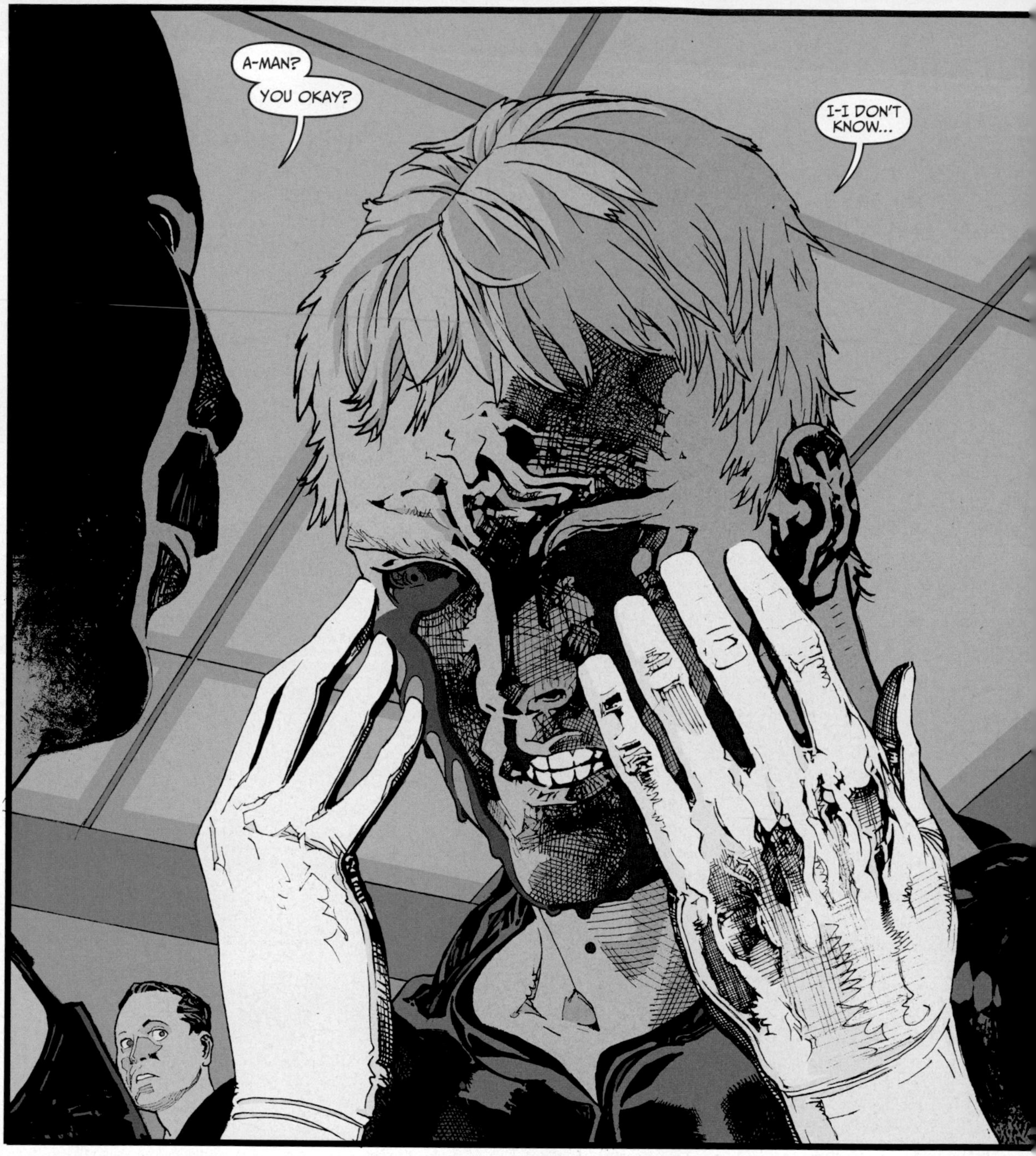
A-MAN?
YOU OKAY?
I-I DON'T KNOW...

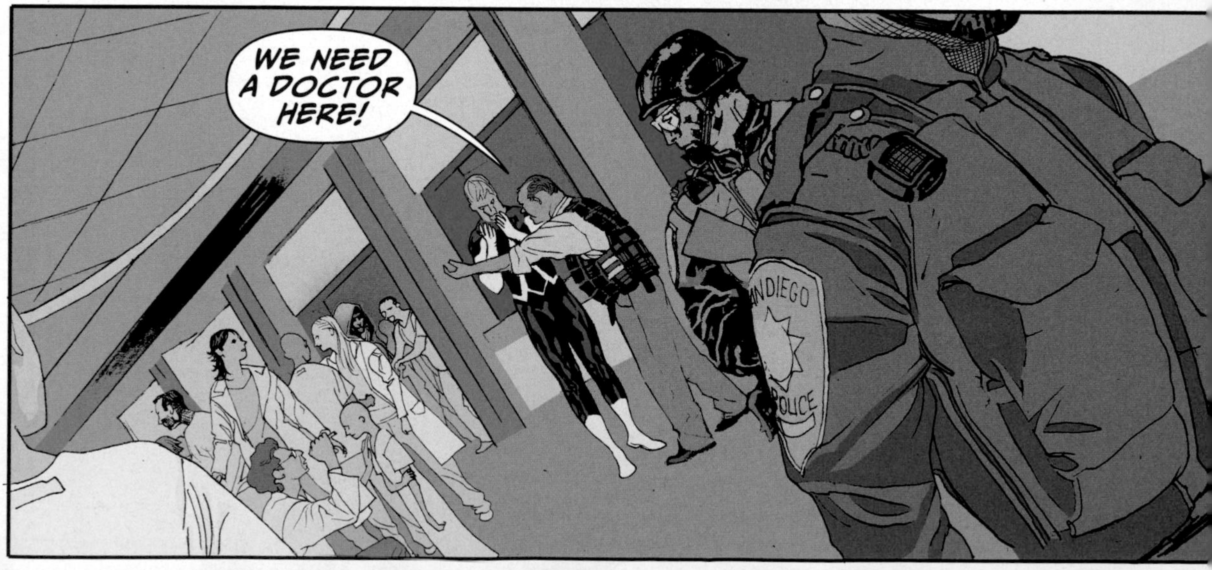
WE NEED A DOCTOR HERE!
SAN DIEGO POLICE

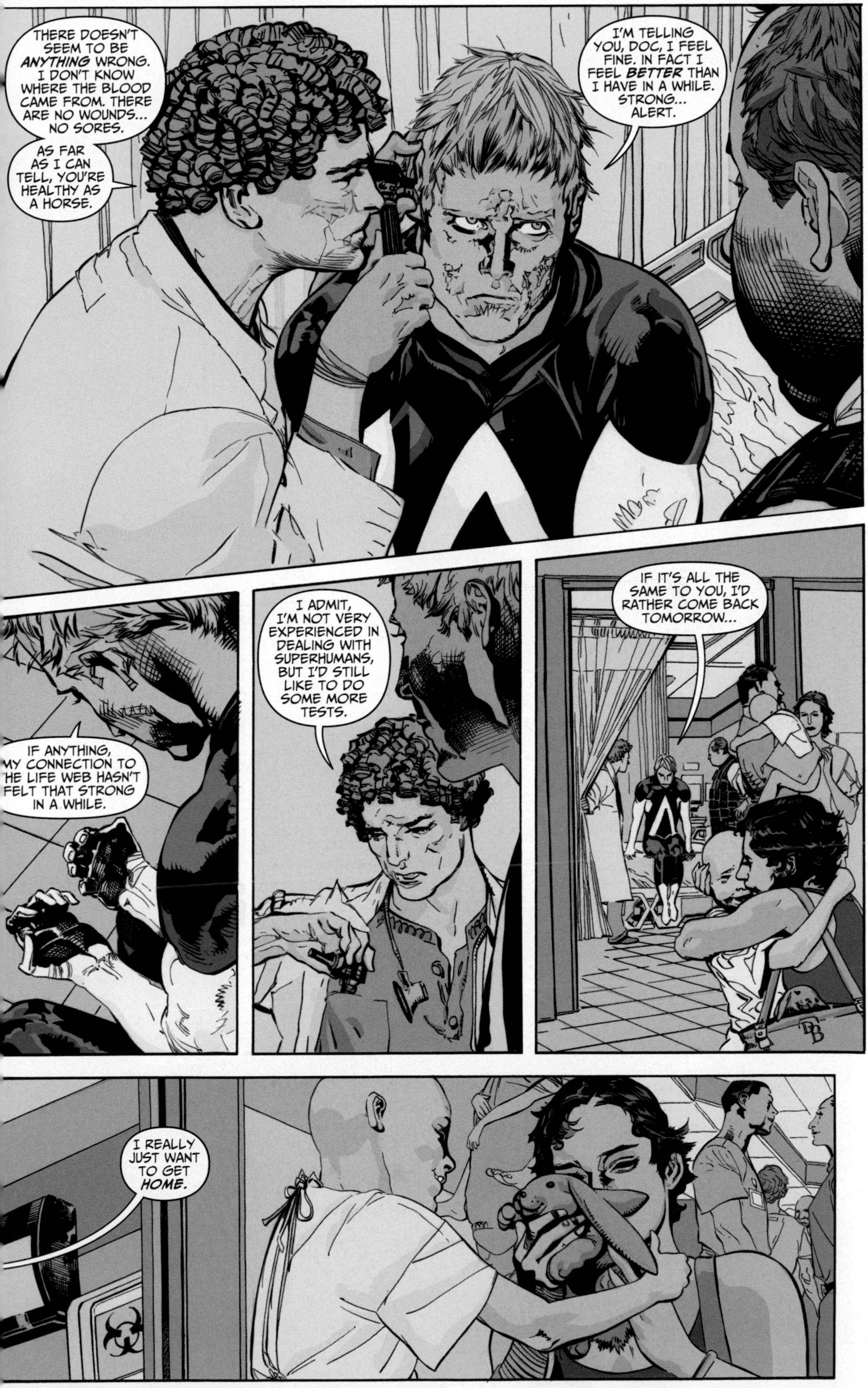
THERE DOESN'T SEEM TO BE ANYTHING WRONG. I DON'T KNOW WHERE THE BLOOD CAME FROM. THERE ARE NO WOUNDS... NO SORES.
AS FAR AS I CAN TELL, YOU'RE HEALTHY AS A HORSE.
I'M TELLING YOU, DOC, I FEEL FINE. IN FACT I FEEL BETTER THAN I HAVE IN A WHILE. STRONG... ALERT.
IF ANYTHING, MY CONNECTION TO THE LIFE WEB HASN'T FELT THAT STRONG IN A WHILE.
I ADMIT, I'M NOT VERY EXPERIENCED IN DEALING WITH SUPERHUMANS, BUT I'D STILL LIKE TO DO SOME MORE TESTS.
IF IT'S ALL THE SAME TO YOU, I'D RATHER COME BACK TOMORROW...
I REALLY JUST WANT TO GET HOME.

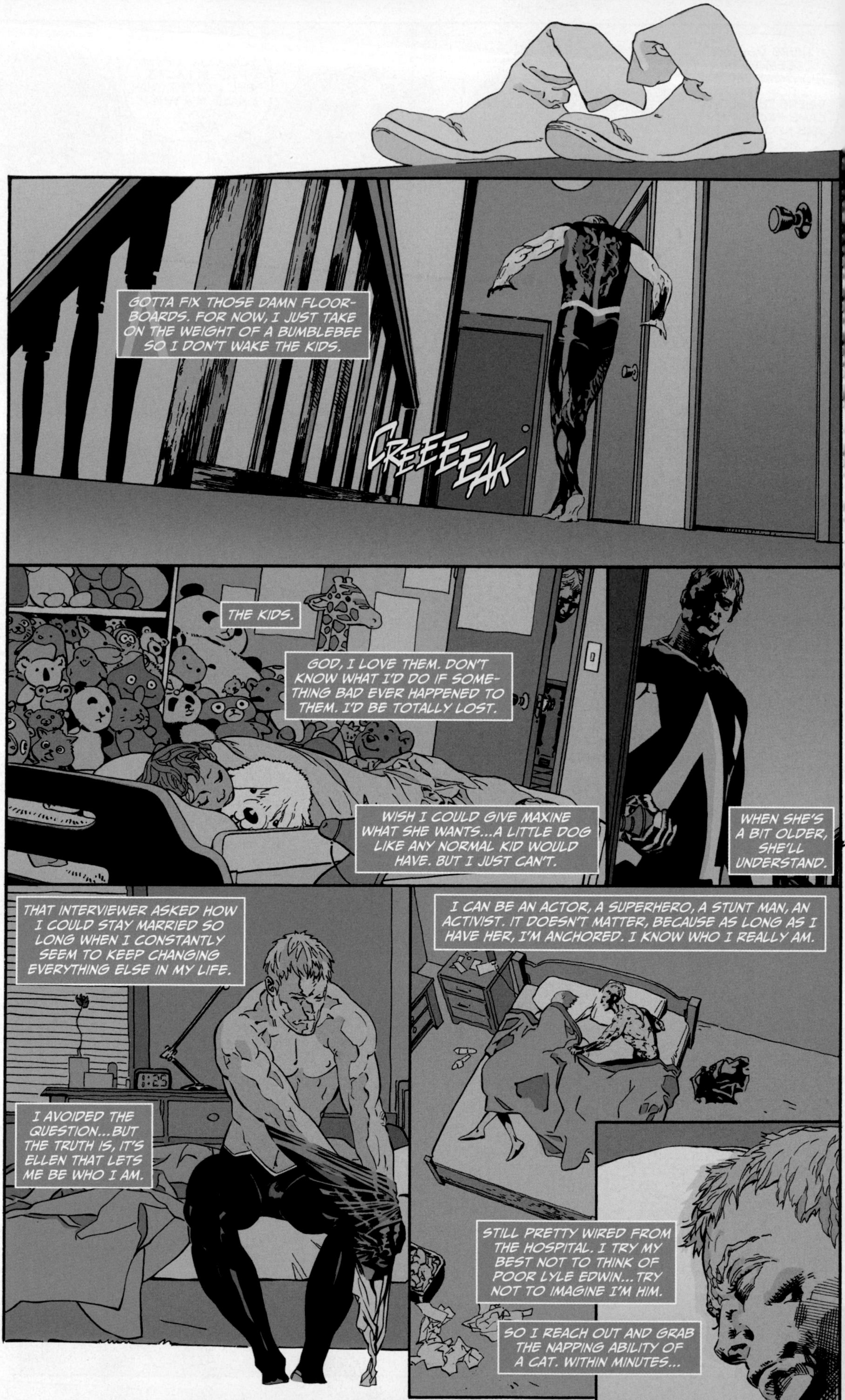
GOTTA FIX THOSE DAMN FLOOR-BOARDS. FOR NOW, I JUST TAKE ON THE WEIGHT OF A BUMBLEBEE SO I DON'T WAKE THE KIDS.
CREEEEEAK
THE KIDS.
GOD, I LOVE THEM. DON'T KNOW WHAT I'D DO IF SOME-THING BAD EVER HAPPENED TO THEM. I'D BE TOTALLY LOST.
WISH I COULD GIVE MAXINE WHAT SHE WANTS...A LITTLE DOG LIKE ANY NORMAL KID WOULD HAVE. BUT I JUST CAN'T.
WHEN SHE'S A BIT OLDER, SHE'LL UNDERSTAND.
THAT INTERVIEWER ASKED HOW I COULD STAY MARRIED SO LONG WHEN I CONSTANTLY SEEM TO KEEP CHANGING EVERYTHING ELSE IN MY LIFE.
I AVOIDED THE QUESTION...BUT THE TRUTH IS, IT'S ELLEN THAT LETS ME BE WHO I AM.
I CAN BE AN ACTOR, A SUPERHERO, A STUNT MAN, AN ACTIVIST. IT DOESN'T MATTER, BECAUSE AS LONG AS I HAVE HER, I'M ANCHORED. I KNOW WHO I REALLY AM.
STILL PRETTY WIRED FROM THE HOSPITAL. I TRY MY BEST NOT TO THINK OF POOR LYLE EDWIN...TRY NOT TO IMAGINE I'M HIM.
SO I REACH OUT AND GRAB THE NAPPING ABILITY OF A CAT. WITHIN MINUTES...

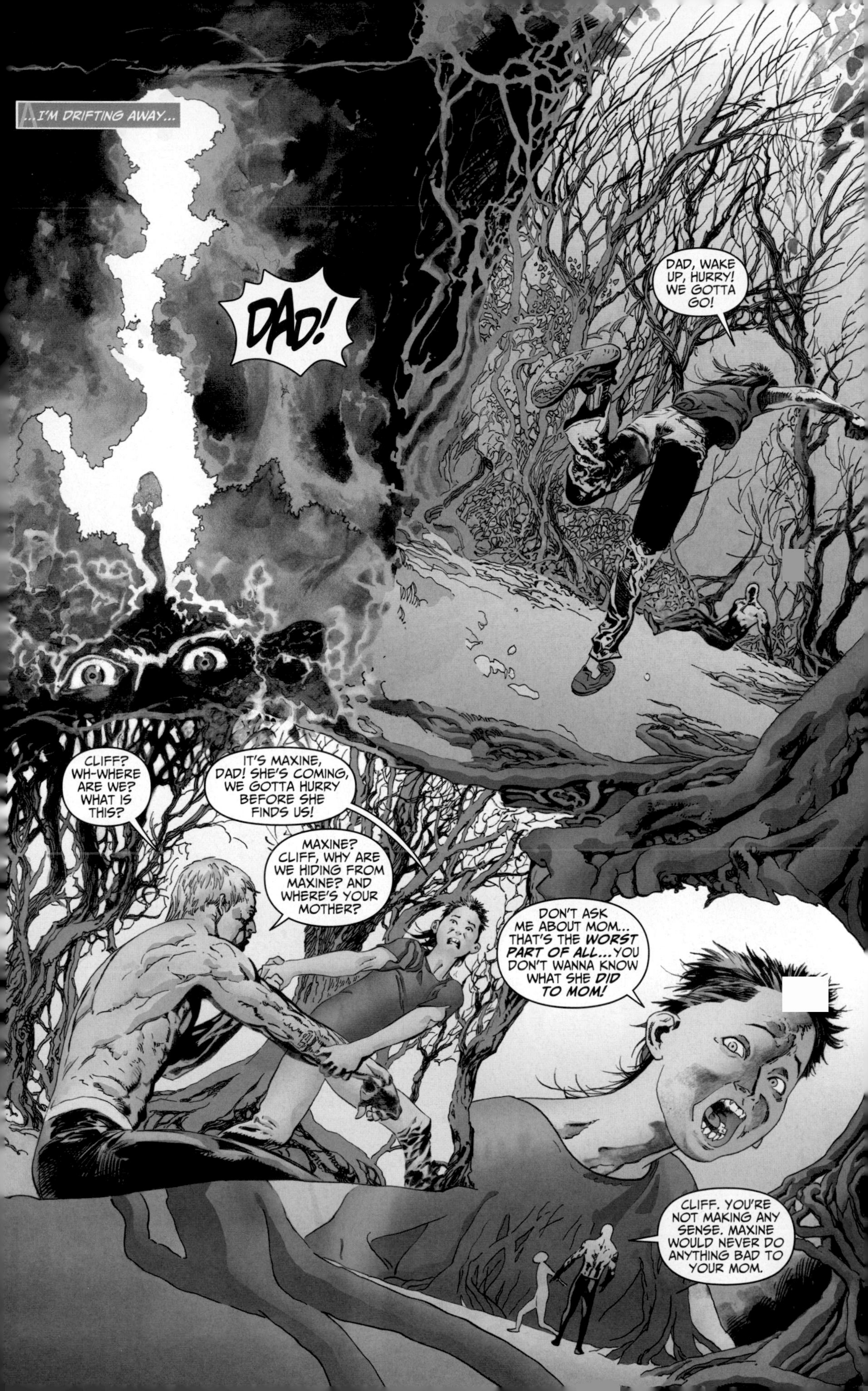
...I'M DRIFTING AWAY...
DAD!
DAD, WAKE UP, HURRY! WE GOTTA GO!
CLIFF? WH-WHERE ARE WE? WHAT IS THIS?
IT'S MAXINE, DAD! SHE'S COMING, WE GOTTA HURRY BEFORE SHE FINDS US!
MAXINE? CLIFF, WHY ARE WE HIDING FROM MAXINE? AND WHERE'S YOUR MOTHER?
DON'T ASK ME ABOUT MOM... THAT'S THE **WORST PART OF ALL...** YOU DON'T WANNA KNOW WHAT SHE ***DID TO MOM!***
CLIFF. YOU'RE NOT MAKING ANY SENSE. MAXINE WOULD NEVER DO ANYTHING BAD TO YOUR MOM.

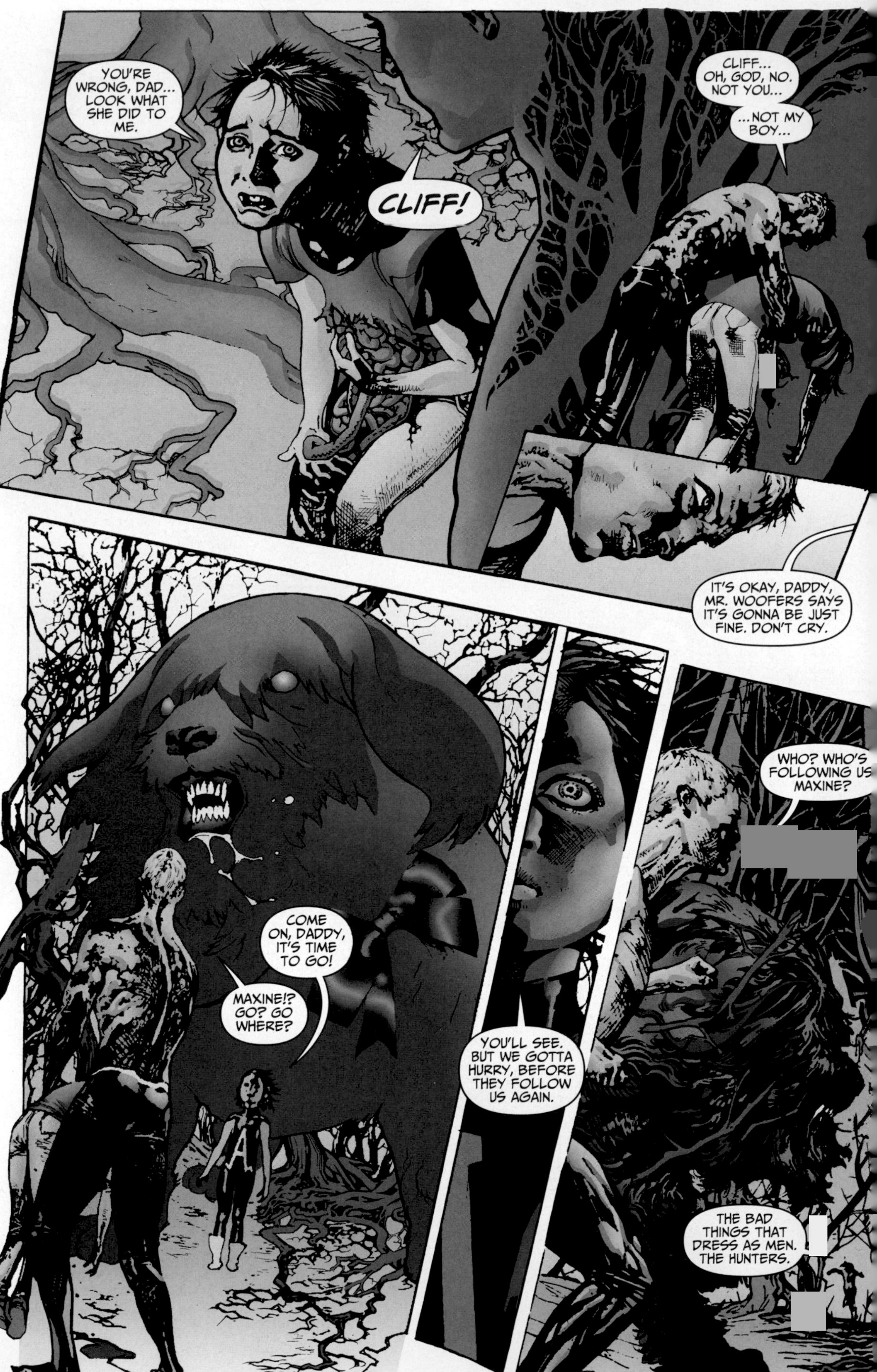
YOU'RE WRONG, DAD... LOOK WHAT SHE DID TO ME.
CLIFF!
CLIFF... OH, GOD, NO. NOT YOU...
...NOT MY BOY...
IT'S OKAY, DADDY, MR. WOOFERS SAYS IT'S GONNA BE JUST FINE. DON'T CRY.
COME ON, DADDY, IT'S TIME TO GO!
MAXINE!? GO? GO WHERE?
YOU'LL SEE. BUT WE GOTTA HURRY, BEFORE THEY FOLLOW US AGAIN.
WHO? WHO'S FOLLOWING US MAXINE?
THE BAD THINGS THAT DRESS AS MEN. THE HUNTERS.

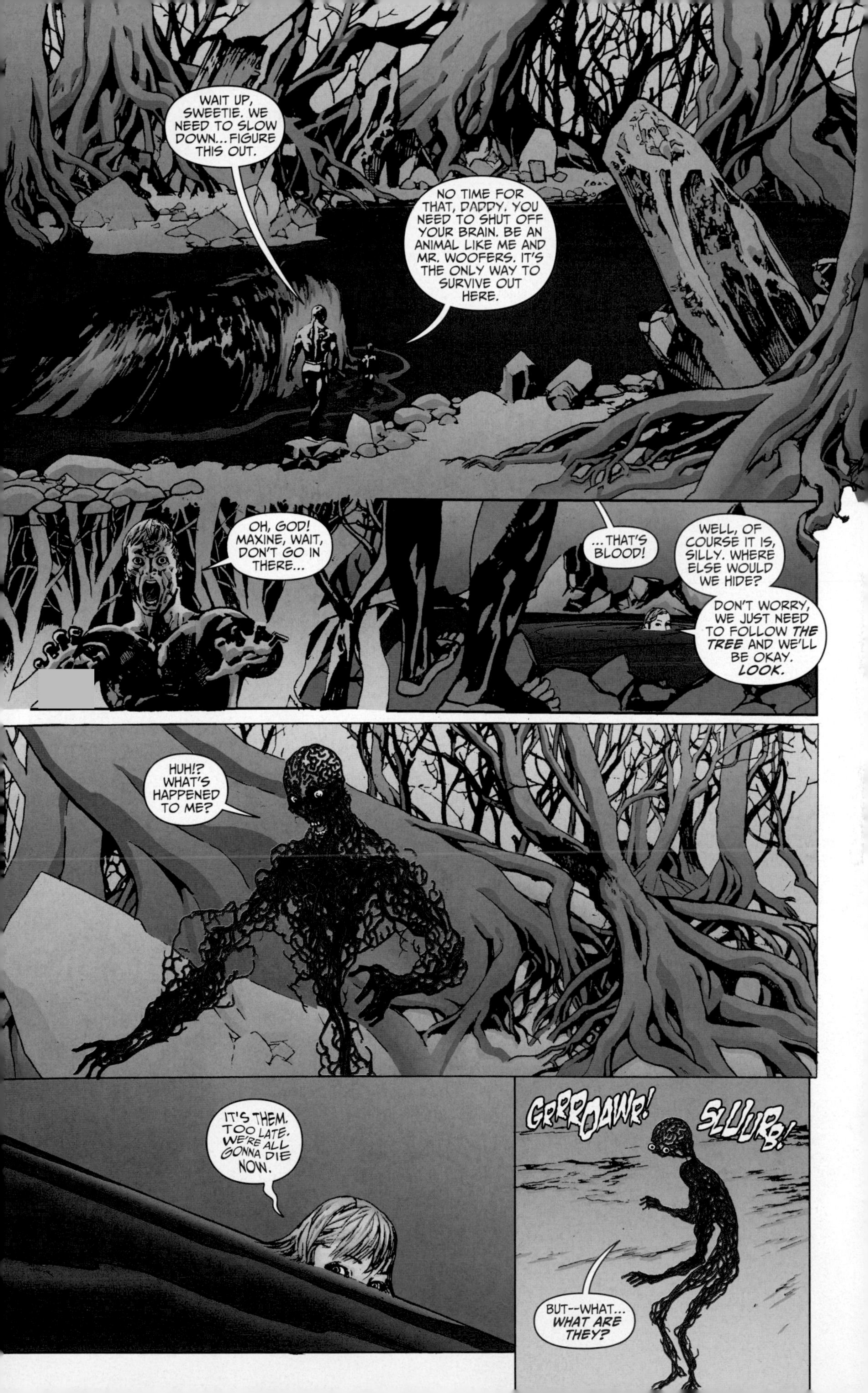
WAIT UP, SWEETIE. WE NEED TO SLOW DOWN... FIGURE THIS OUT.
NO TIME FOR THAT, DADDY. YOU NEED TO SHUT OFF YOUR BRAIN. BE AN ANIMAL LIKE ME AND MR. WOOFERS. IT'S THE ONLY WAY TO SURVIVE OUT HERE.
OH, GOD! MAXINE, WAIT, DON'T GO IN THERE...
...THAT'S BLOOD!
WELL, OF COURSE IT IS, SILLY. WHERE ELSE WOULD WE HIDE?
DON'T WORRY, WE JUST NEED TO FOLLOW THE TREE AND WE'LL BE OKAY. LOOK.
HUH!? WHAT'S HAPPENED TO ME?
IT'S THEM. TOO LATE. WE'RE ALL GONNA DIE NOW.
GRRROAWR!
SLUURB!
BUT--WHAT... WHAT ARE THEY?

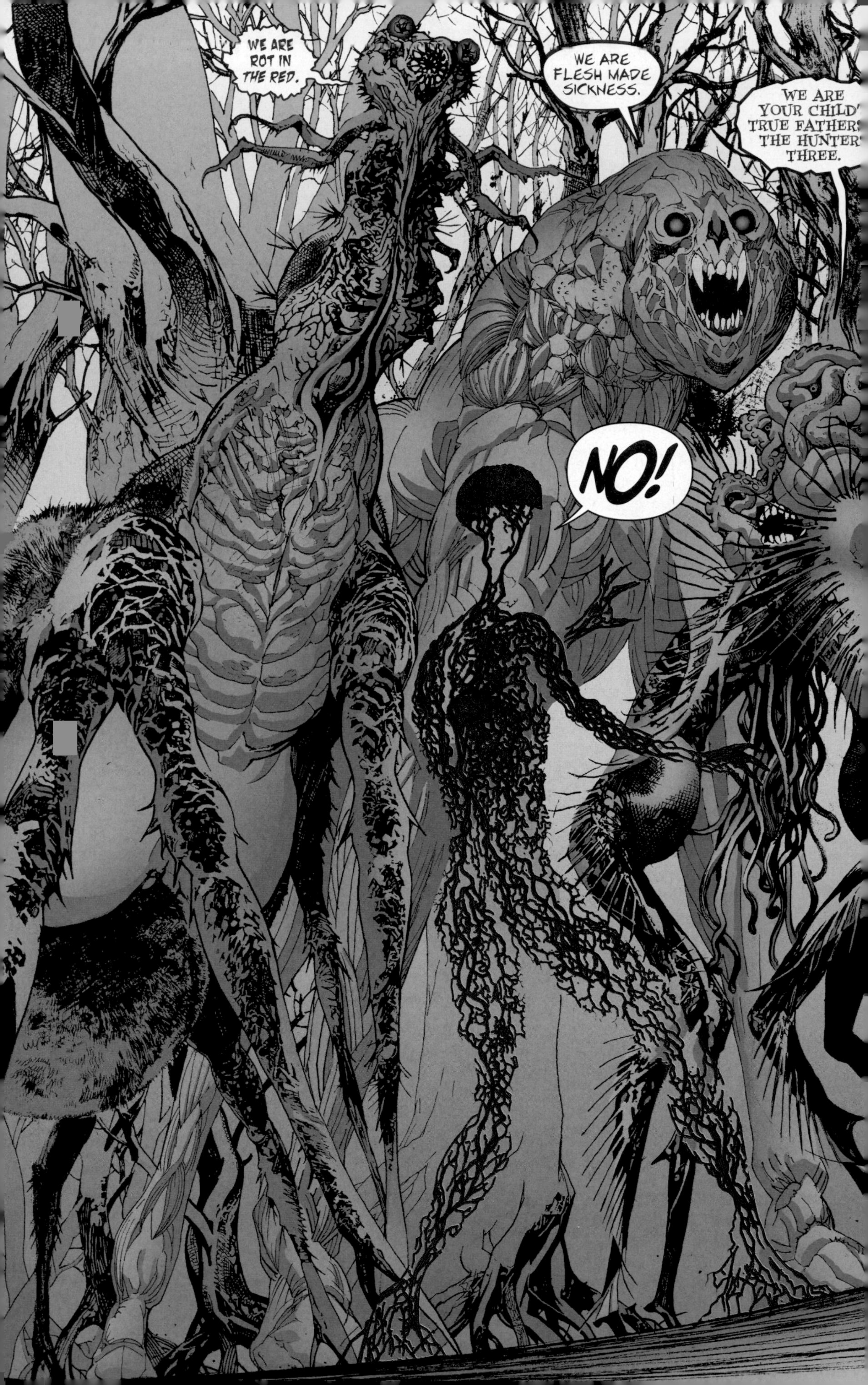
WE ARE ROT IN THE RED.
WE ARE FLESH MADE SICKNESS.
WE ARE YOUR CHILD' TRUE FATHERS THE HUNTER' THREE.
NO!

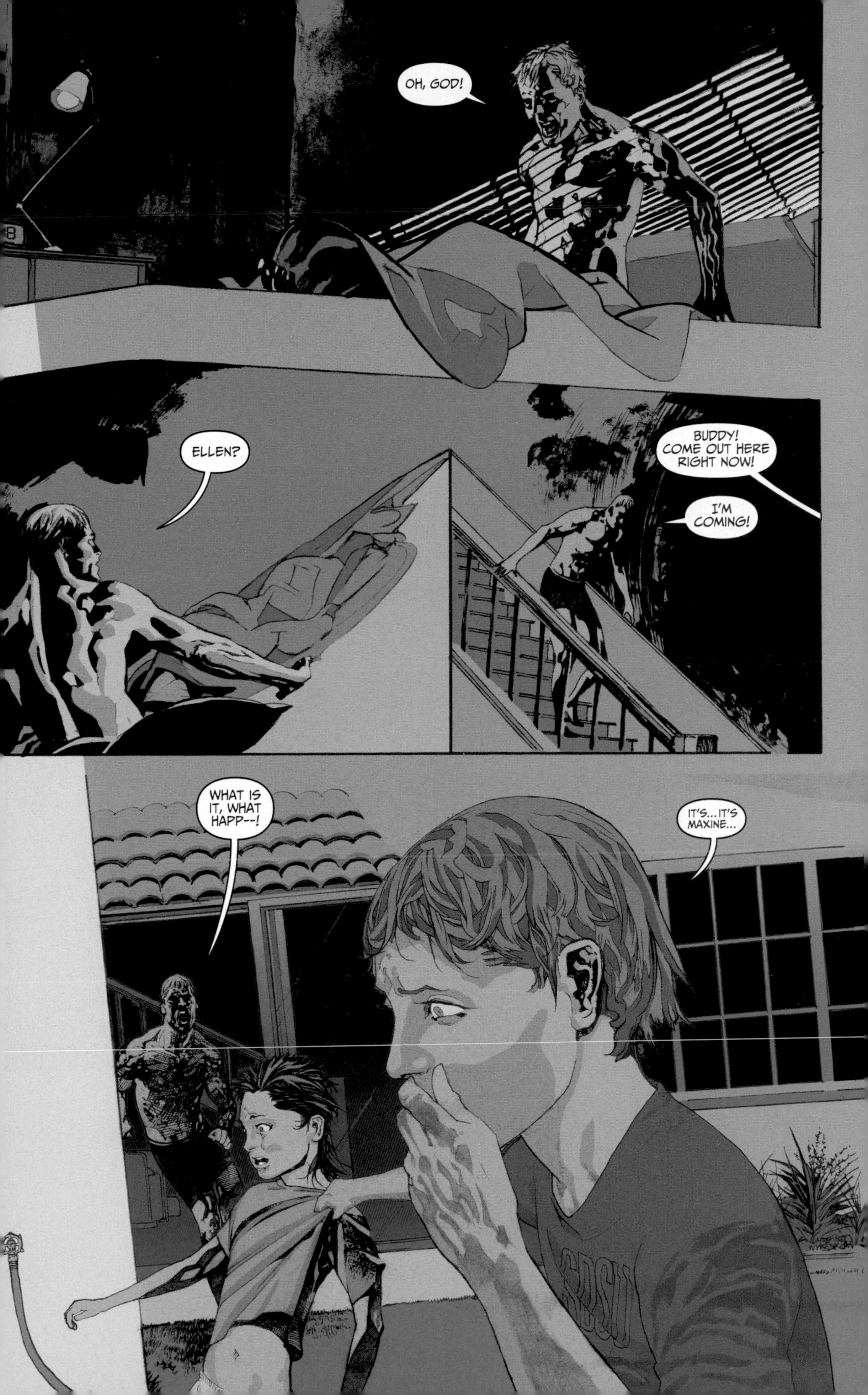
OH, GOD!
ELLEN?
BUDDY! COME OUT HERE RIGHT NOW!
I'M COMING!
WHAT IS IT, WHAT HAPP--!
IT'S...IT'S MAXINE...

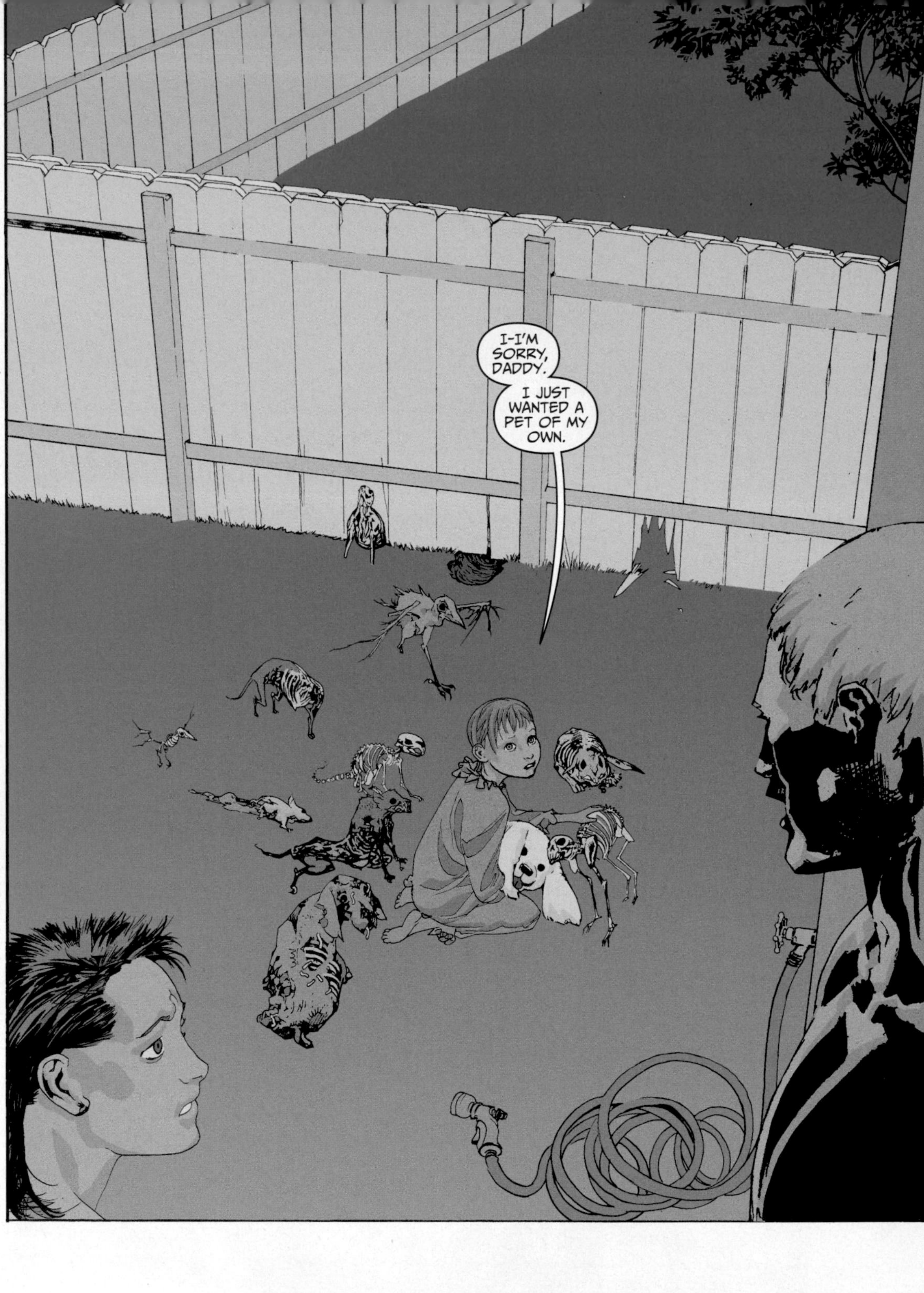
I-I'M SORRY, DADDY.
I JUST WANTED A PET OF MY OWN.

the hunt

part one

WARNING FROM THE RED

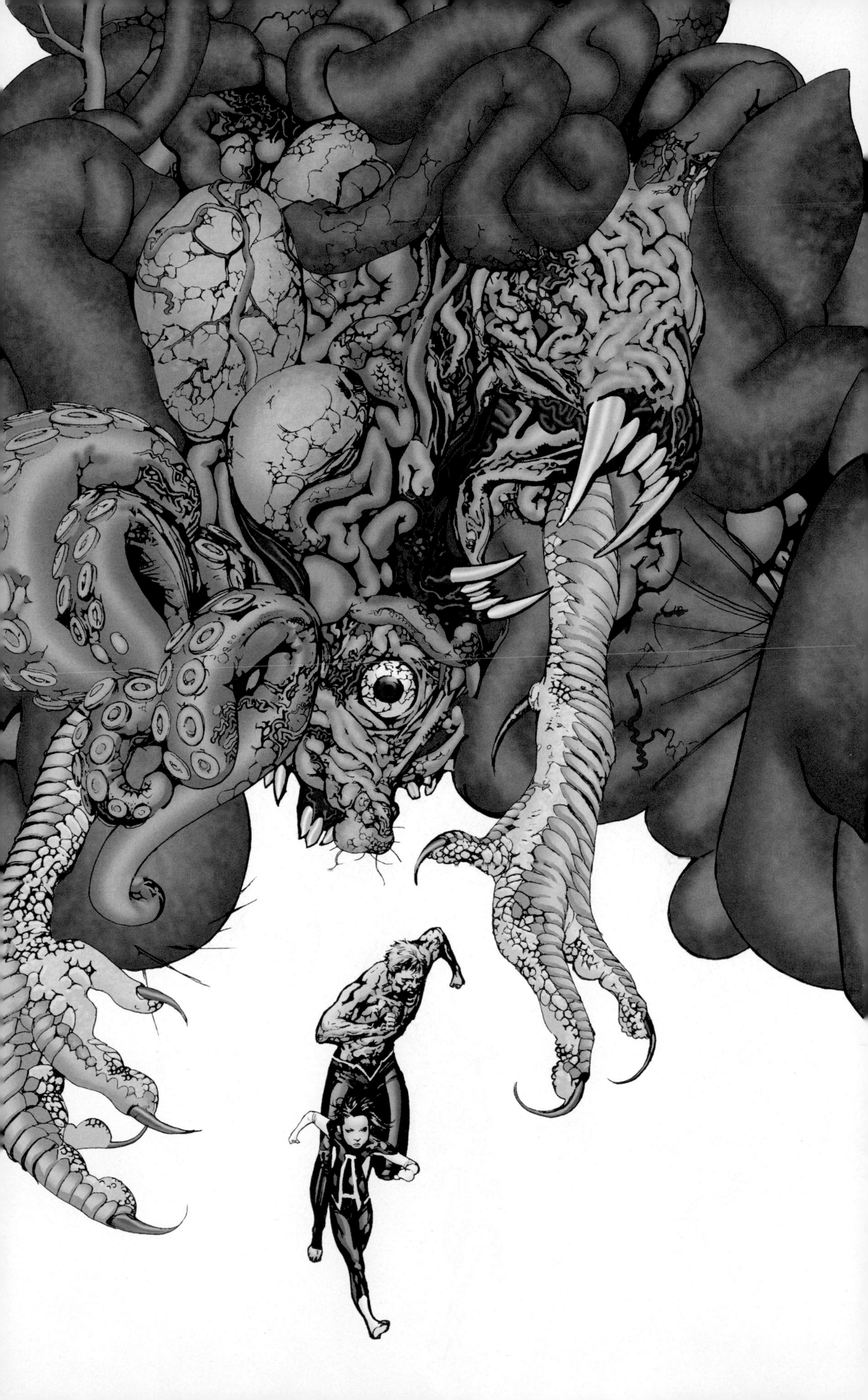

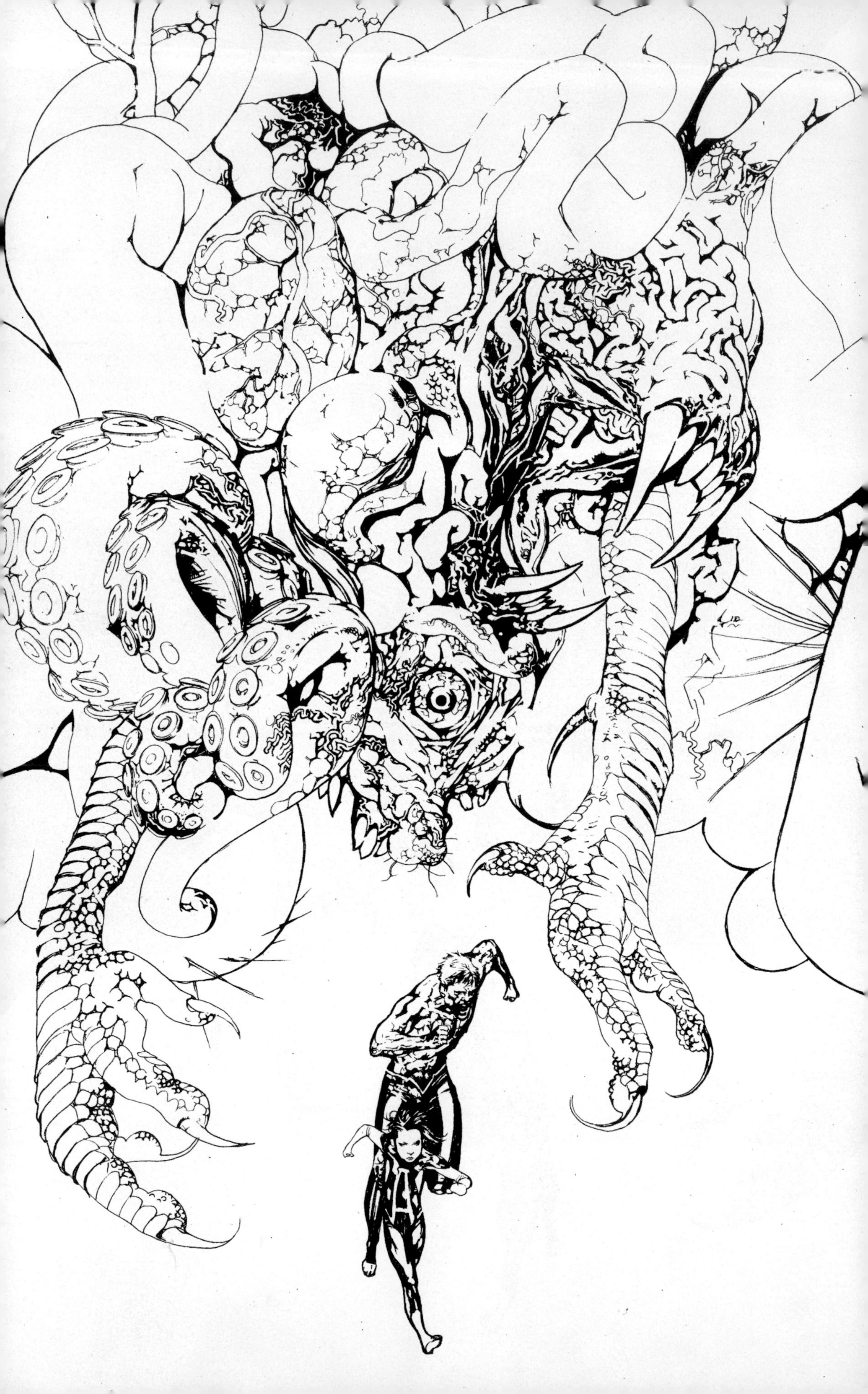

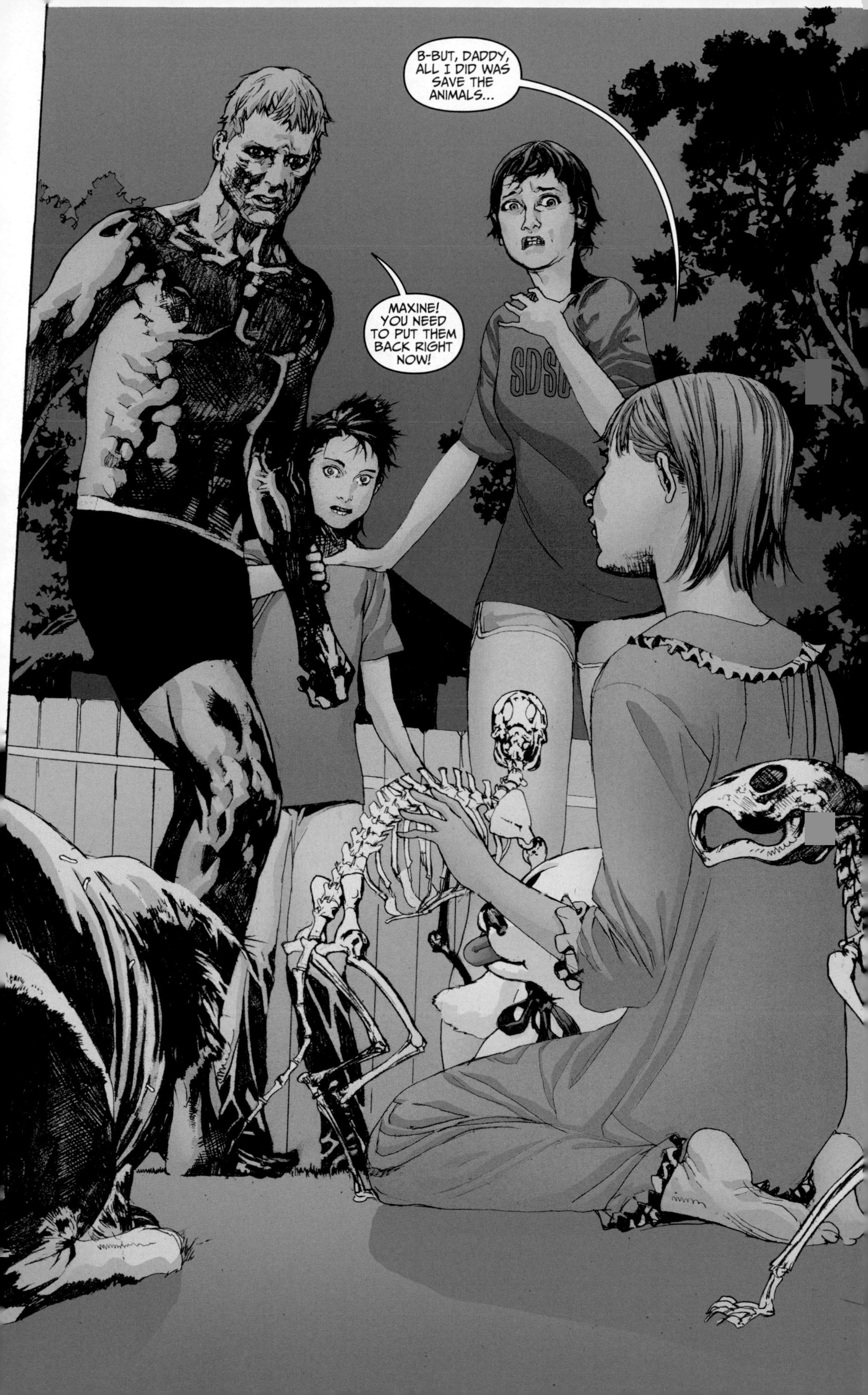
B-BUT, DADDY, ALL I DID WAS SAVE THE ANIMALS...
MAXINE! YOU NEED TO PUT THEM BACK RIGHT NOW!
SDSU

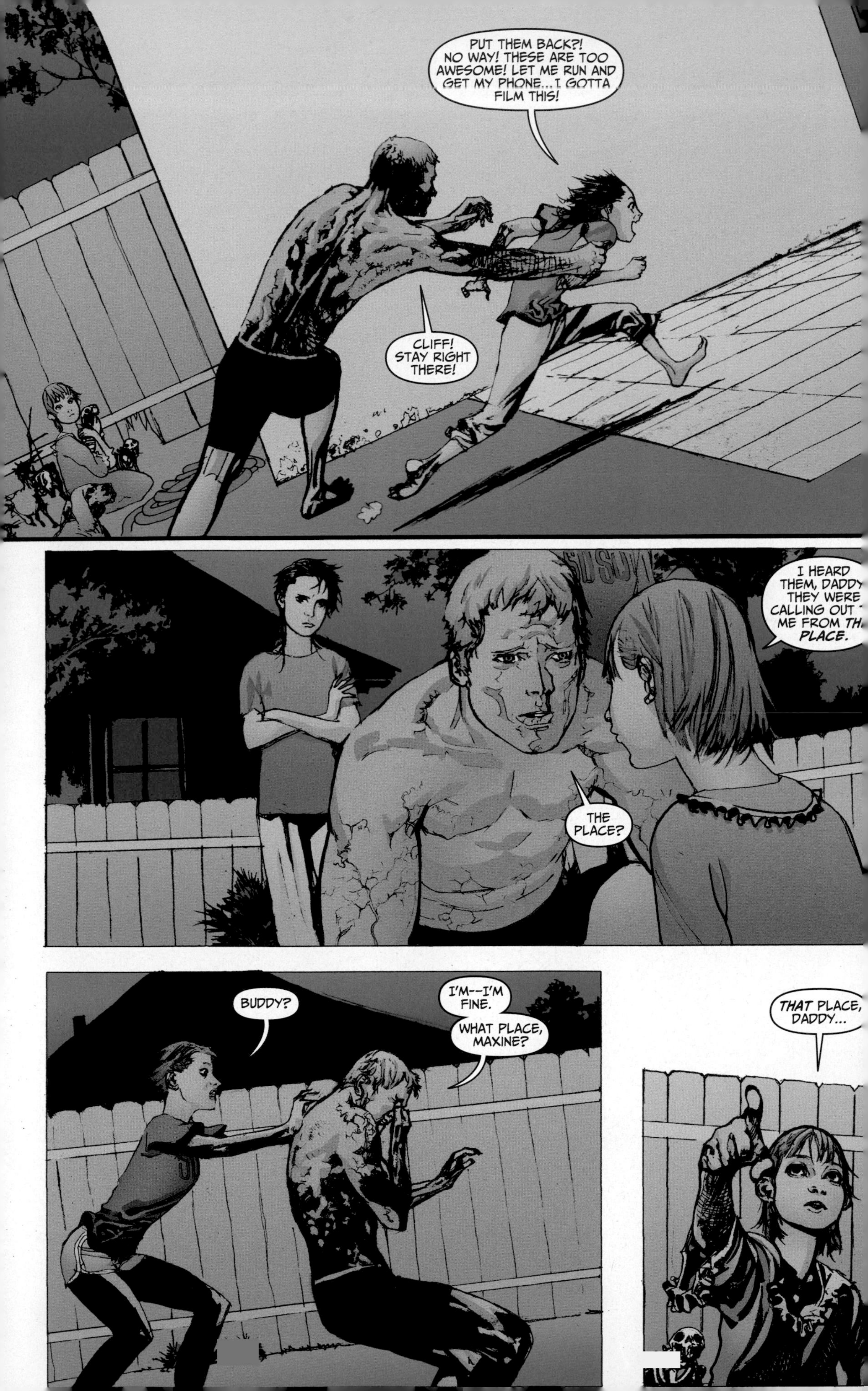
PUT THEM BACK?! NO WAY! THESE ARE TOO AWESOME! LET ME RUN AND GET MY PHONE... I GOTTA FILM THIS!
CLIFF! STAY RIGHT THERE!
I HEARD THEM, DADDY THEY WERE CALLING OUT ME FROM TH PLACE.
THE PLACE?
BUDDY?
I'M--I'M FINE.
WHAT PLACE, MAXINE?
THAT PLACE, DADDY...

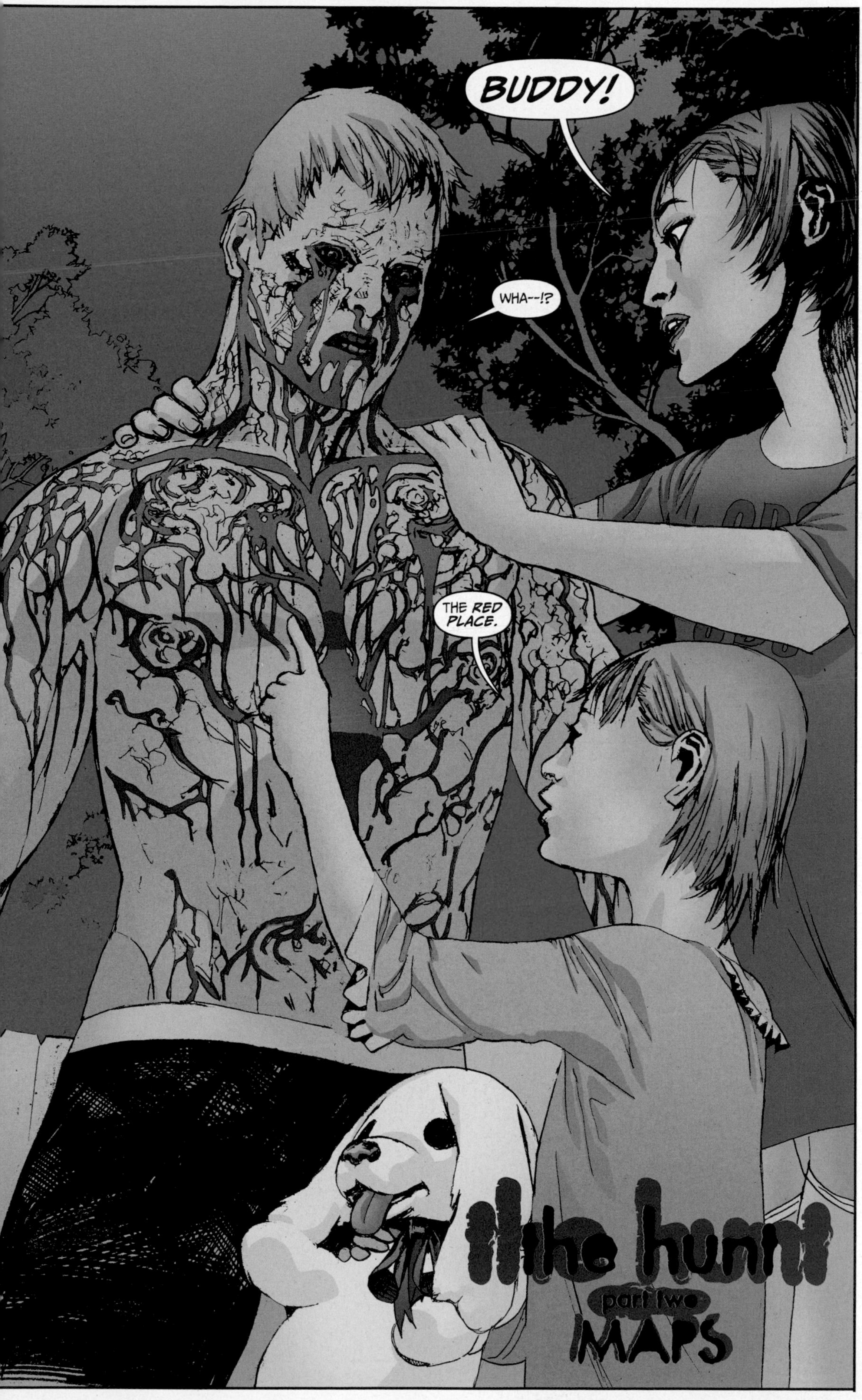
BUDDY!
WHA--!?
THE RED PLACE.
the hunt
part two
MAPS

THIS IS *SO* BADASS!

I DON'T KNOW, BUDDY...IT'S LIKE IT'S A PART OF YOUR SKIN.

HSSSSs!

CLIFF, PUT THAT AWAY AND GO AND GET DRESSED!

I NEED YOU TO GET OUT THERE AND DO YOUR BEST TO COVER UP ALL THE GRAVES THESE THINGS UPTURNED BEFORE IT GETS LIGHT OUT.

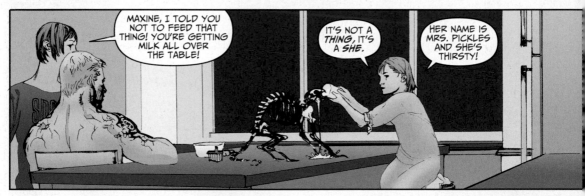

MAXINE, I TOLD YOU NOT TO FEED THAT THING! YOU'RE GETTING MILK ALL OVER THE TABLE!

IT'S NOT A *THING*, IT'S A *SHE*.

HER NAME IS MRS. PICKLES AND SHE'S THIRSTY!

I DON'T CARE WHAT IT IS, JUST GET IT OFF MY TABLE, NOW!

BACK IN A MINUTE!

IT'S NO USE, HON...THESE THINGS ARE NOT COMING OFF.

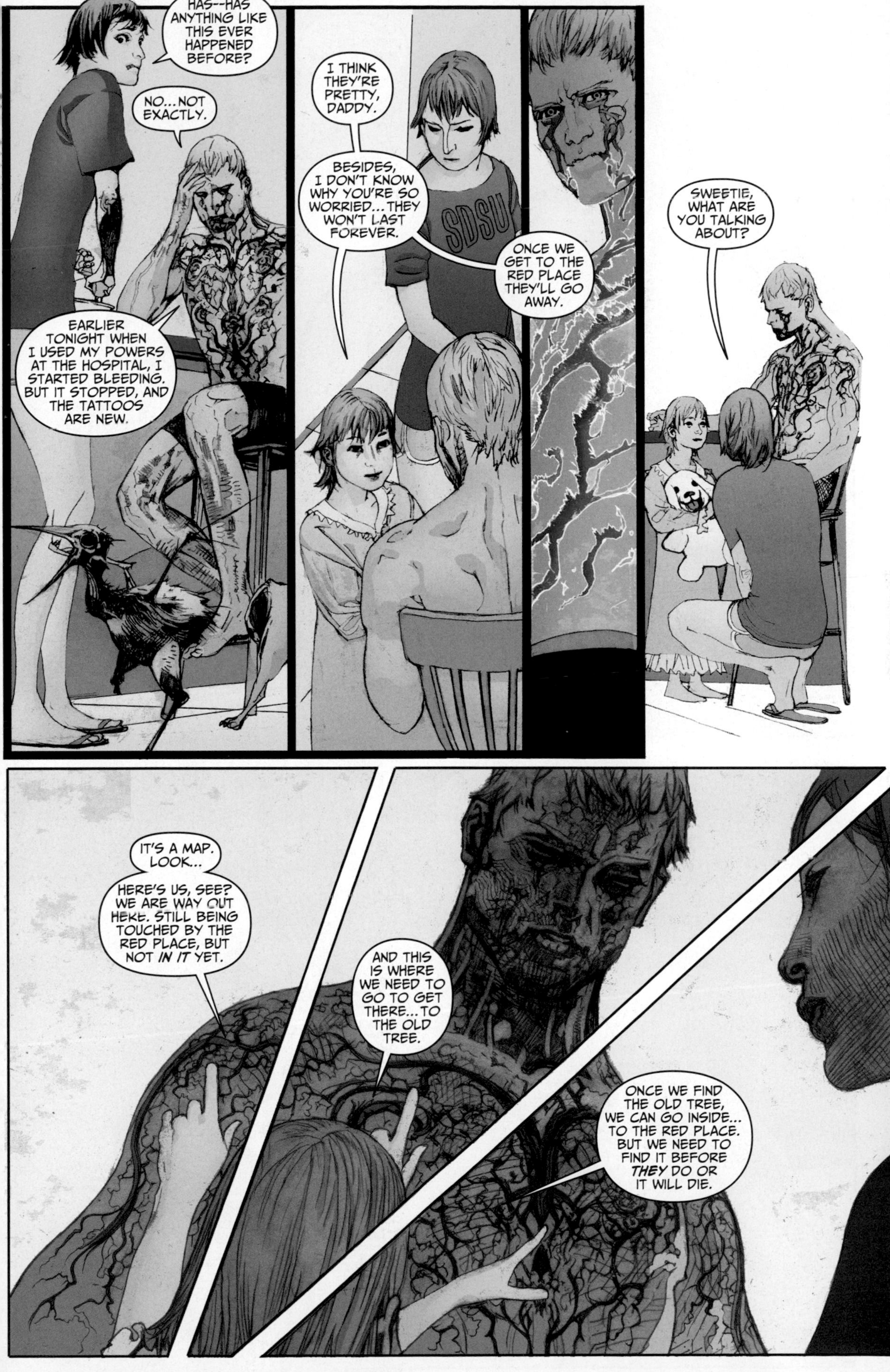
HAS--HAS ANYTHING LIKE THIS EVER HAPPENED BEFORE?
NO...NOT EXACTLY.
EARLIER TONIGHT WHEN I USED MY POWERS AT THE HOSPITAL, I STARTED BLEEDING. BUT IT STOPPED, AND THE TATTOOS ARE NEW.
I THINK THEY'RE PRETTY, DADDY.
BESIDES, I DON'T KNOW WHY YOU'RE SO WORRIED... THEY WON'T LAST FOREVER.
ONCE WE GET TO THE RED PLACE THEY'LL GO AWAY.
SWEETIE, WHAT ARE YOU TALKING ABOUT?
IT'S A MAP. LOOK...
HERE'S US, SEE? WE ARE WAY OUT HERE. STILL BEING TOUCHED BY THE RED PLACE, BUT NOT *IN IT* YET.
AND THIS IS WHERE WE NEED TO GO TO GET THERE... TO THE OLD TREE.
ONCE WE FIND THE OLD TREE, WE CAN GO INSIDE... TO THE RED PLACE. BUT WE NEED TO FIND IT BEFORE *THEY* DO OR IT WILL DIE.

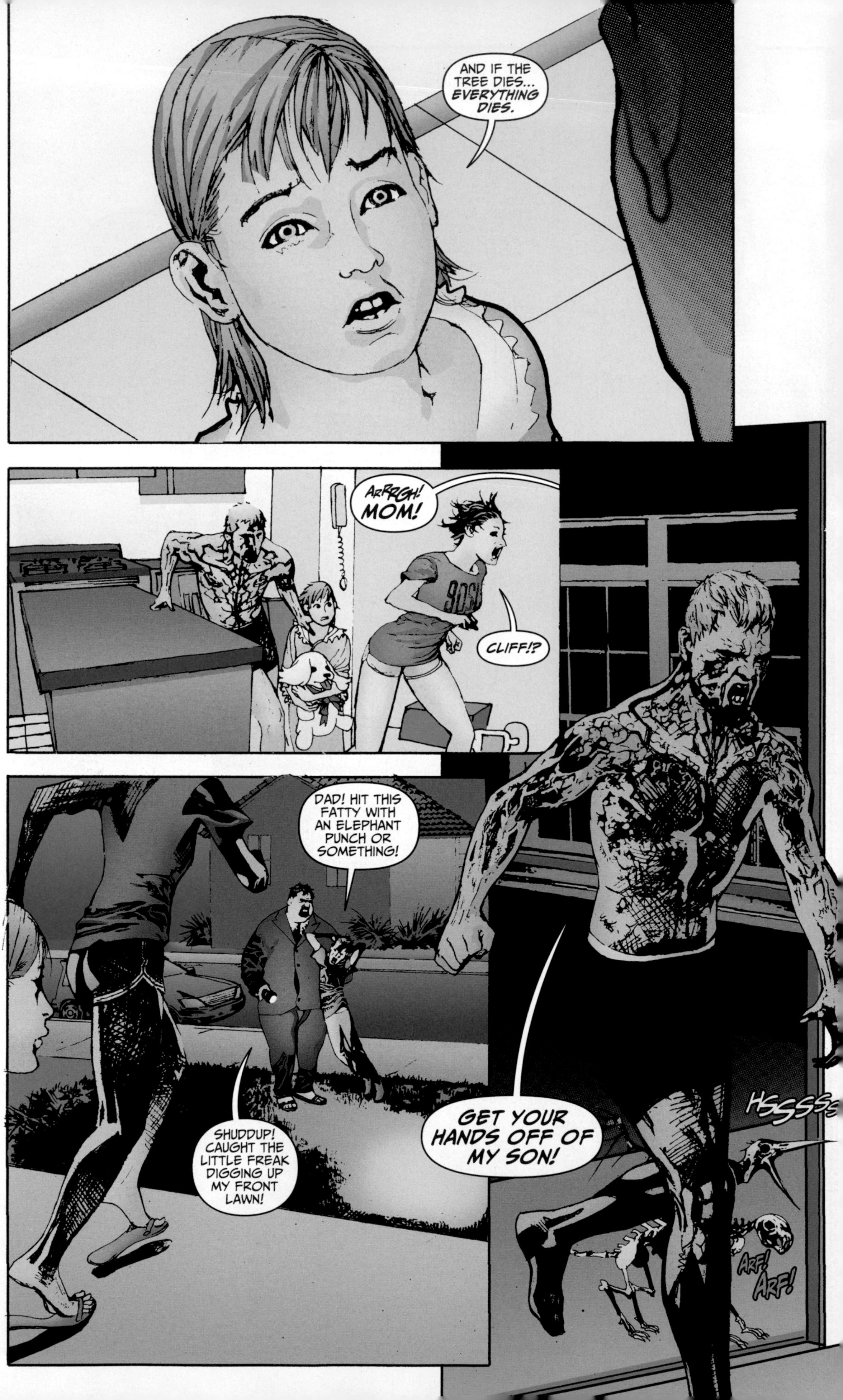
AND IF THE TREE DIES... EVERYTHING DIES.
ARRRGH! MOM!
CLIFF!?
DAD! HIT THIS FATTY WITH AN ELEPHANT PUNCH OR SOMETHING!
SHUDDUP! CAUGHT THE LITTLE FREAK DIGGING UP MY FRONT LAWN!
GET YOUR HANDS OFF OF MY SON!
HSSSSS
ARF! ARF!

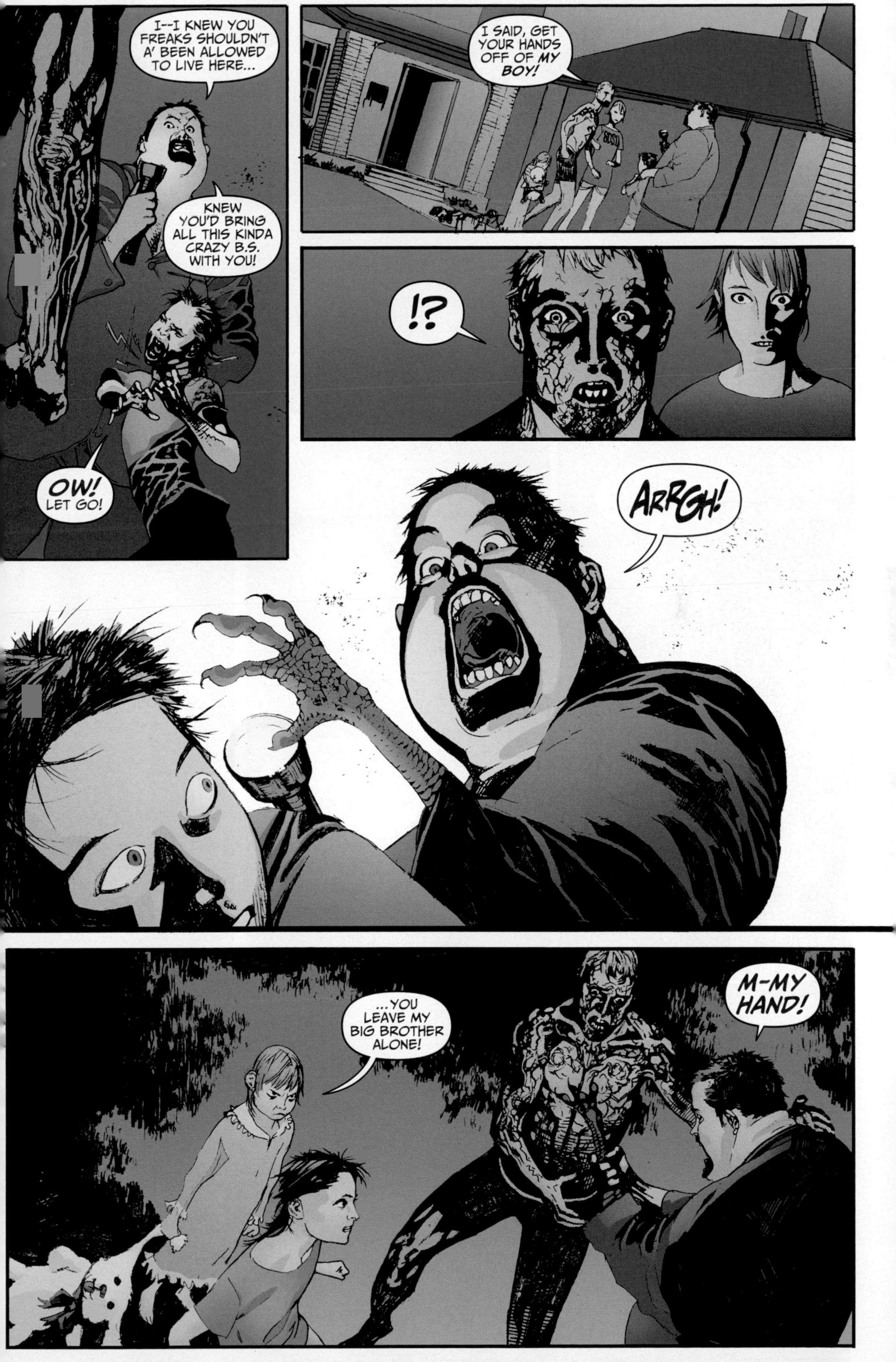
I--I KNEW YOU FREAKS SHOULDN'T A' BEEN ALLOWED TO LIVE HERE...
KNEW YOU'D BRING ALL THIS KINDA CRAZY B.S. WITH YOU!
OW! LET GO!
I SAID, GET YOUR HANDS OFF OF MY BOY!
!?
ARRGH!
...YOU LEAVE MY BIG BROTHER ALONE!
M-MY HAND!

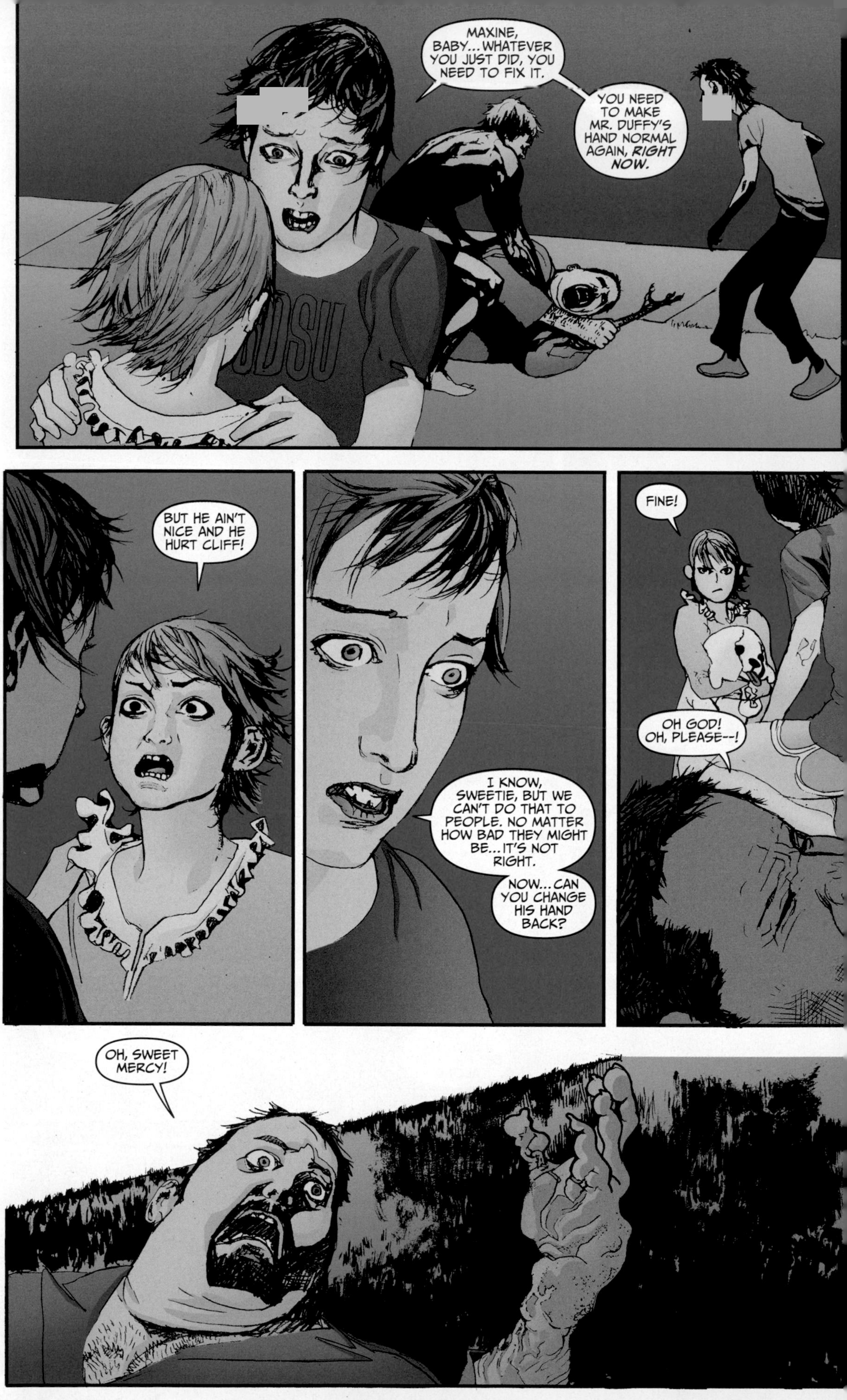
MAXINE, BABY...WHATEVER YOU JUST DID, YOU NEED TO FIX IT.
YOU NEED TO MAKE MR. DUFFY'S HAND NORMAL AGAIN, *RIGHT NOW.*
BUT HE AIN'T NICE AND HE HURT CLIFF!
I KNOW, SWEETIE, BUT WE CAN'T DO THAT TO PEOPLE. NO MATTER HOW BAD THEY MIGHT BE...IT'S NOT RIGHT.
NOW...CAN YOU CHANGE HIS HAND BACK?
FINE!
OH GOD! OH, PLEASE--!
OH, SWEET MERCY!

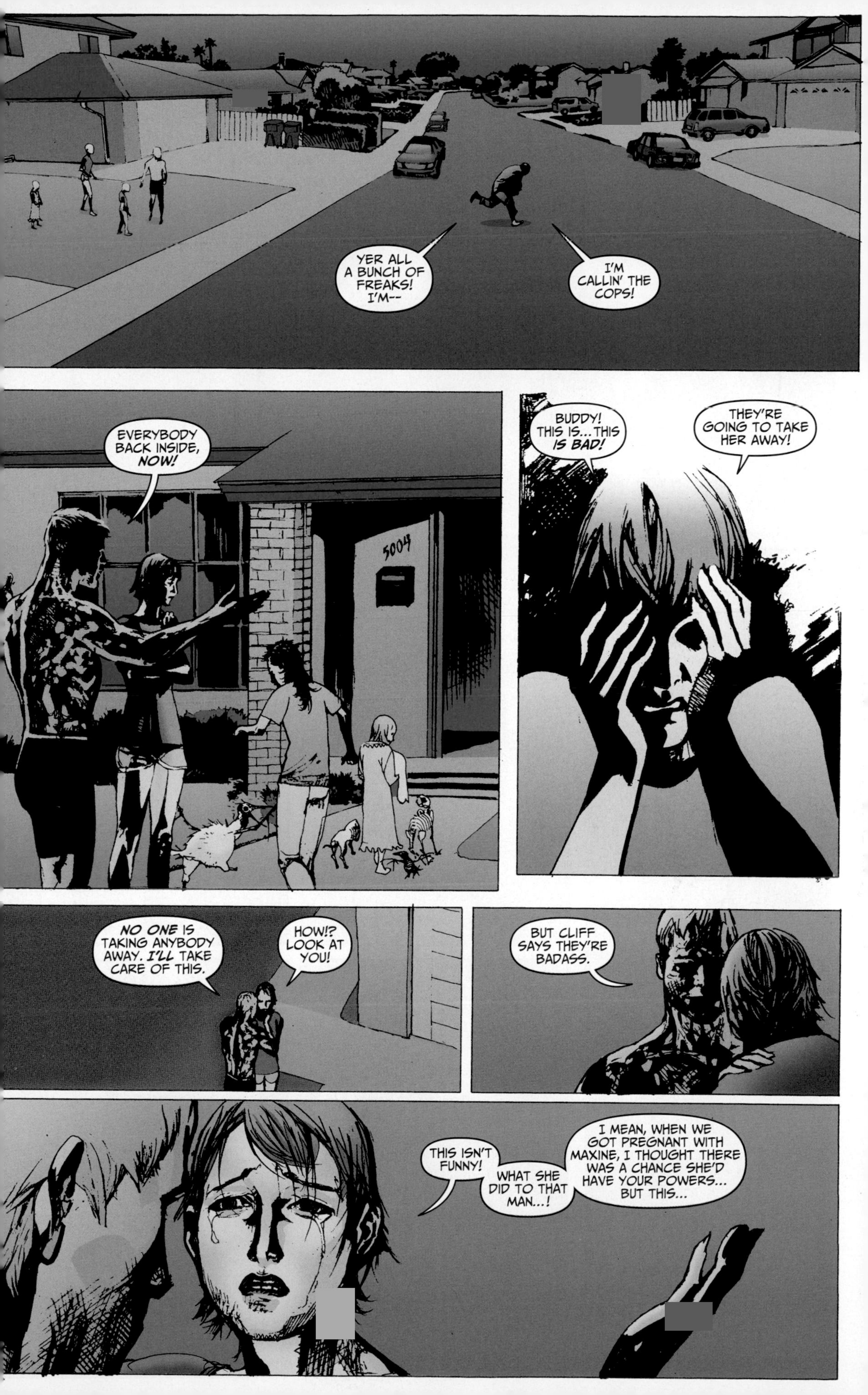

YER ALL A BUNCH OF FREAKS! I'M--
I'M CALLIN' THE COPS!
EVERYBODY BACK INSIDE, *NOW!*
BUDDY! THIS IS... THIS *IS BAD!*
THEY'RE GOING TO TAKE HER AWAY!
NO ONE IS TAKING ANYBODY AWAY. *I'LL* TAKE CARE OF THIS.
HOW!? LOOK AT YOU!
BUT CLIFF SAYS THEY'RE BADASS.
THIS ISN'T FUNNY!
WHAT SHE DID TO THAT MAN...!
I MEAN, WHEN WE GOT PREGNANT WITH MAXINE, I THOUGHT THERE WAS A CHANCE SHE'D HAVE YOUR POWERS... BUT THIS...
5004

WHATEVER THIS IS, WE'RE GOING TO GET THROUGH IT. I PROMISE.

LOOK, I DON'T KNOW WHAT'S GOING ON WITH MAXINE, BUT *SHE SEEMS TO.*

I THINK WE NEED TO LISTEN TO HER... FOLLOW *THIS* WITH HER.

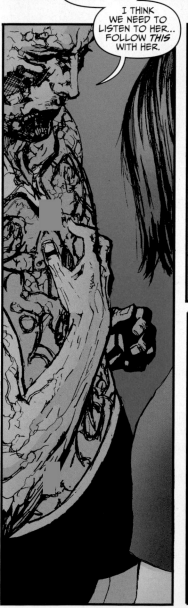

BUT WE CAN'T ALL JUST LEAVE... THE COPS WILL BE HERE SOON.

I KNOW... BUT THERE'S NO PROOF THAT MAXINE DID ANYTHING TO DUFFY. IT'LL JUST BE HIS CRAZED WORD AGAINST YOURS.

MINE? WAIT--

ELLEN, WHATEVER'S HAPPENING... WHEREVER MAXINE AND I ARE HEADED... I DON'T THINK CLIFF AND YOU WILL BE ABLE TO FOLLOW, EVEN IF I WANTED YOU TO.

LOOK, I'M GOING TO GIVE YOU THE NUMBER OF A COP I KNOW, KRENSHAW. HE'S A GOOD MAN. CALL HIM. HE'LL TAKE CARE OF ALL OF THIS.

ELLEN? SAY SOMETHING...

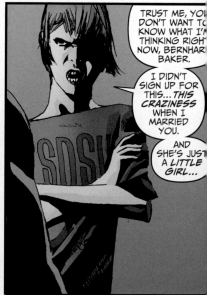

TRUST ME, YOU DON'T WANT TO KNOW WHAT I'M THINKING RIGHT NOW, BERNHARD BAKER.

I DIDN'T SIGN UP FOR THIS...*THIS CRAZINESS* WHEN I MARRIED YOU.

AND SHE'S JUST A *LITTLE GIRL...*

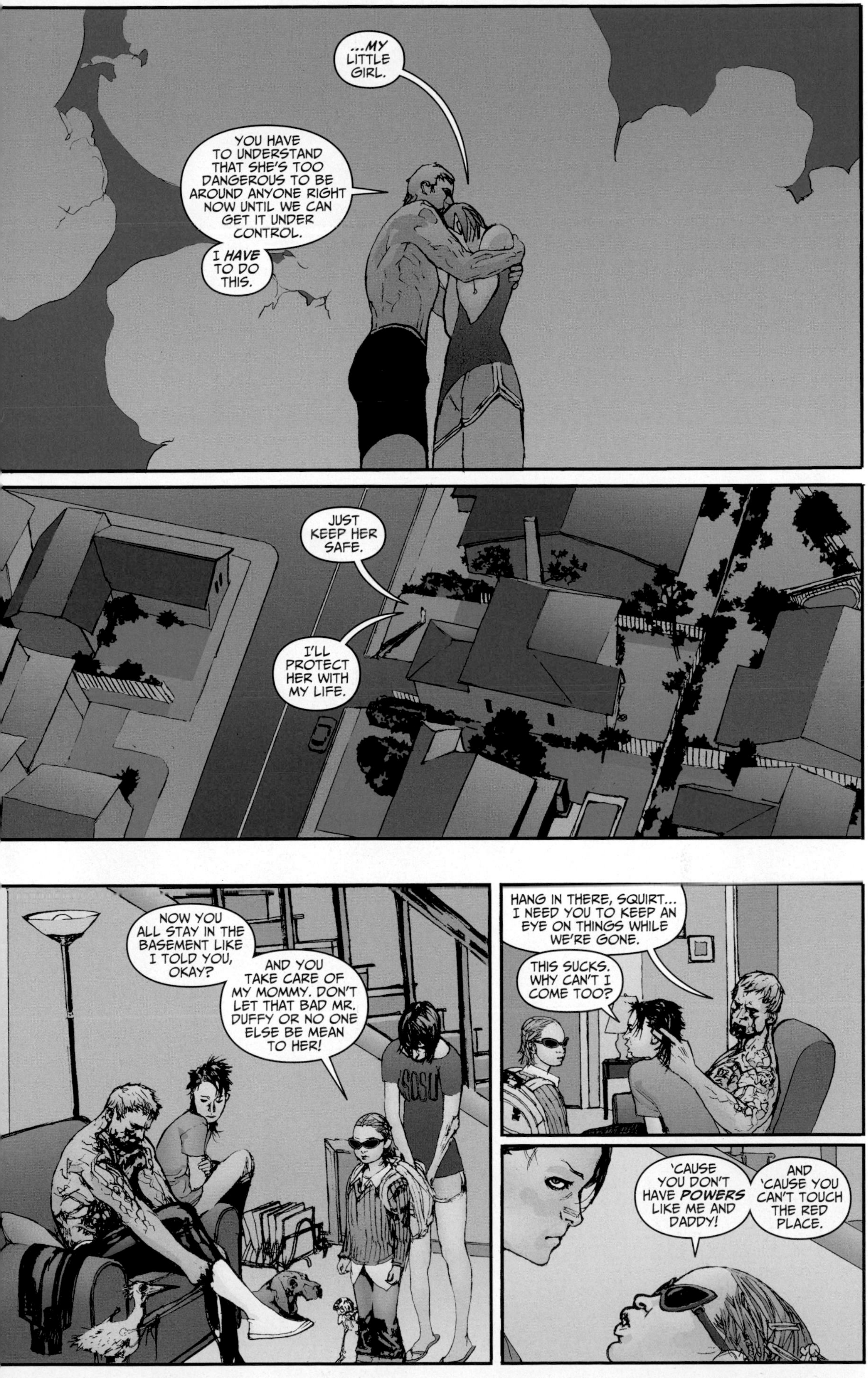
...MY LITTLE GIRL.
YOU HAVE TO UNDERSTAND THAT SHE'S TOO DANGEROUS TO BE AROUND ANYONE RIGHT NOW UNTIL WE CAN GET IT UNDER CONTROL.
I *HAVE* TO DO THIS.
JUST KEEP HER SAFE.
I'LL PROTECT HER WITH MY LIFE.
NOW YOU ALL STAY IN THE BASEMENT LIKE I TOLD YOU, OKAY?
AND YOU TAKE CARE OF MY MOMMY. DON'T LET THAT BAD MR. DUFFY OR NO ONE ELSE BE MEAN TO HER!
HANG IN THERE, SQUIRT... I NEED YOU TO KEEP AN EYE ON THINGS WHILE WE'RE GONE.
THIS SUCKS. WHY CAN'T I COME TOO?
'CAUSE YOU DON'T HAVE *POWERS* LIKE ME AND DADDY!
AND 'CAUSE YOU CAN'T TOUCH THE RED PLACE.

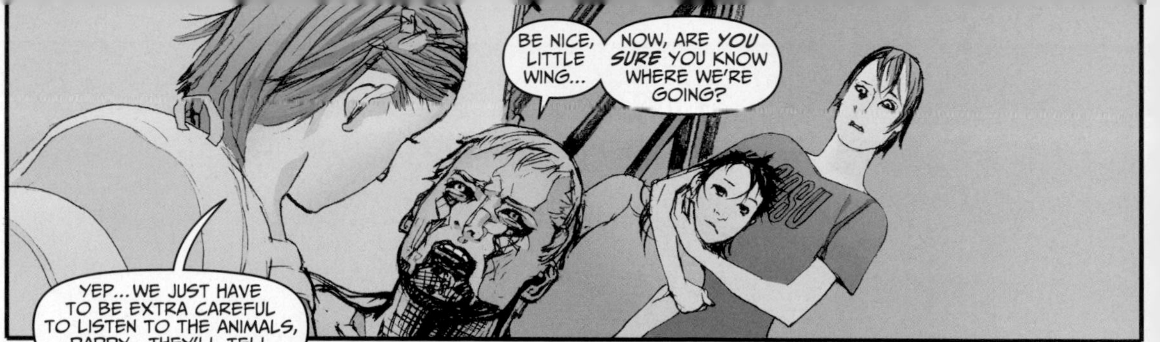
BE NICE, LITTLE WING...
NOW, ARE YOU SURE YOU KNOW WHERE WE'RE GOING?
YEP... WE JUST HAVE TO BE EXTRA CAREFUL TO LISTEN TO THE ANIMALS, DADDY... THEY'LL TELL US WHERE TO GO.

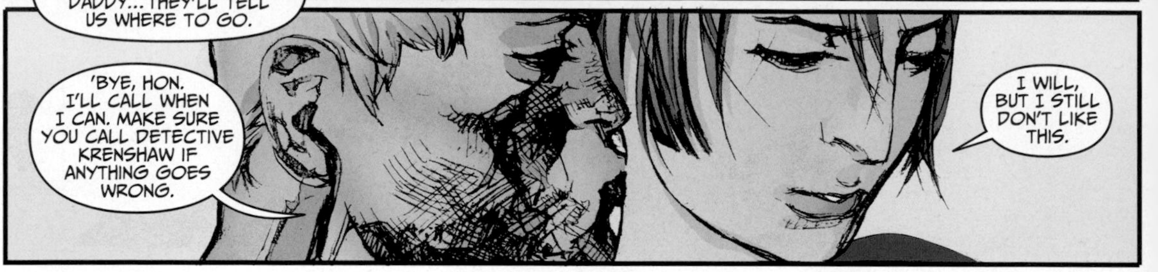
'BYE, HON. I'LL CALL WHEN I CAN. MAKE SURE YOU CALL DETECTIVE KRENSHAW IF ANYTHING GOES WRONG.
I WILL, BUT I STILL DON'T LIKE THIS.

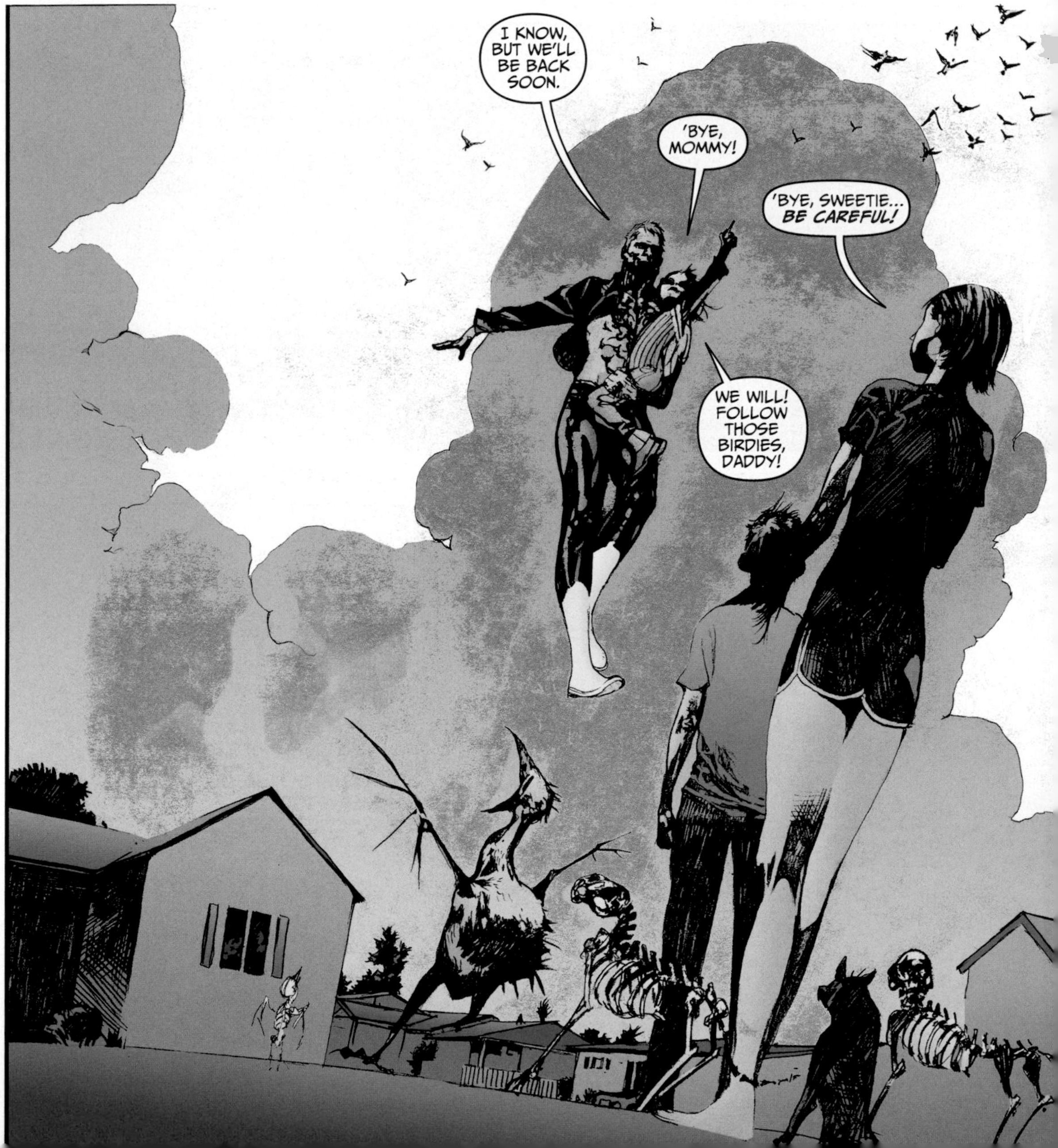
I KNOW, BUT WE'LL BE BACK SOON.
'BYE, MOMMY!
'BYE, SWEETIE... BE CAREFUL!
WE WILL! FOLLOW THOSE BIRDIES, DADDY!

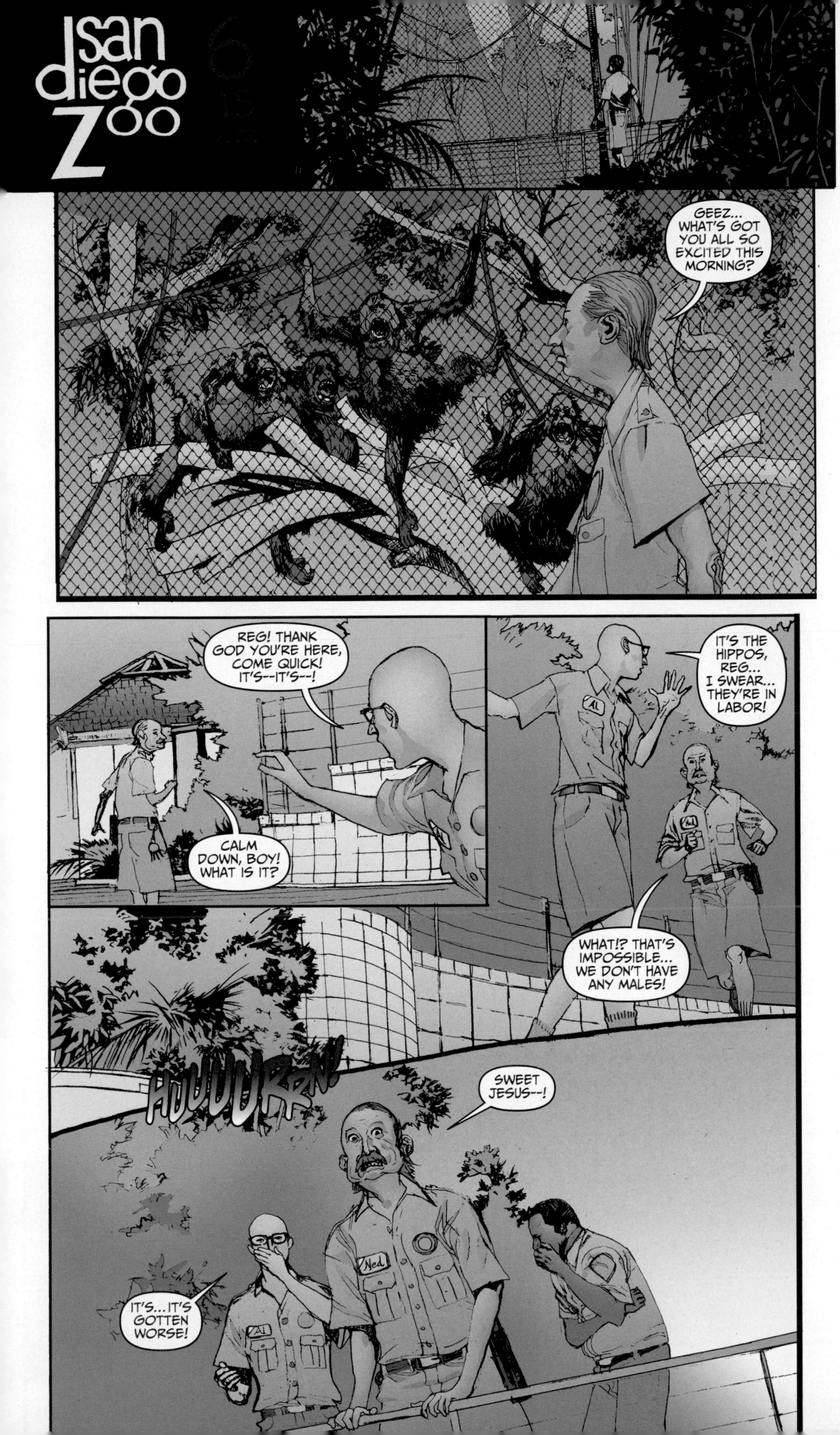
San Diego Zoo
6 15
GEEZ... WHAT'S GOT YOU ALL SO EXCITED THIS MORNING?
REG! THANK GOD YOU'RE HERE, COME QUICK! IT'S--IT'S--!
CALM DOWN, BOY! WHAT IS IT?
IT'S THE HIPPOS, REG... I SWEAR... THEY'RE IN LABOR!
WHAT!? THAT'S IMPOSSIBLE... WE DON'T HAVE ANY MALES!
HUUURRN!
SWEET JESUS--!
IT'S...IT'S GOTTEN WORSE!
AL
NED

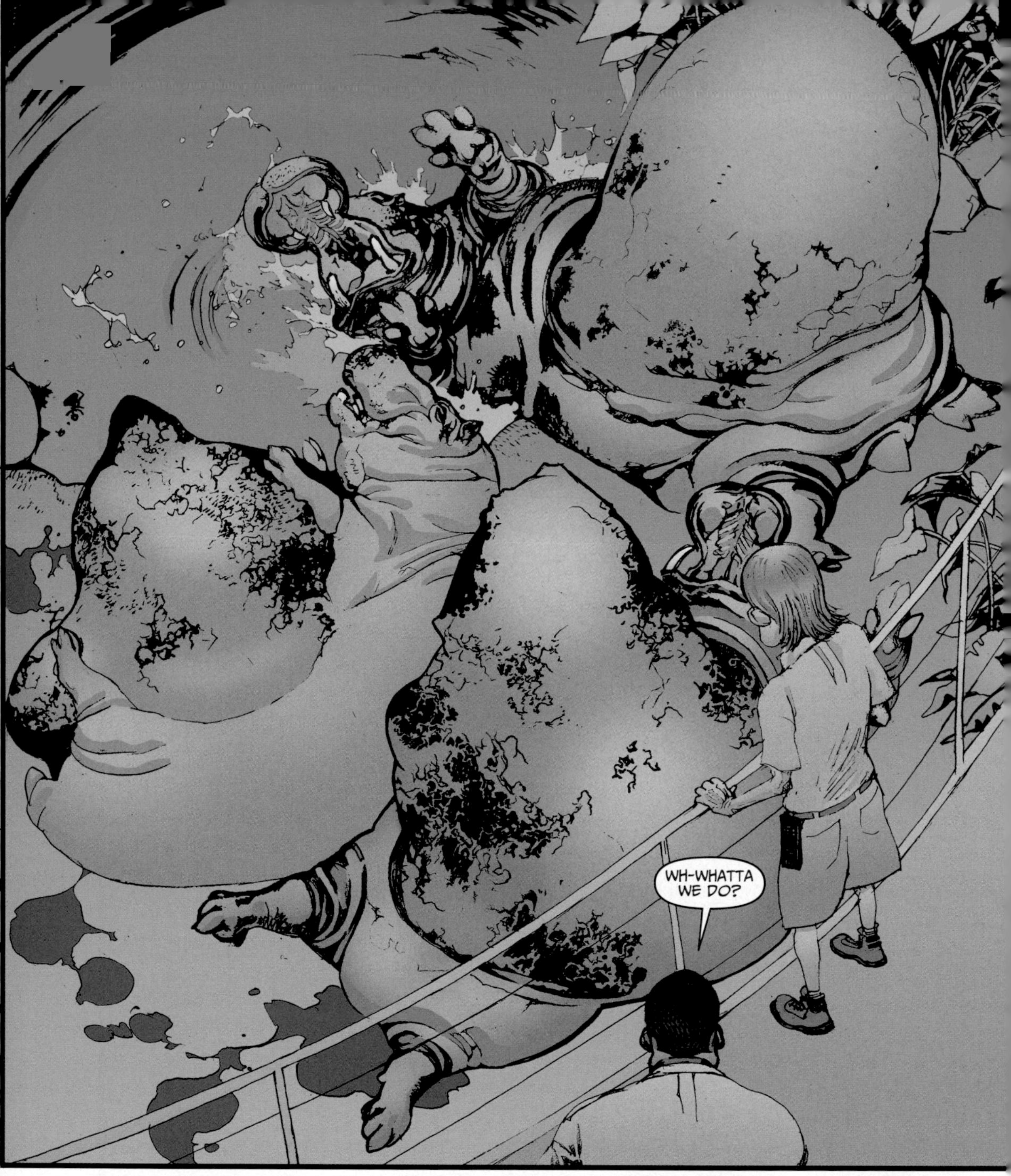
WH-WHATTA WE DO?

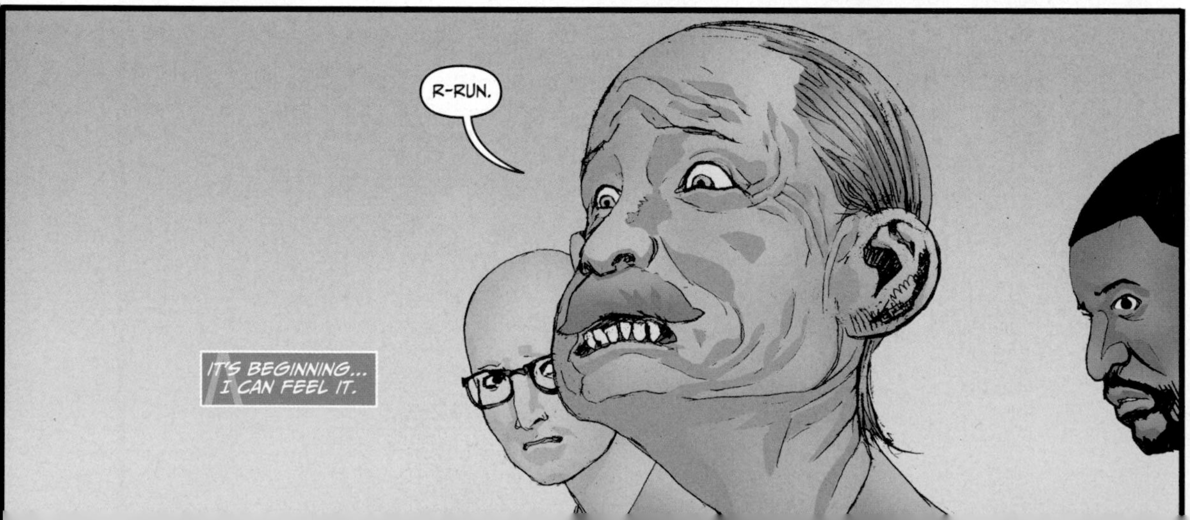
R-RUN.
IT'S BEGINNING... I CAN FEEL IT.

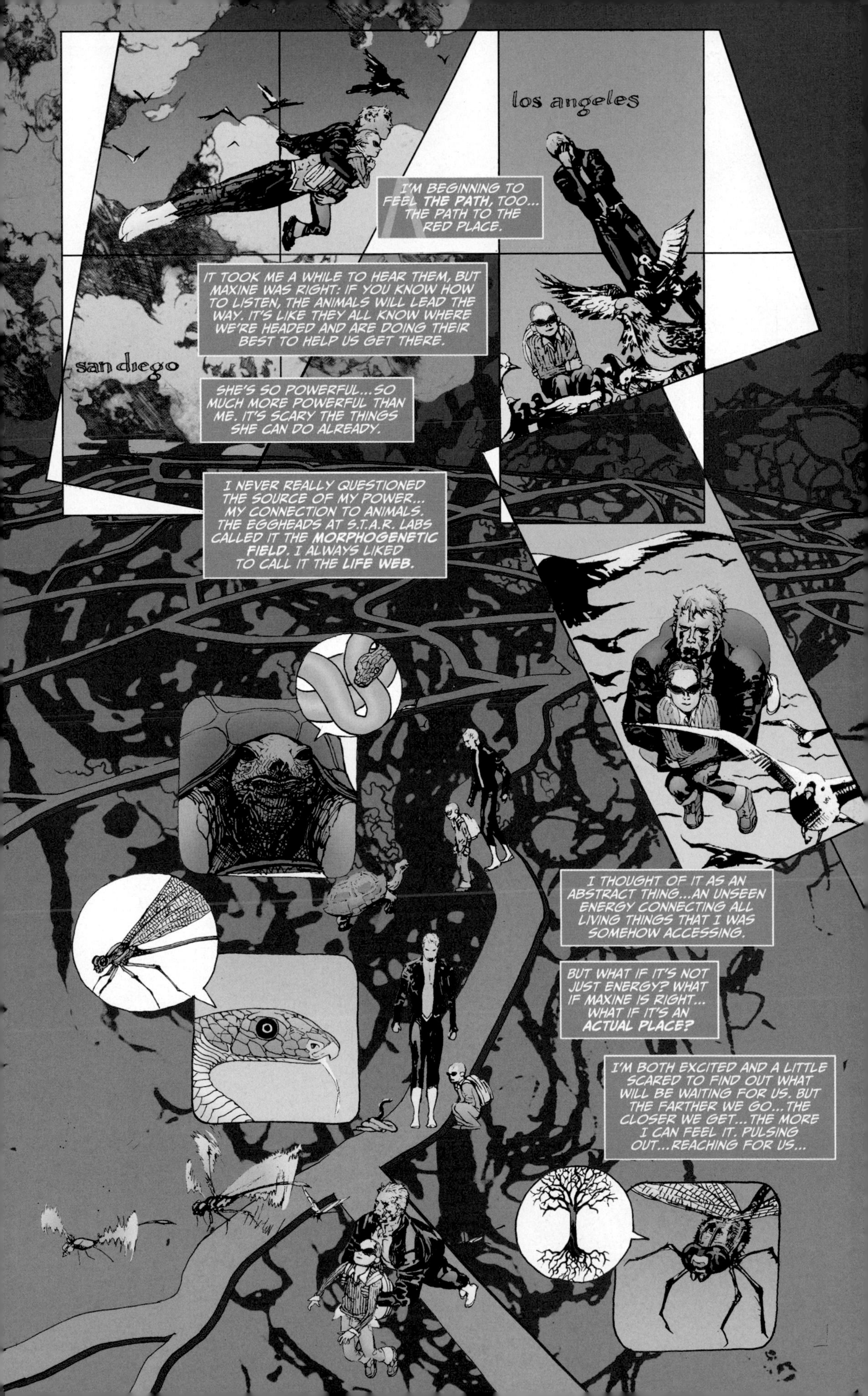

los angeles
I'M BEGINNING TO FEEL THE PATH, TOO... THE PATH TO THE RED PLACE.
IT TOOK ME A WHILE TO HEAR THEM, BUT MAXINE WAS RIGHT: IF YOU KNOW HOW TO LISTEN, THE ANIMALS WILL LEAD THE WAY. IT'S LIKE THEY ALL KNOW WHERE WE'RE HEADED AND ARE DOING THEIR BEST TO HELP US GET THERE.
san diego
SHE'S SO POWERFUL...SO MUCH MORE POWERFUL THAN ME. IT'S SCARY THE THINGS SHE CAN DO ALREADY.
I NEVER REALLY QUESTIONED THE SOURCE OF MY POWER... MY CONNECTION TO ANIMALS. THE EGGHEADS AT S.T.A.R. LABS CALLED IT THE MORPHOGENETIC FIELD. I ALWAYS LIKED TO CALL IT THE LIFE WEB.
I THOUGHT OF IT AS AN ABSTRACT THING...AN UNSEEN ENERGY CONNECTING ALL LIVING THINGS THAT I WAS SOMEHOW ACCESSING.
BUT WHAT IF IT'S NOT JUST ENERGY? WHAT IF MAXINE IS RIGHT... WHAT IF IT'S AN ACTUAL PLACE?
I'M BOTH EXCITED AND A LITTLE SCARED TO FIND OUT WHAT WILL BE WAITING FOR US. BUT THE FARTHER WE GO...THE CLOSER WE GET...THE MORE I CAN FEEL IT. PULSING OUT...REACHING FOR US...

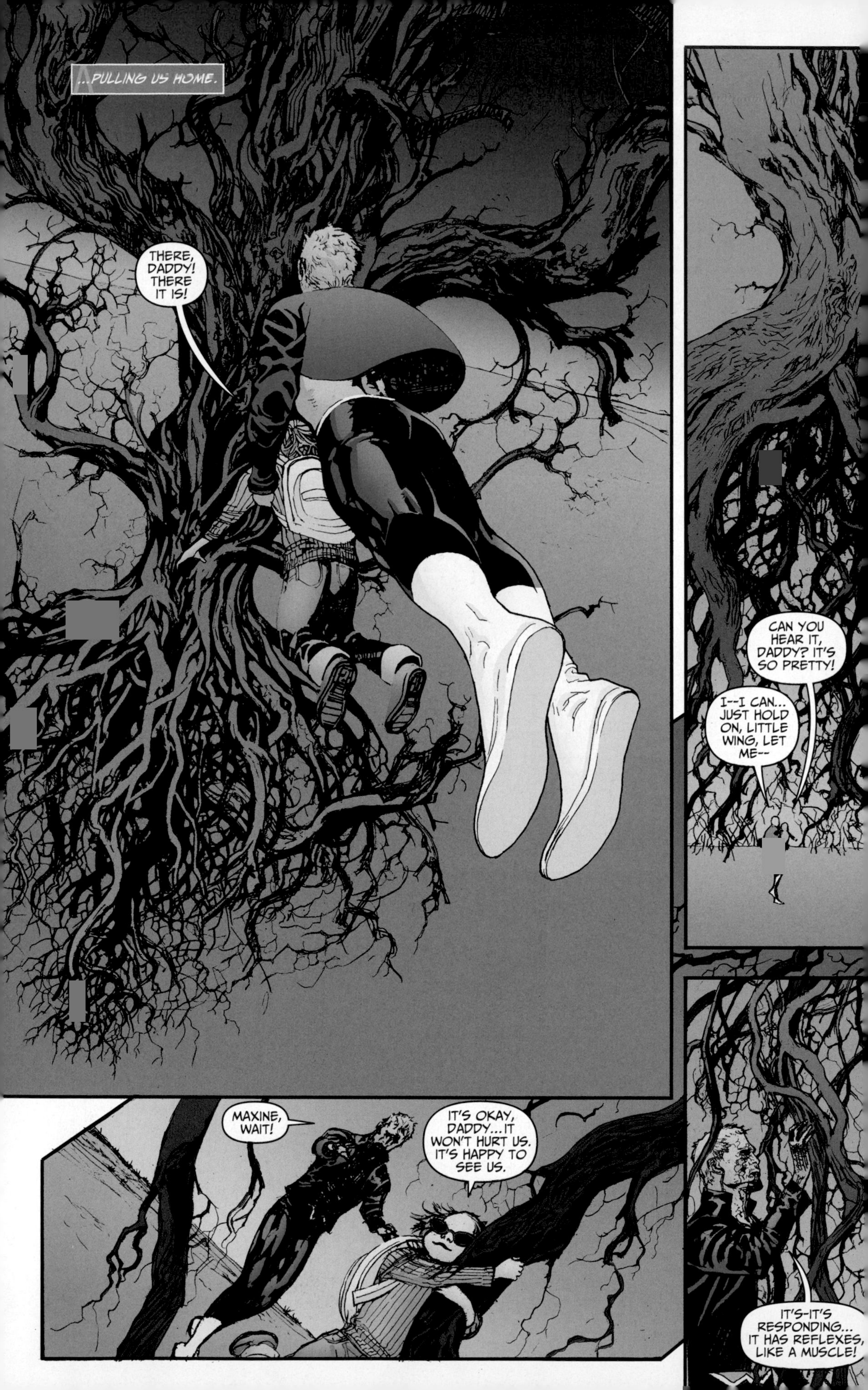
...PULLING US HOME.
THERE, DADDY! THERE IT IS!
CAN YOU HEAR IT, DADDY? IT'S SO PRETTY!
I--I CAN... JUST HOLD ON, LITTLE WING, LET ME--
MAXINE, WAIT!
IT'S OKAY, DADDY... IT WON'T HURT US. IT'S HAPPY TO SEE US.
IT'S-IT'S RESPONDING... IT HAS REFLEXES, LIKE A MUSCLE!

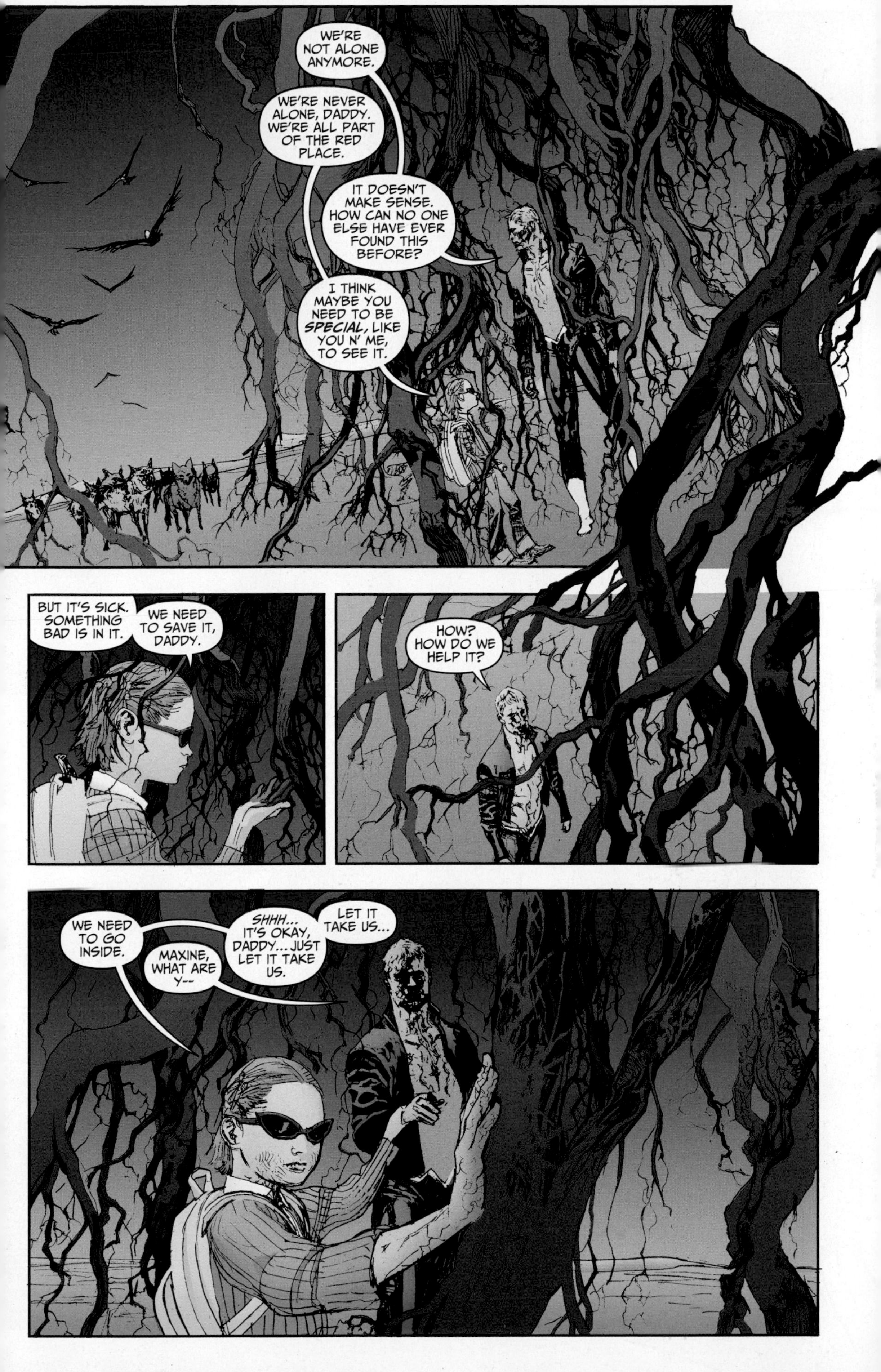
WE'RE NOT ALONE ANYMORE.
WE'RE NEVER ALONE, DADDY. WE'RE ALL PART OF THE RED PLACE.
IT DOESN'T MAKE SENSE. HOW CAN NO ONE ELSE HAVE EVER FOUND THIS BEFORE?
I THINK MAYBE YOU NEED TO BE ***SPECIAL,*** LIKE YOU N' ME, TO SEE IT.
BUT IT'S SICK. SOMETHING BAD IS IN IT.
WE NEED TO SAVE IT, DADDY.
HOW? HOW DO WE HELP IT?
WE NEED TO GO INSIDE.
MAXINE, WHAT ARE Y--
SHHH... IT'S OKAY, DADDY... JUST LET IT TAKE US.
LET IT TAKE US...

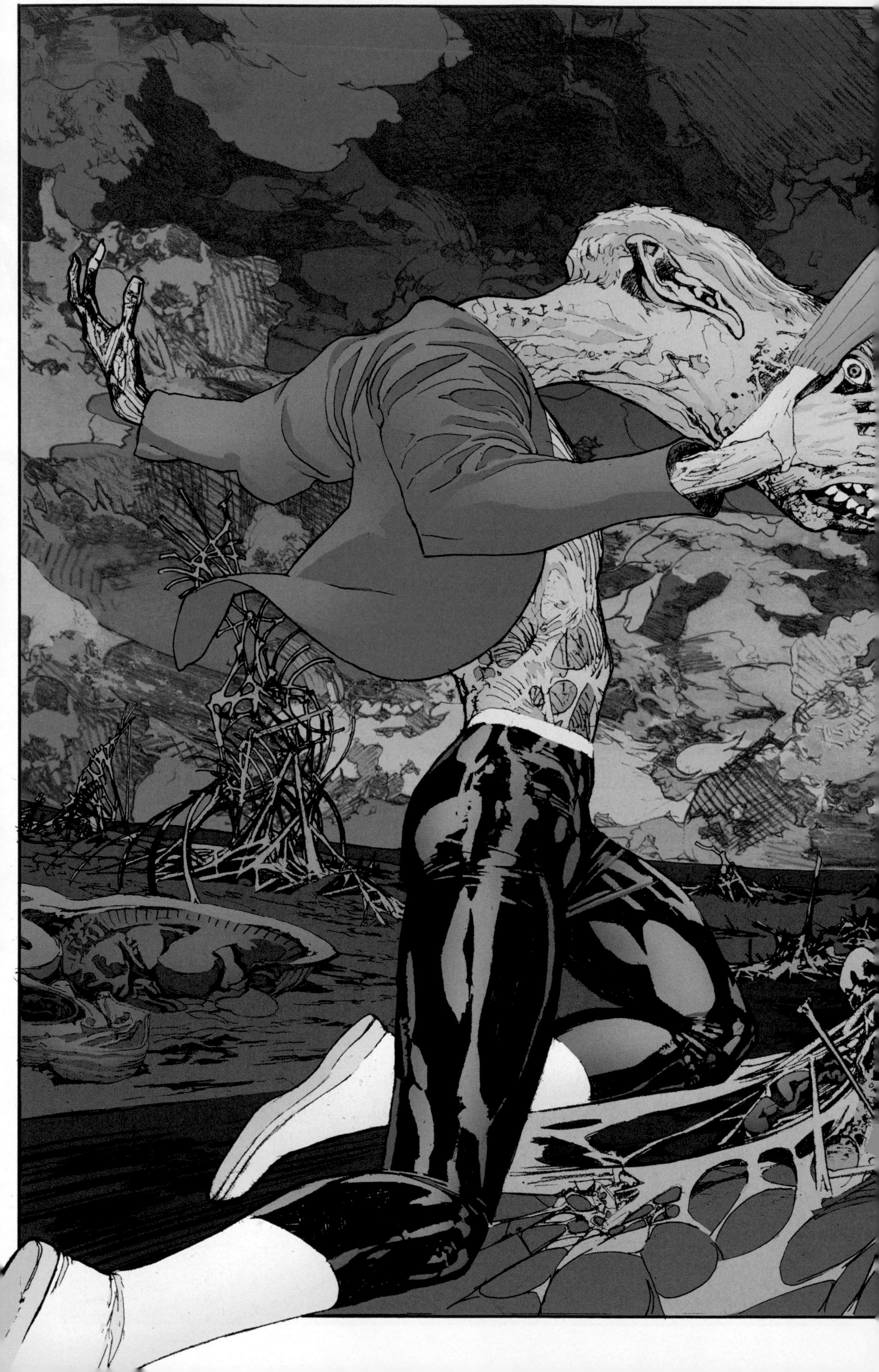

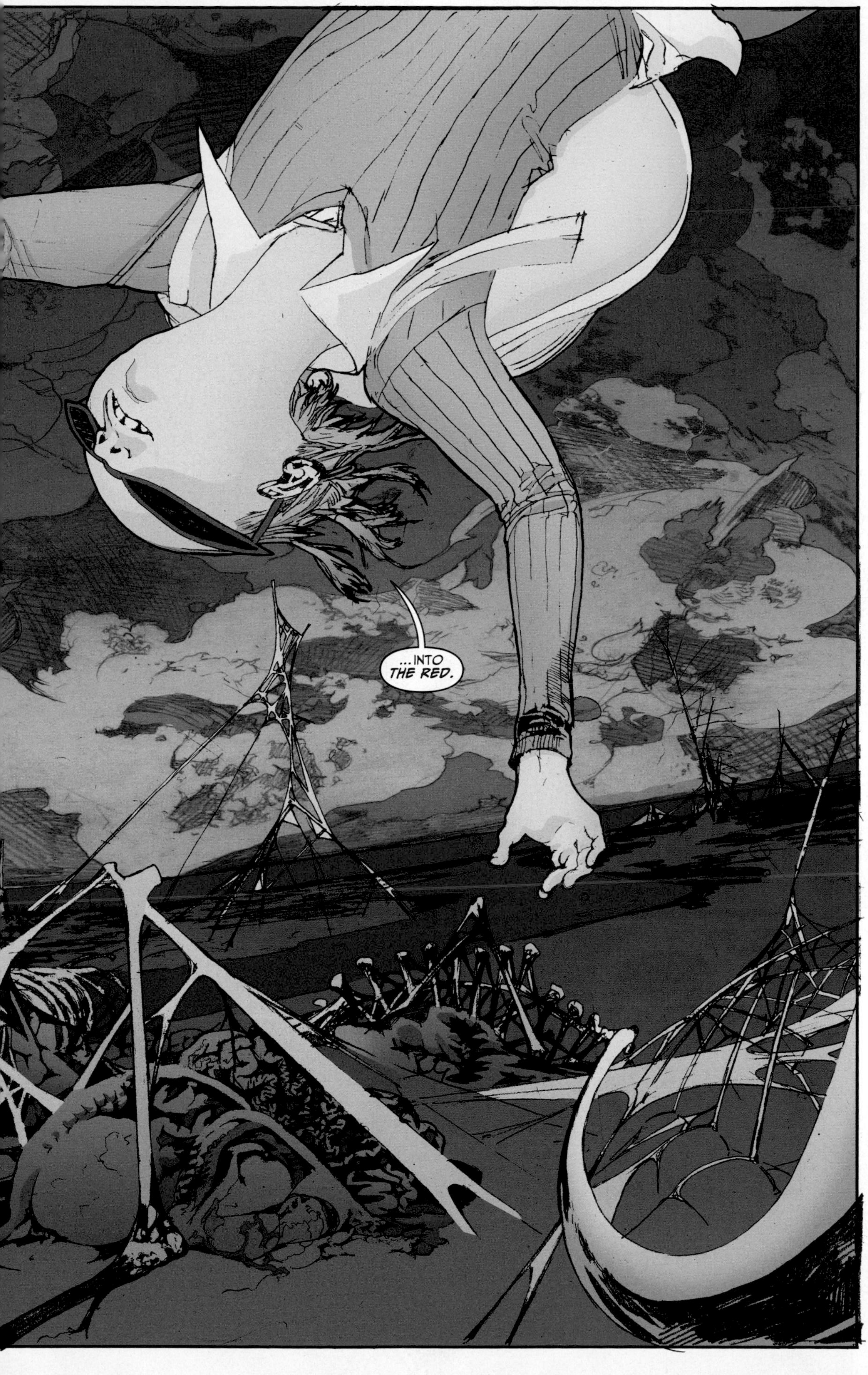
...INTO THE RED.

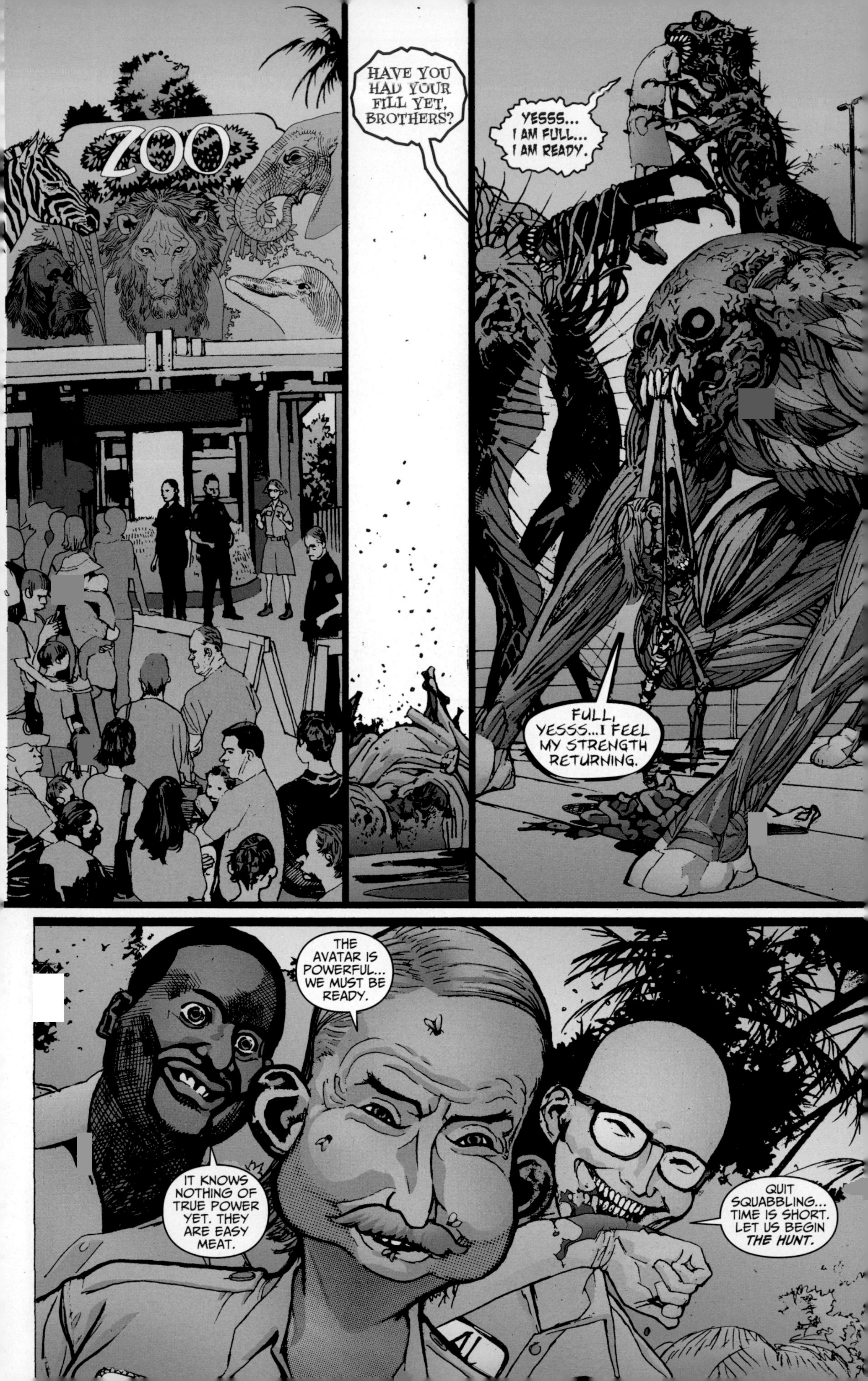
ZOO
HAVE YOU HAD YOUR FILL YET, BROTHERS?
YESSS... I AM FULL... I AM READY.
FULL, YESSS...I FEEL MY STRENGTH RETURNING.
THE AVATAR IS POWERFUL... WE MUST BE READY.
IT KNOWS NOTHING OF TRUE POWER YET. THEY ARE EASY MEAT.
QUIT SQUABBLING... TIME IS SHORT. LET US BEGIN *THE HUNT*.

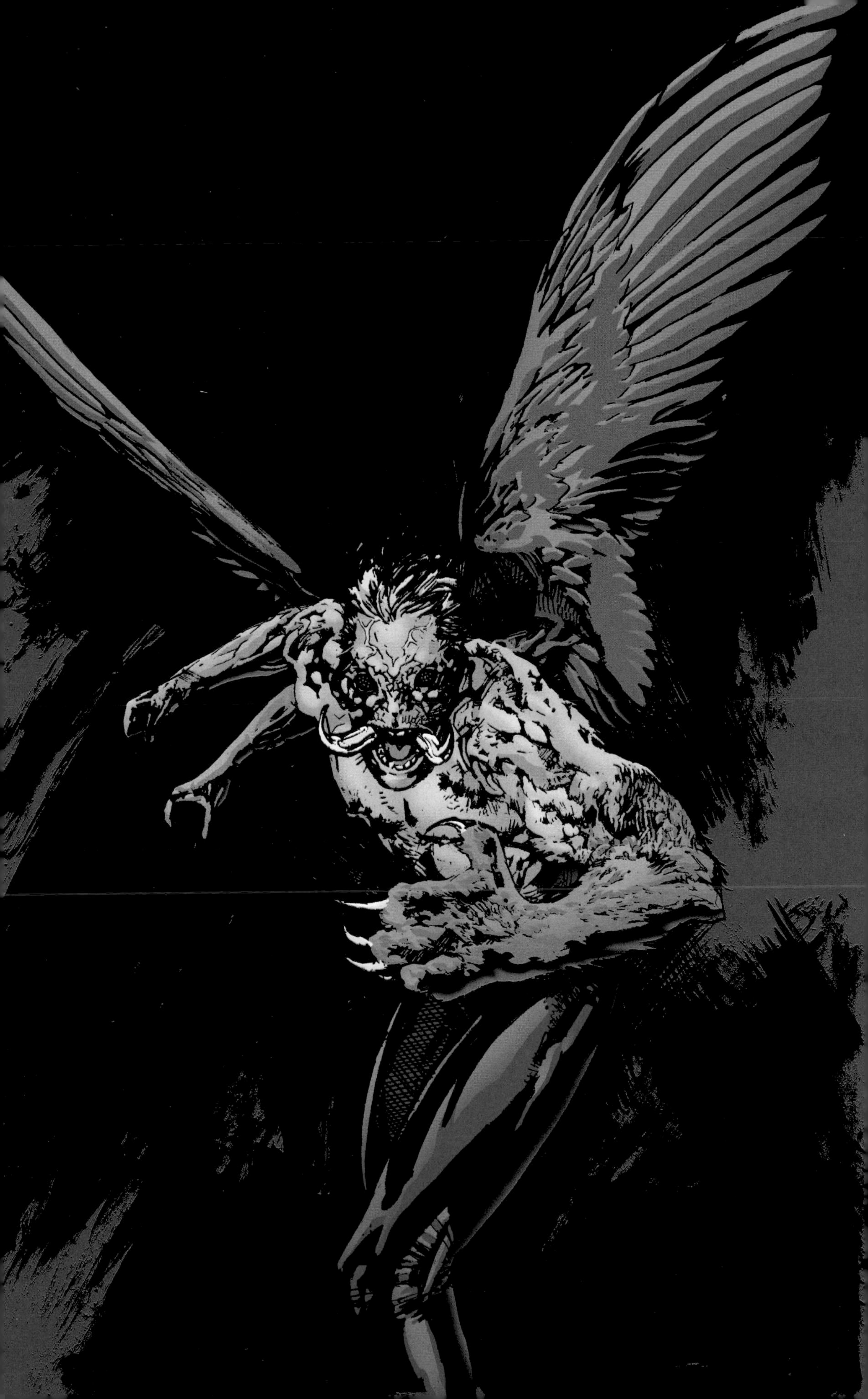

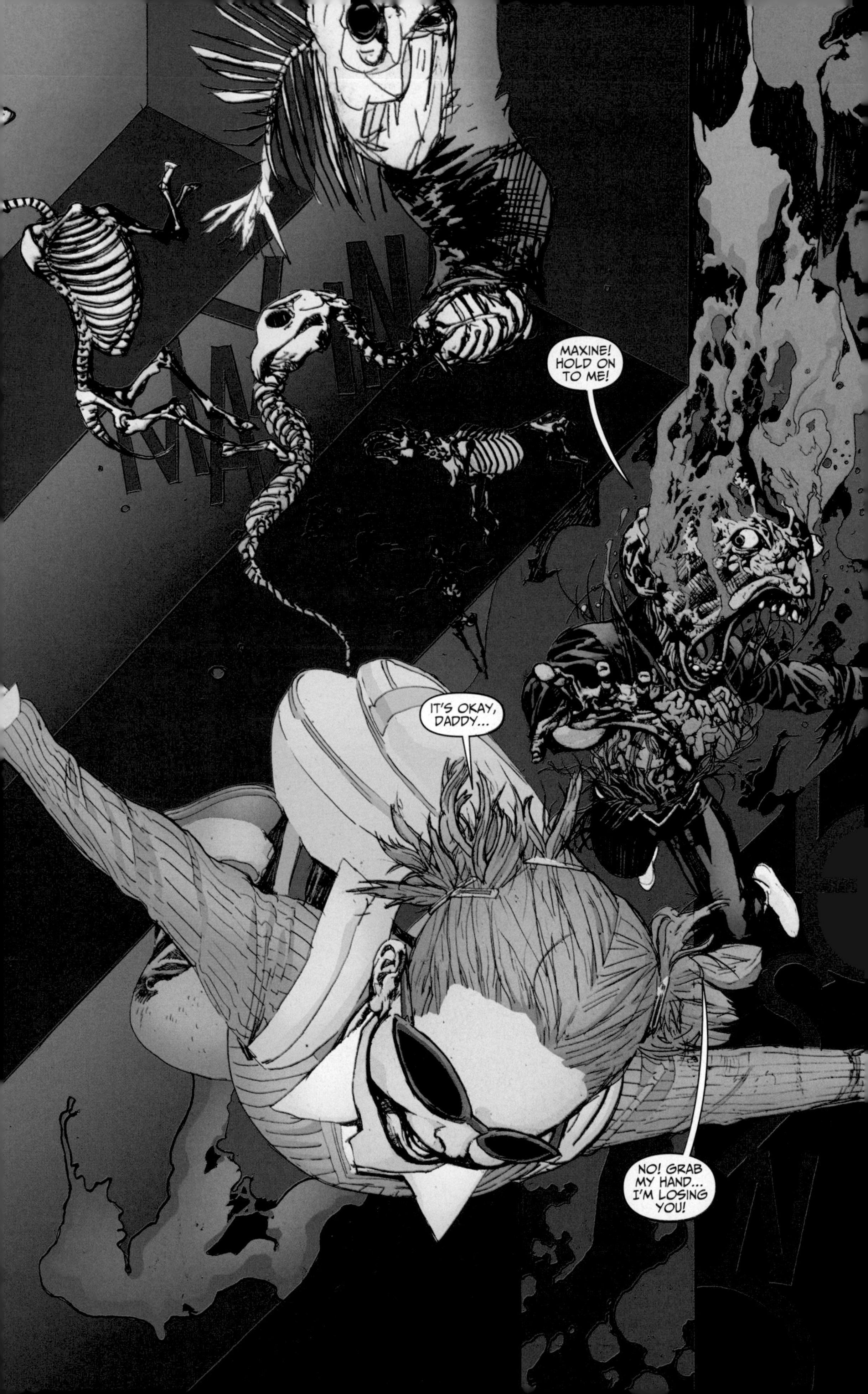
MAXINE! HOLD ON TO ME!
IT'S OKAY, DADDY...
NO! GRAB MY HAND... I'M LOSING YOU!

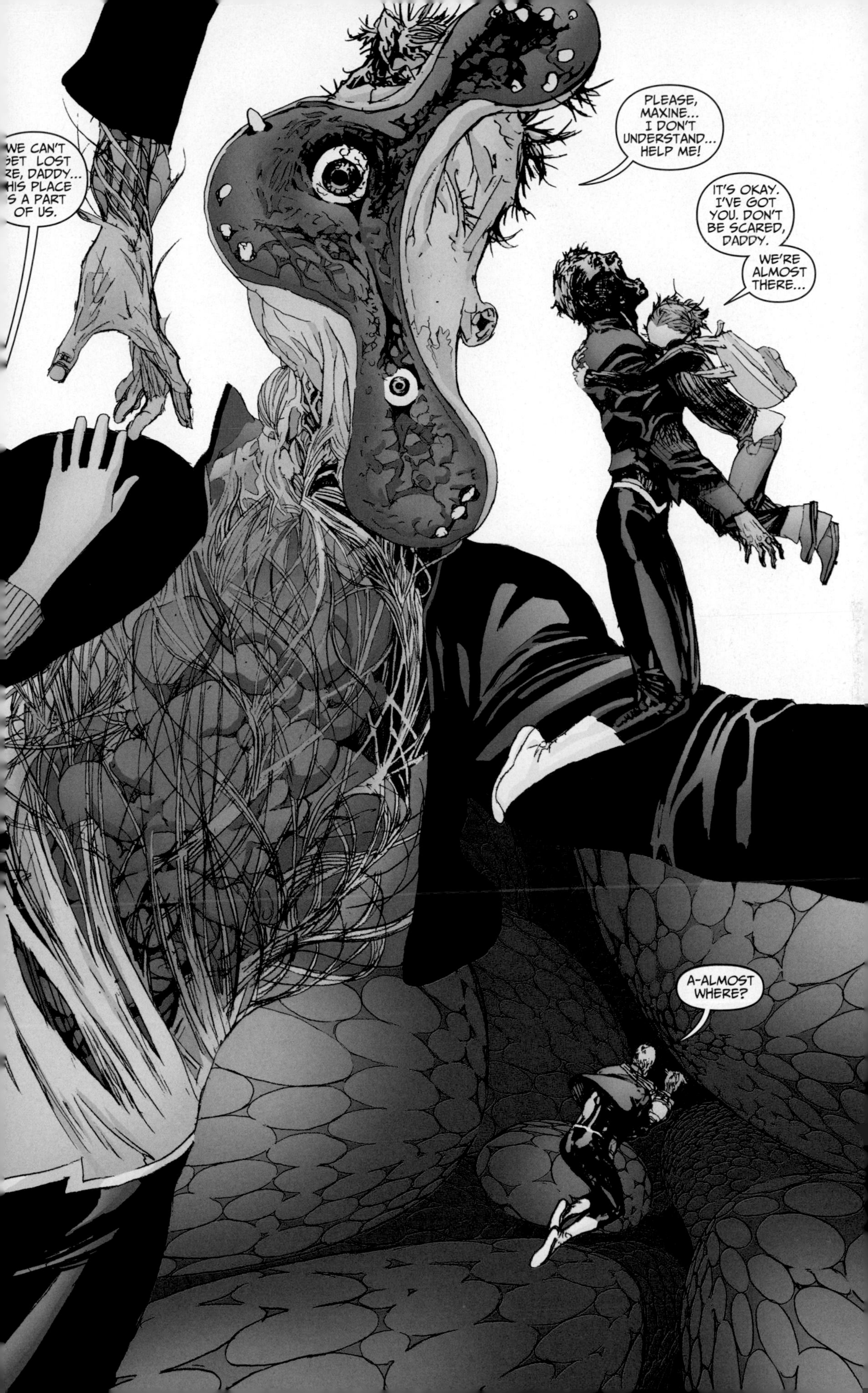
WE CAN'T GET LOST RE, DADDY... HIS PLACE S A PART OF US.
PLEASE, MAXINE... I DON'T UNDERSTAND... HELP ME!
IT'S OKAY. I'VE GOT YOU. DON'T BE SCARED, DADDY.
WE'RE ALMOST THERE...
A-ALMOST WHERE?

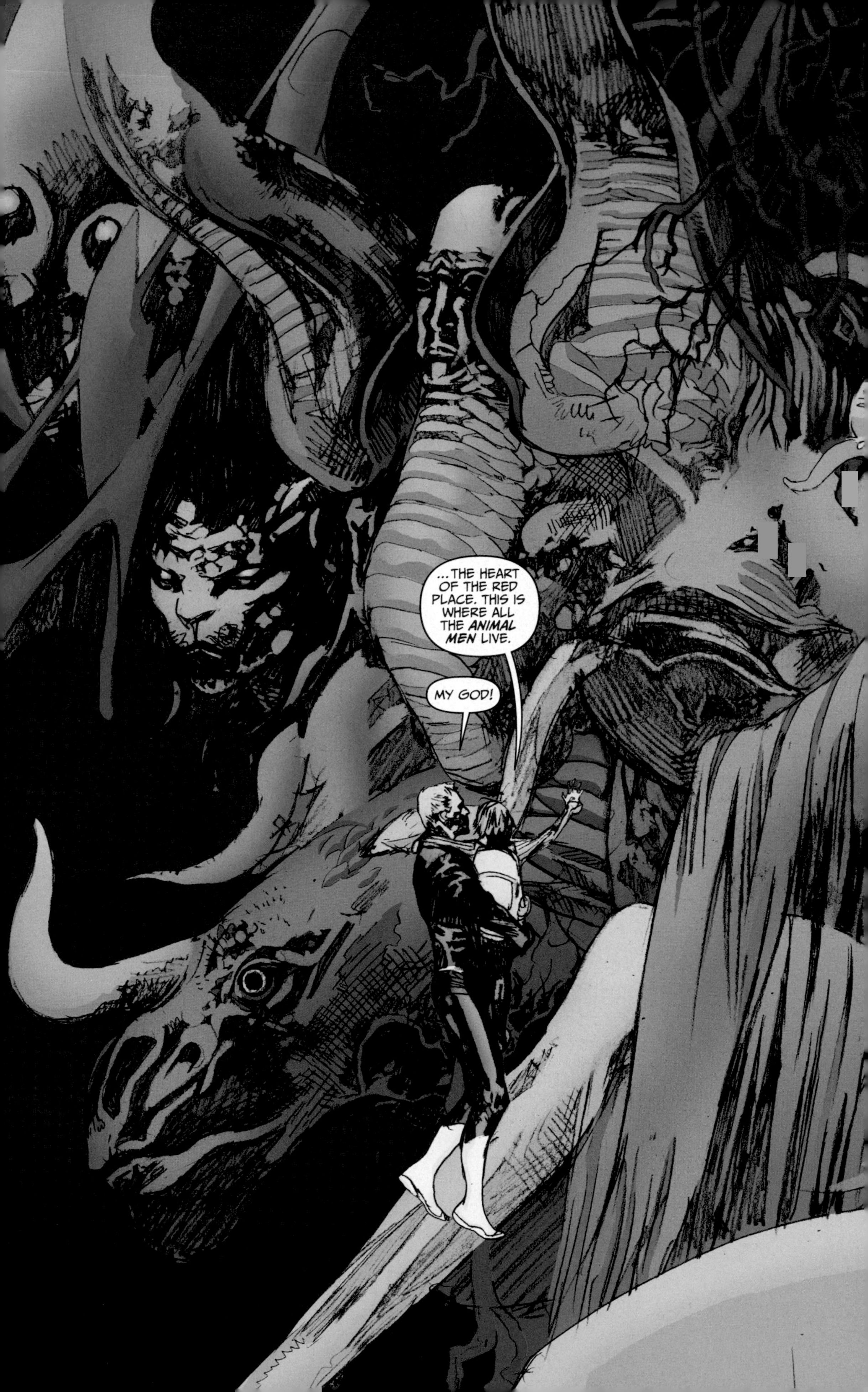
...THE HEART OF THE RED PLACE. THIS IS WHERE ALL THE ANIMAL MEN LIVE.
MY GOD!

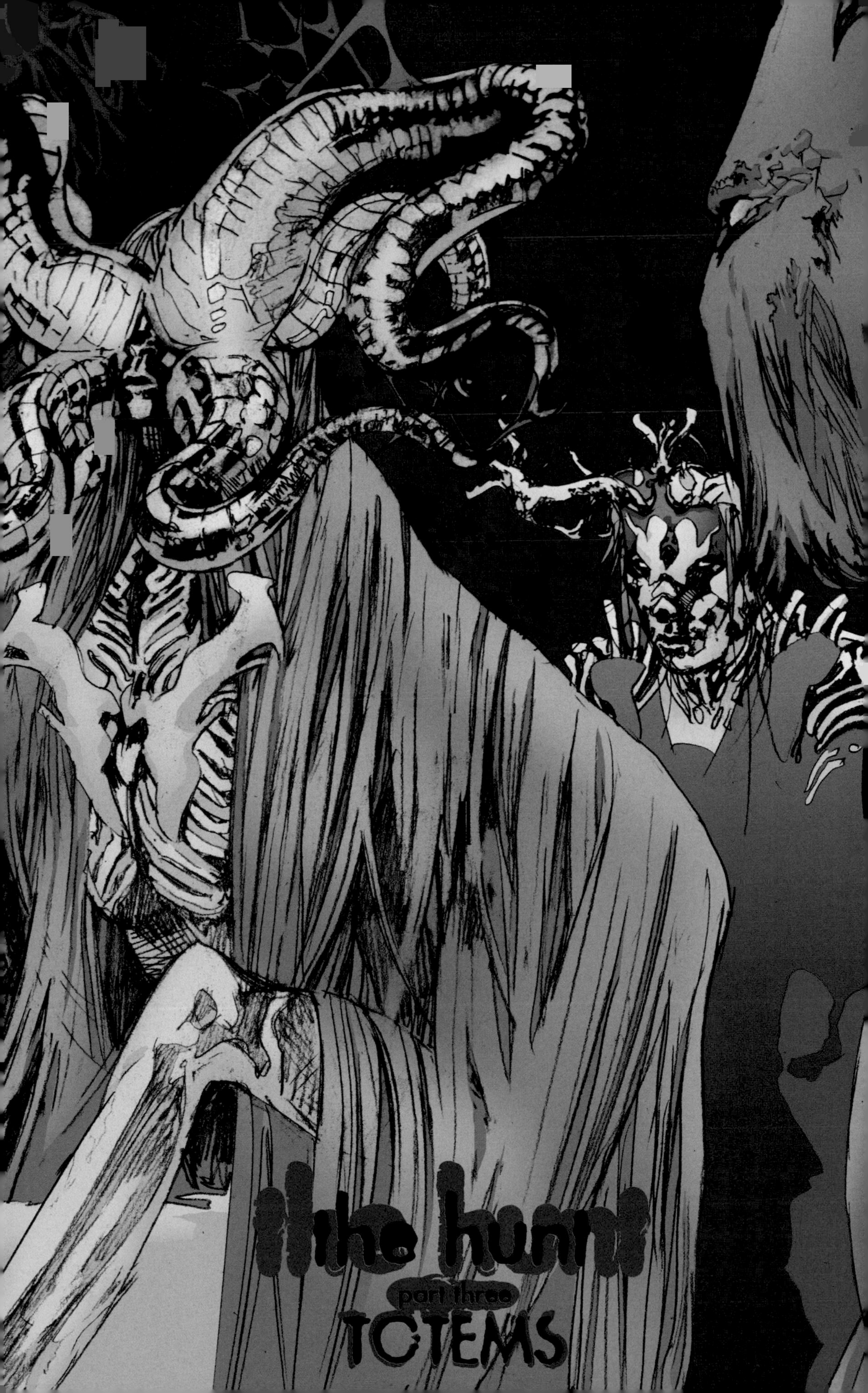

the hunt
part three
TOTEMS

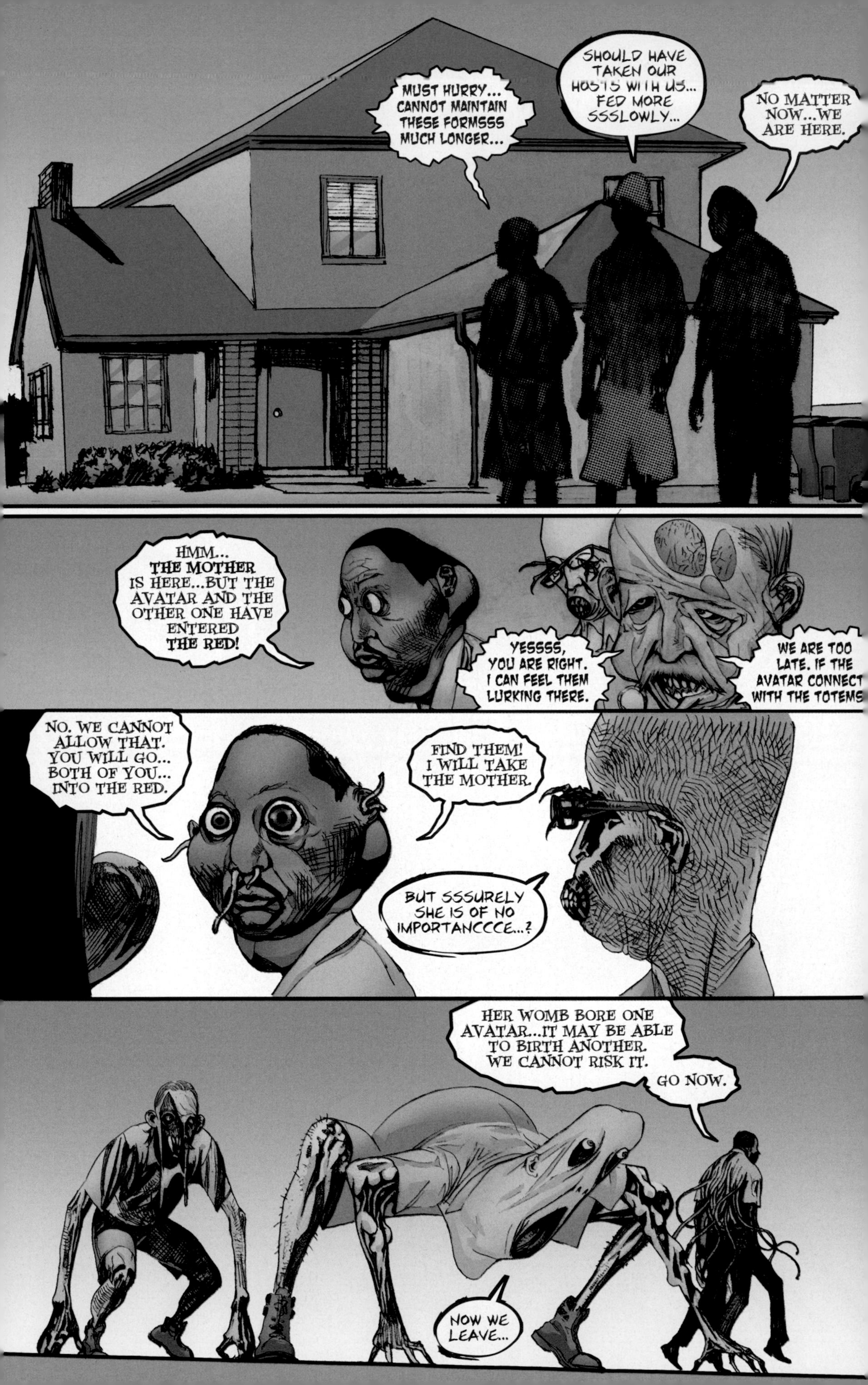
MUST HURRY... CANNOT MAINTAIN THESE FORMSSS MUCH LONGER...
SHOULD HAVE TAKEN OUR HOSTS WITH US... FED MORE SSSLOWLY...
NO MATTER NOW...WE ARE HERE.
HMM... THE MOTHER IS HERE...BUT THE AVATAR AND THE OTHER ONE HAVE ENTERED THE RED!
YESSSS, YOU ARE RIGHT. I CAN FEEL THEM LURKING THERE.
WE ARE TOO LATE. IF THE AVATAR CONNECT WITH THE TOTEMS
NO. WE CANNOT ALLOW THAT. YOU WILL GO... BOTH OF YOU... INTO THE RED.
FIND THEM! I WILL TAKE THE MOTHER.
BUT SSSURELY SHE IS OF NO IMPORTANCCCE...?
HER WOMB BORE ONE AVATAR...IT MAY BE ABLE TO BIRTH ANOTHER. WE CANNOT RISK IT.
GO NOW.
NOW WE LEAVE...

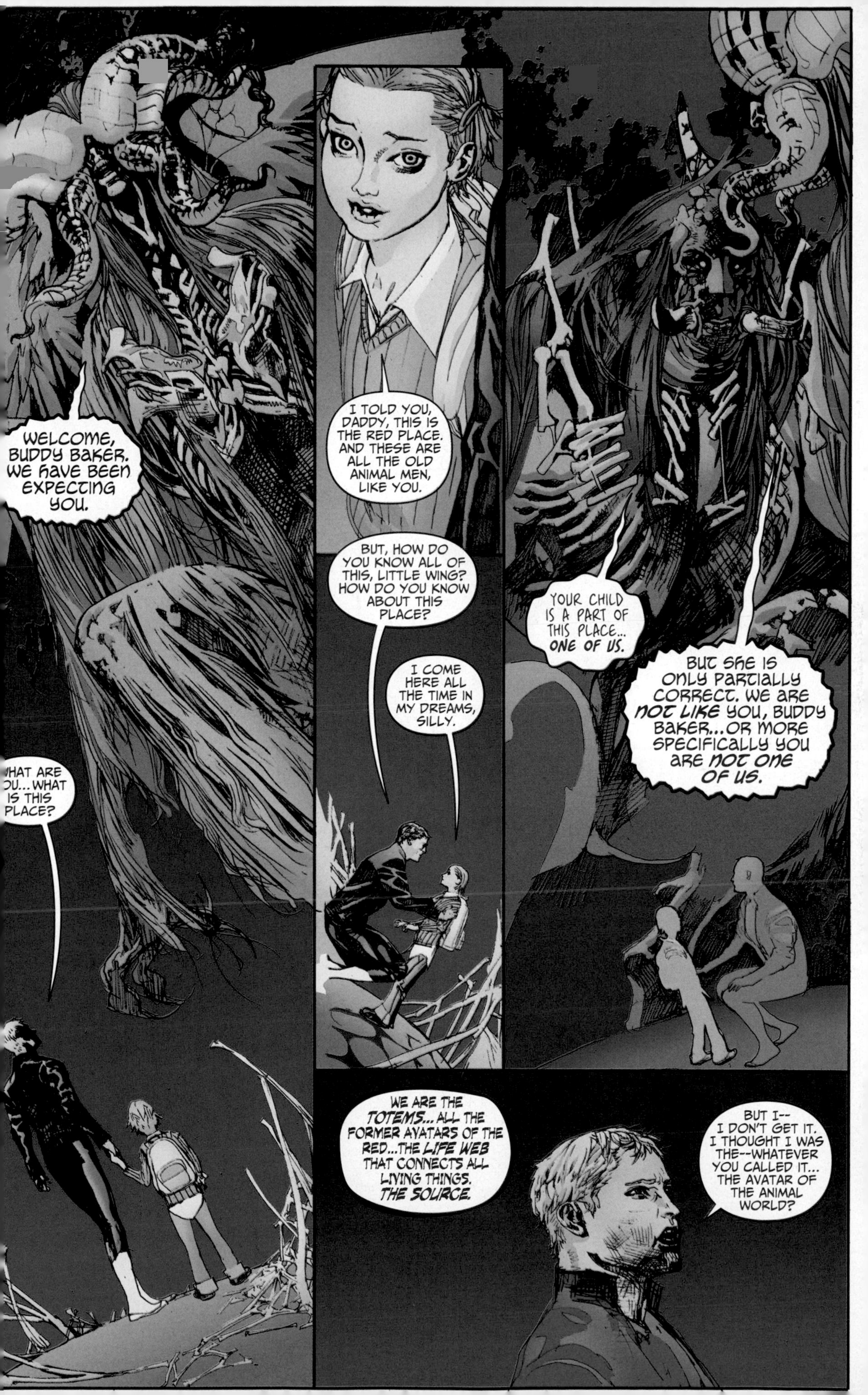
WELCOME, BUDDY BAKER. WE HAVE BEEN EXPECTING YOU.
I TOLD YOU, DADDY, THIS IS THE RED PLACE. AND THESE ARE ALL THE OLD ANIMAL MEN, LIKE YOU.
YOUR CHILD IS A PART OF THIS PLACE... ONE OF US.
BUT SHE IS ONLY PARTIALLY CORRECT. WE ARE NOT LIKE YOU, BUDDY BAKER...OR MORE SPECIFICALLY YOU ARE NOT ONE OF US.
WHAT ARE YOU...WHAT IS THIS PLACE?
BUT, HOW DO YOU KNOW ALL OF THIS, LITTLE WING? HOW DO YOU KNOW ABOUT THIS PLACE?
I COME HERE ALL THE TIME IN MY DREAMS, SILLY.
WE ARE THE TOTEMS... ALL THE FORMER AVATARS OF THE RED...THE LIFE WEB THAT CONNECTS ALL LIVING THINGS. THE SOURCE.
BUT I-- I DON'T GET IT. I THOUGHT I WAS THE--WHATEVER YOU CALLED IT... THE AVATAR OF THE ANIMAL WORLD?

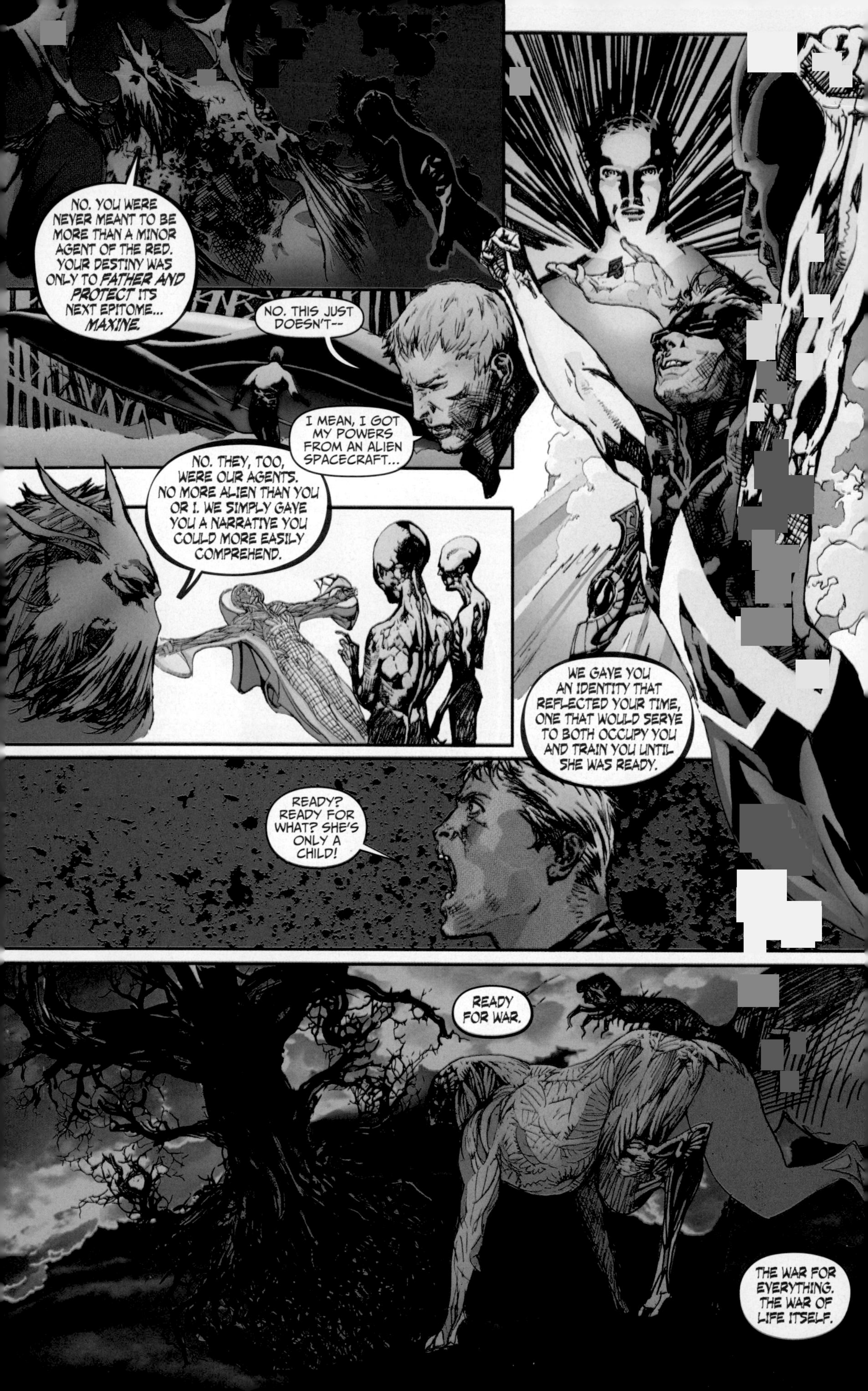
NO. YOU WERE NEVER MEANT TO BE MORE THAN A MINOR AGENT OF THE RED. YOUR DESTINY WAS ONLY TO *FATHER AND PROTECT* ITS NEXT EPITOME... *MAXINE.*
NO. THIS JUST DOESN'T--
I MEAN, I GOT MY POWERS FROM AN ALIEN SPACECRAFT...
NO. THEY, TOO, WERE OUR AGENTS. NO MORE ALIEN THAN YOU OR I. WE SIMPLY GAVE YOU A NARRATIVE YOU COULD MORE EASILY COMPREHEND.
WE GAVE YOU AN IDENTITY THAT REFLECTED YOUR TIME, ONE THAT WOULD SERVE TO BOTH OCCUPY YOU AND TRAIN YOU UNTIL SHE WAS READY.
READY? READY FOR WHAT? SHE'S ONLY A CHILD!
READY FOR WAR.
THE WAR FOR EVERYTHING. THE WAR OF LIFE ITSELF.

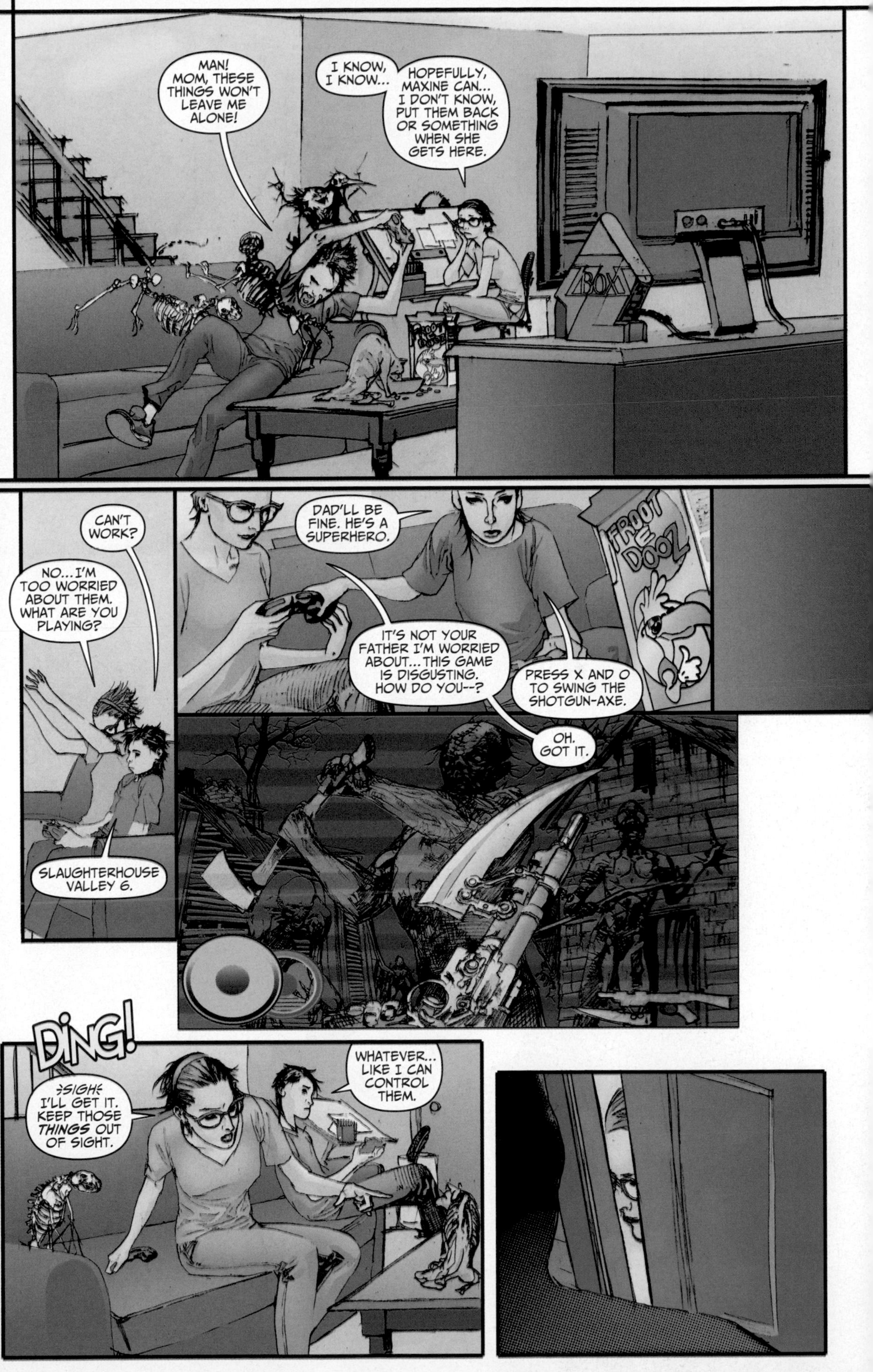

MAN! MOM, THESE THINGS WON'T LEAVE ME ALONE!
I KNOW, I KNOW...
HOPEFULLY, MAXINE CAN... I DON'T KNOW, PUT THEM BACK OR SOMETHING WHEN SHE GETS HERE.
ZBOX
CAN'T WORK?
NO... I'M TOO WORRIED ABOUT THEM. WHAT ARE YOU PLAYING?
SLAUGHTERHOUSE VALLEY 6.
DAD'LL BE FINE. HE'S A SUPERHERO.
FROOT DOOZ
IT'S NOT YOUR FATHER I'M WORRIED ABOUT... THIS GAME IS DISGUSTING. HOW DO YOU--?
PRESS X AND O TO SWING THE SHOTGUN-AXE.
OH. GOT IT.
DING!
SIGH I'LL GET IT. KEEP THOSE *THINGS* OUT OF SIGHT.
WHATEVER... LIKE I CAN CONTROL THEM.

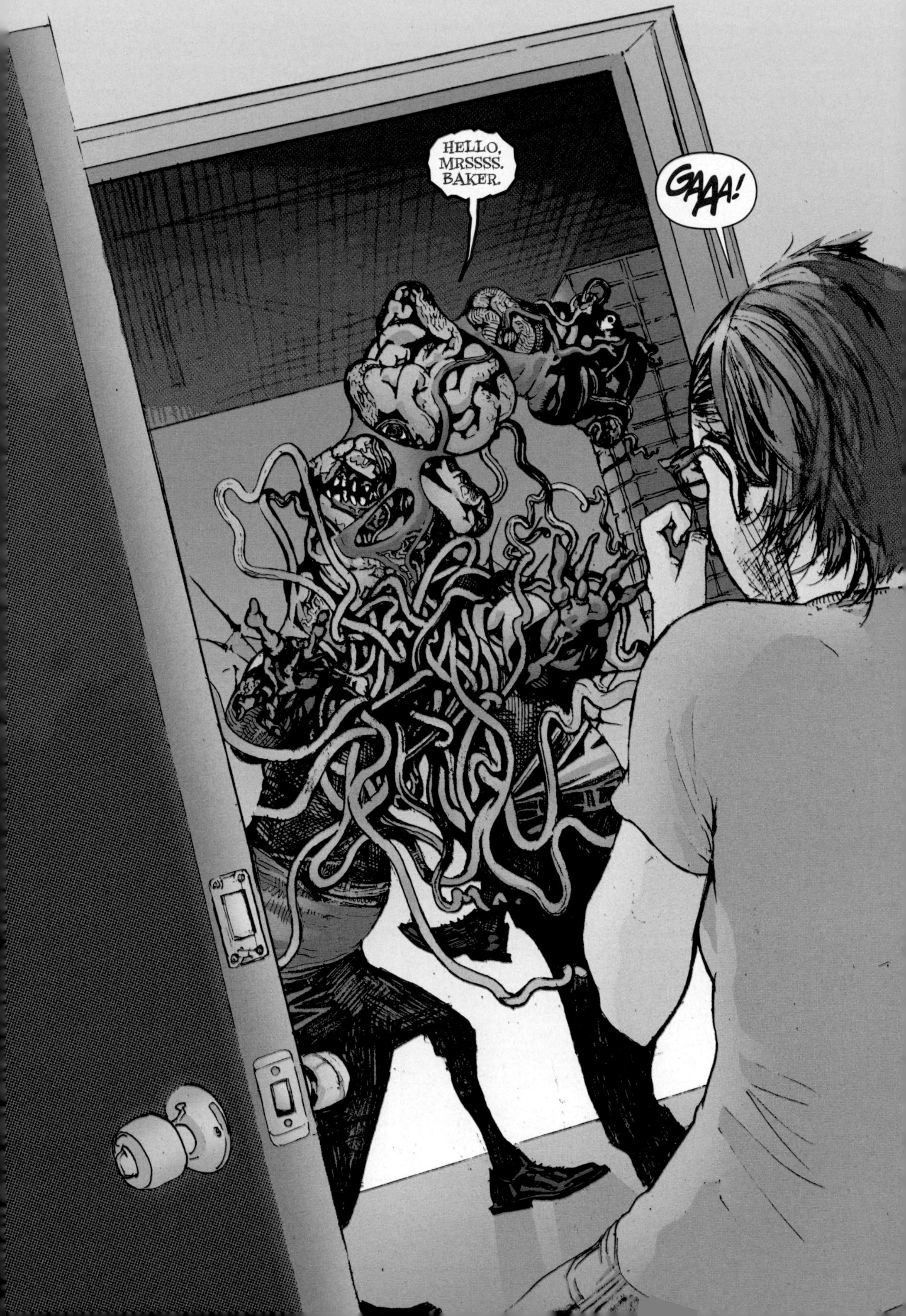
HELLO, MRSSSS. BAKER.
GAAAA!

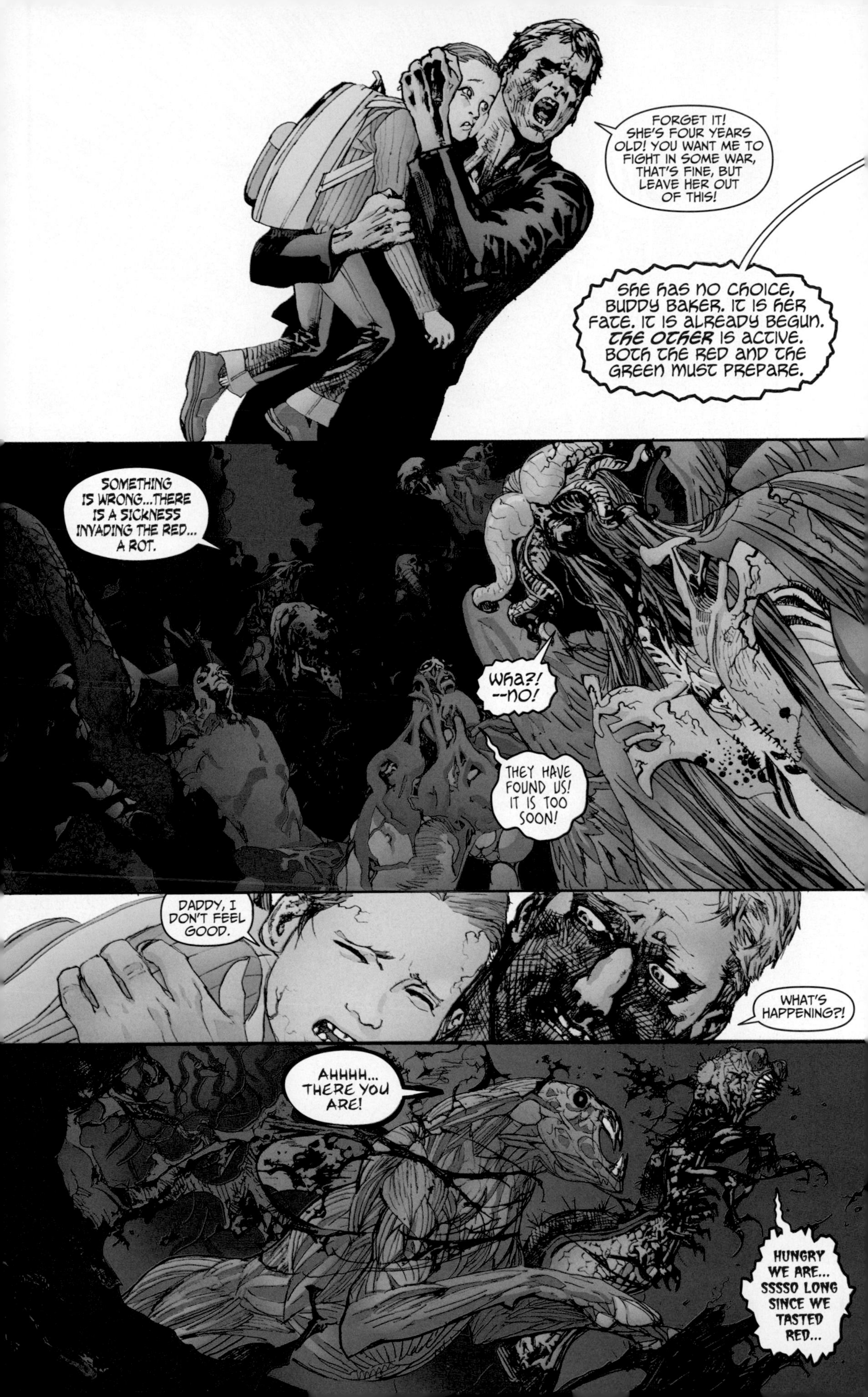
FORGET IT! SHE'S FOUR YEARS OLD! YOU WANT ME TO FIGHT IN SOME WAR, THAT'S FINE, BUT LEAVE HER OUT OF THIS!
SHE HAS NO CHOICE, BUDDY BAKER. IT IS HER FATE. IT IS ALREADY BEGUN. *THE OTHER* IS ACTIVE. BOTH THE RED AND THE GREEN MUST PREPARE.
SOMETHING IS WRONG...THERE IS A SICKNESS INVADING THE RED... A ROT.
WHA?! --NO!
THEY HAVE FOUND US! IT IS TOO SOON!
DADDY, I DON'T FEEL GOOD.
WHAT'S HAPPENING?!
AHHHH... THERE YOU ARE!
HUNGRY WE ARE... SSSSO LONG SINCE WE TASTED RED...

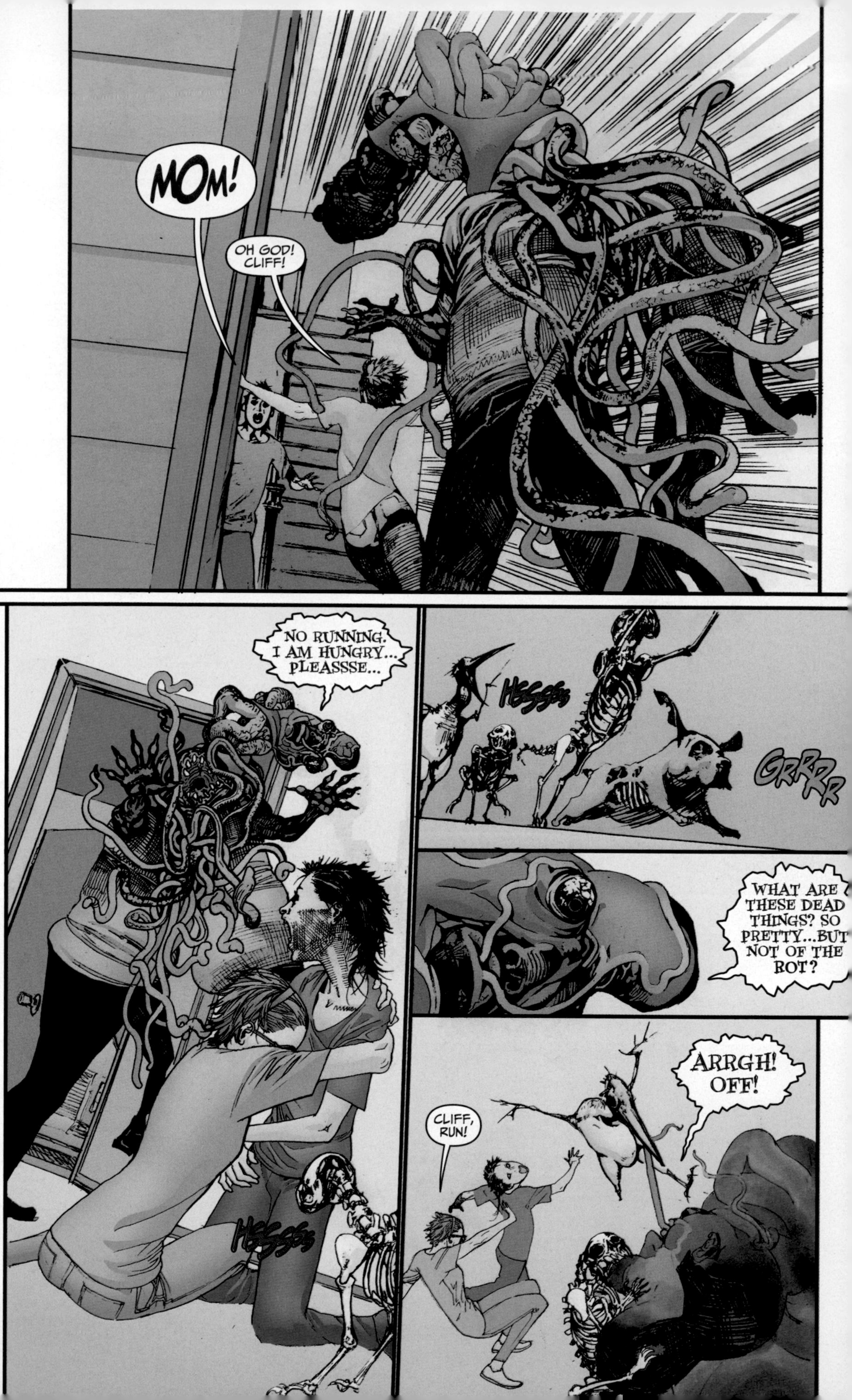
MOM!
OH GOD! CLIFF!
NO RUNNING. I AM HUNGRY... PLEASSSE...
HESSSSS
HESSSS
GRRRR
WHAT ARE THESE DEAD THINGS? SO PRETTY...BUT NOT OF THE ROT?
ARRGH! OFF!
CLIFF, RUN!

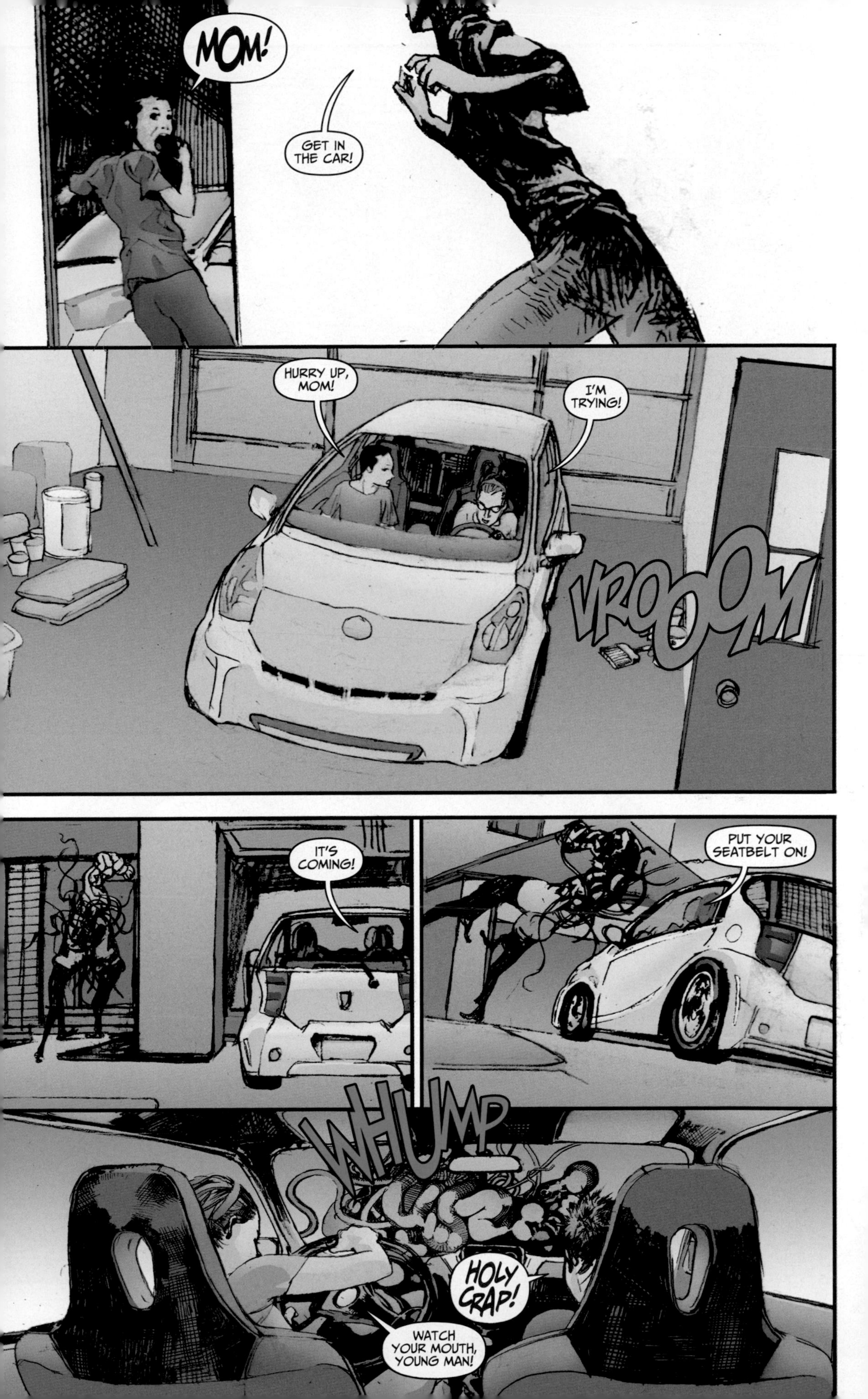
MOM!
GET IN THE CAR!
HURRY UP, MOM!
I'M TRYING!
VROOOM
IT'S COMING!
PUT YOUR SEATBELT ON!
WHUMP
HOLY CRAP!
WATCH YOUR MOUTH, YOUNG MAN!

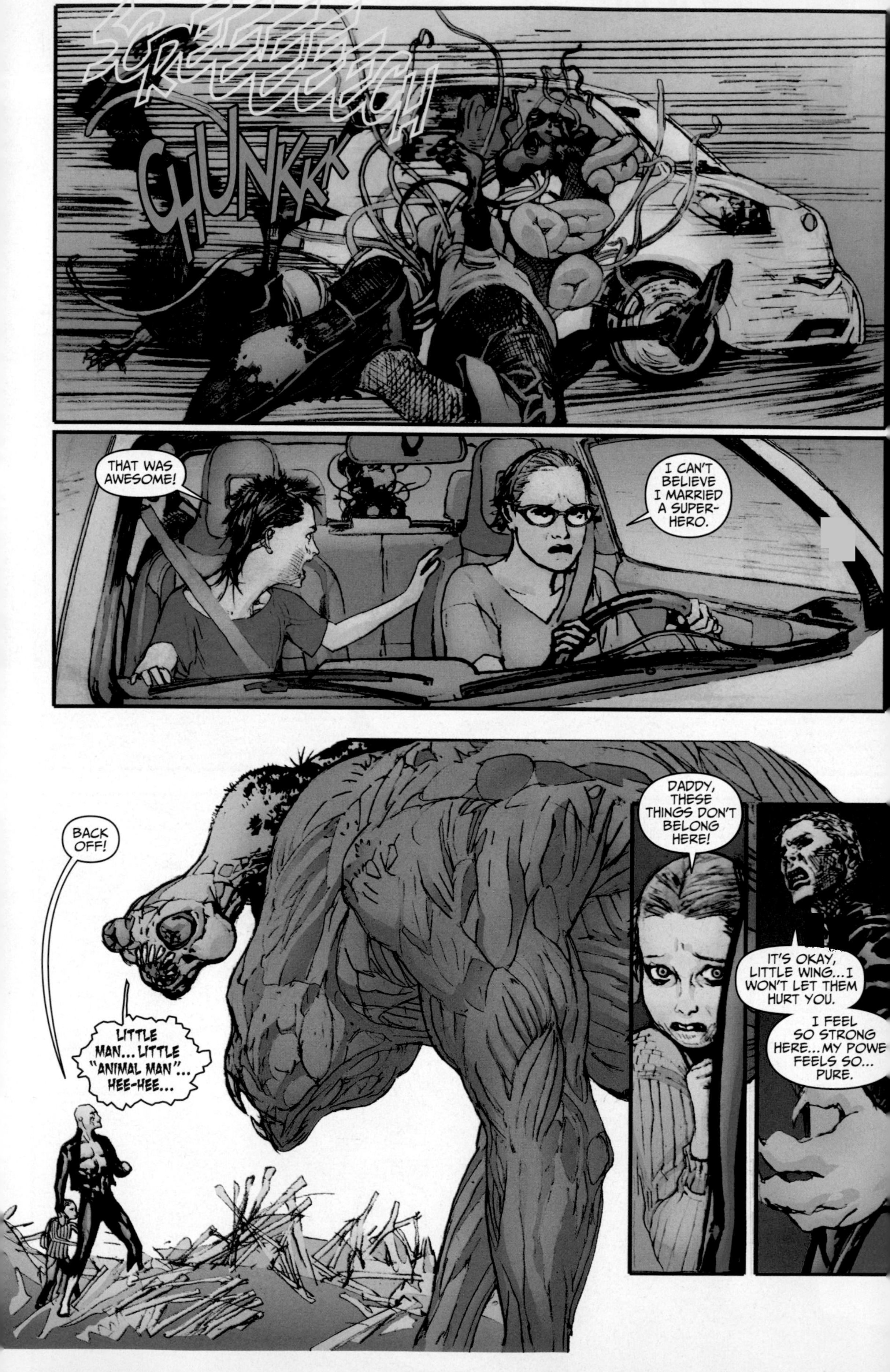
SCREEEEECH
CHUNKKK
THAT WAS AWESOME!
I CAN'T BELIEVE I MARRIED A SUPER-HERO.
BACK OFF!
LITTLE MAN... LITTLE "ANIMAL MAN"... HEE-HEE...
DADDY, THESE THINGS DON'T BELONG HERE!
IT'S OKAY, LITTLE WING... I WON'T LET THEM HURT YOU.
I FEEL SO STRONG HERE... MY POWE FEELS SO... PURE.

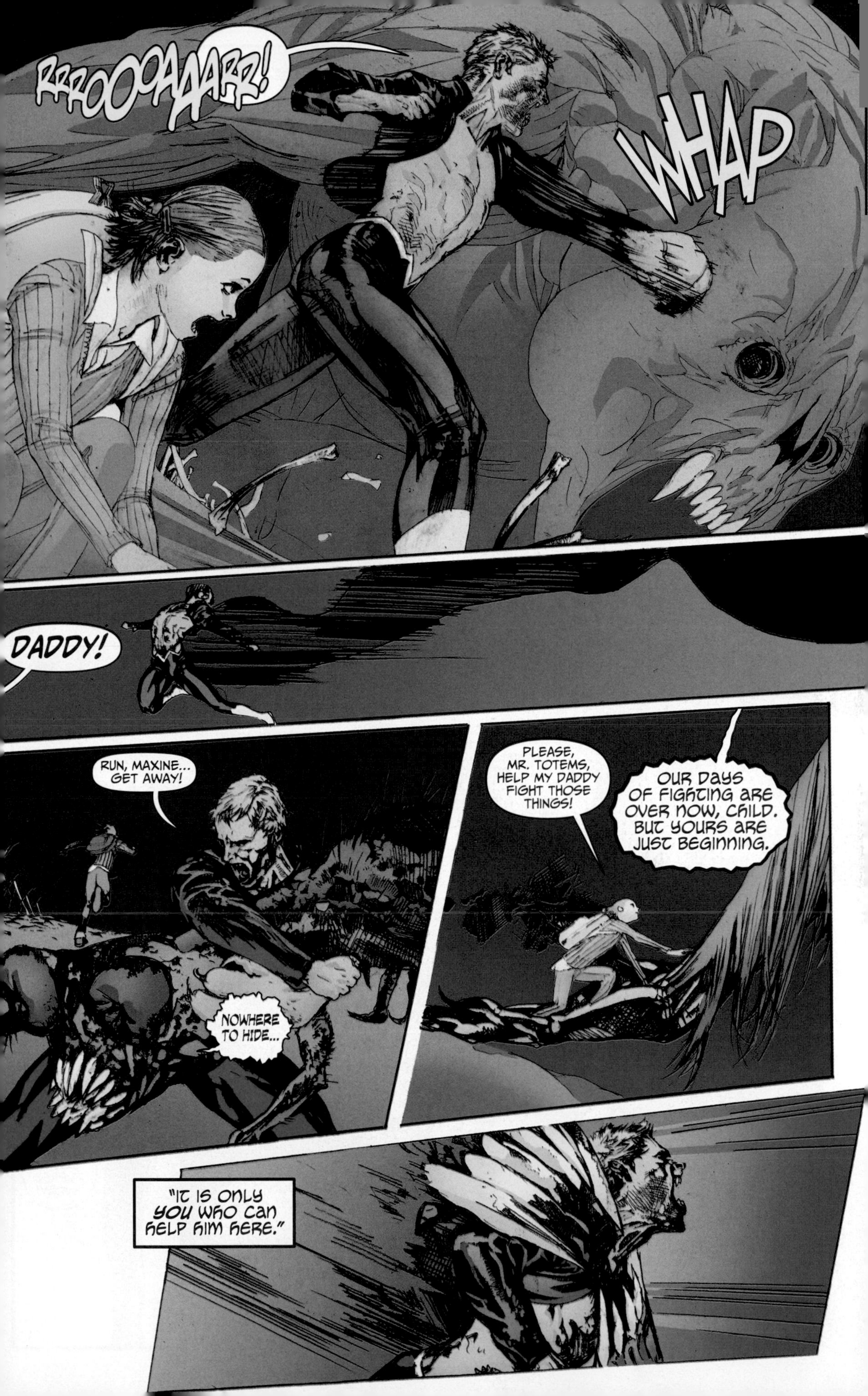
RRROOOAAARR!
WHAP
DADDY!
RUN, MAXINE... GET AWAY!
NOWHERE TO HIDE...
PLEASE, MR. TOTEMS, HELP MY DADDY FIGHT THOSE THINGS!
OUR DAYS OF FIGHTING ARE OVER NOW, CHILD. BUT YOURS ARE JUST BEGINNING.
"IT IS ONLY YOU WHO CAN HELP HIM HERE."

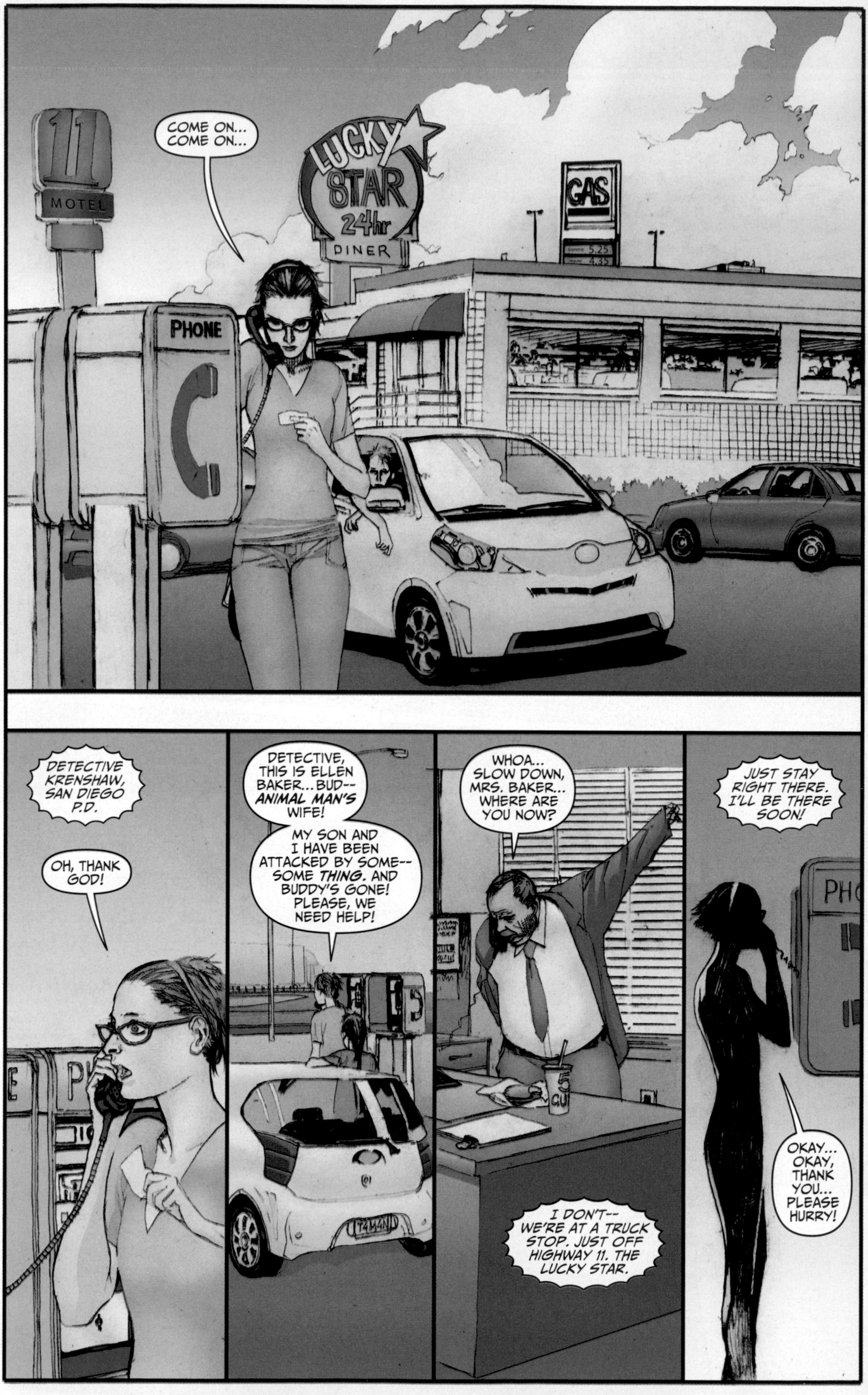
11
MOTEL
LUCKY STAR 24hr DINER
GAS
COME ON... COME ON...
PHONE
DETECTIVE KRENSHAW, SAN DIEGO P.D.
OH, THANK GOD!
DETECTIVE, THIS IS ELLEN BAKER... BUD-- *ANIMAL MAN'S* WIFE!
MY SON AND I HAVE BEEN ATTACKED BY SOME-- SOME *THING*. AND BUDDY'S GONE! PLEASE, WE NEED HELP!
WHOA... SLOW DOWN, MRS. BAKER... WHERE ARE YOU NOW?
I DON'T-- WE'RE AT A TRUCK STOP. JUST OFF HIGHWAY 11. THE LUCKY STAR.
JUST STAY RIGHT THERE. I'LL BE THERE SOON!
OKAY... OKAY, THANK YOU... PLEASE HURRY!

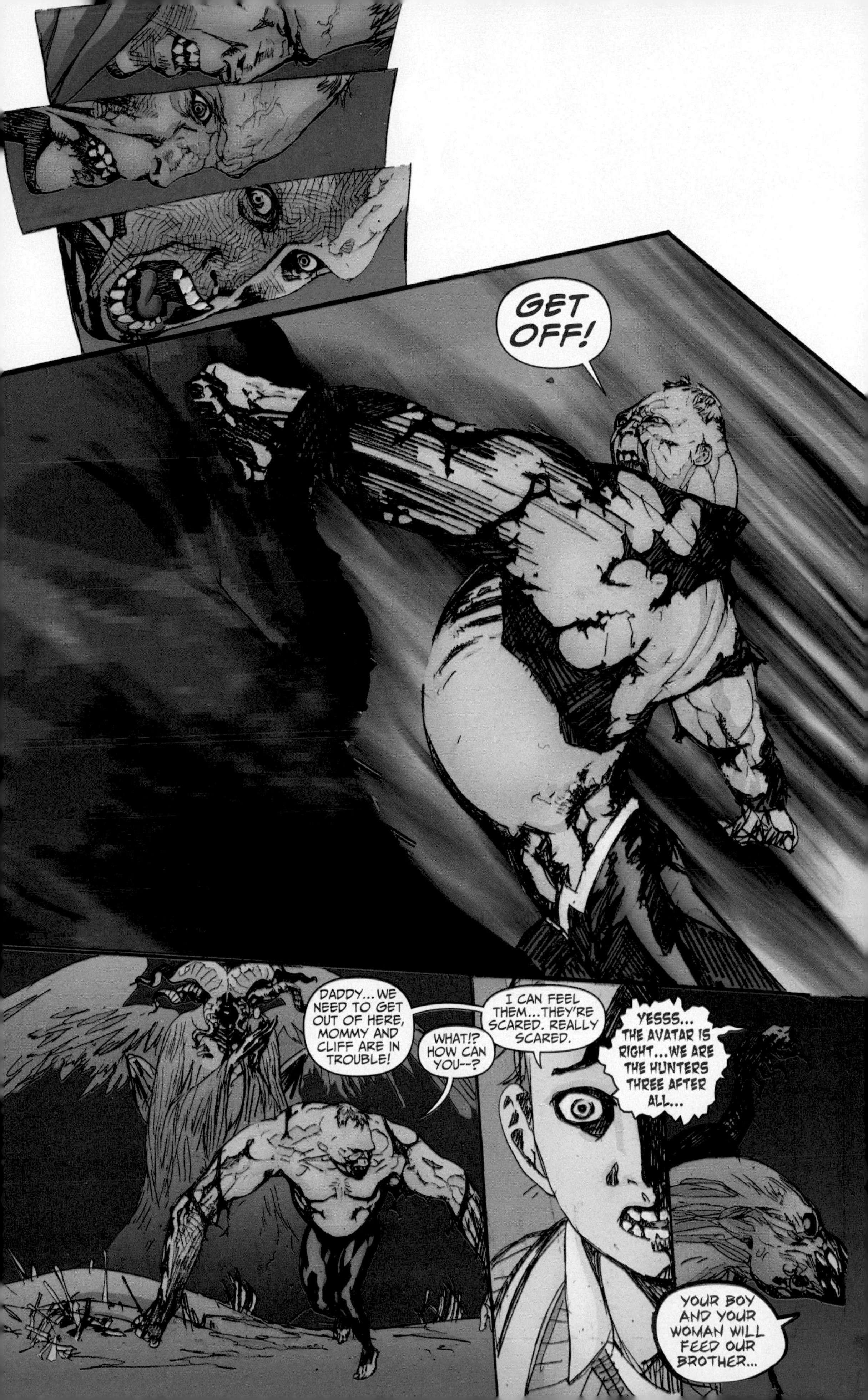
GET OFF!
DADDY... WE NEED TO GET OUT OF HERE, MOMMY AND CLIFF ARE IN TROUBLE!
WHAT!? HOW CAN YOU--?
I CAN FEEL THEM...THEY'RE SCARED. REALLY SCARED.
YESSS... THE AVATAR IS RIGHT...WE ARE THE HUNTERS THREE AFTER ALL...
YOUR BOY AND YOUR WOMAN WILL FEED OUR BROTHER...

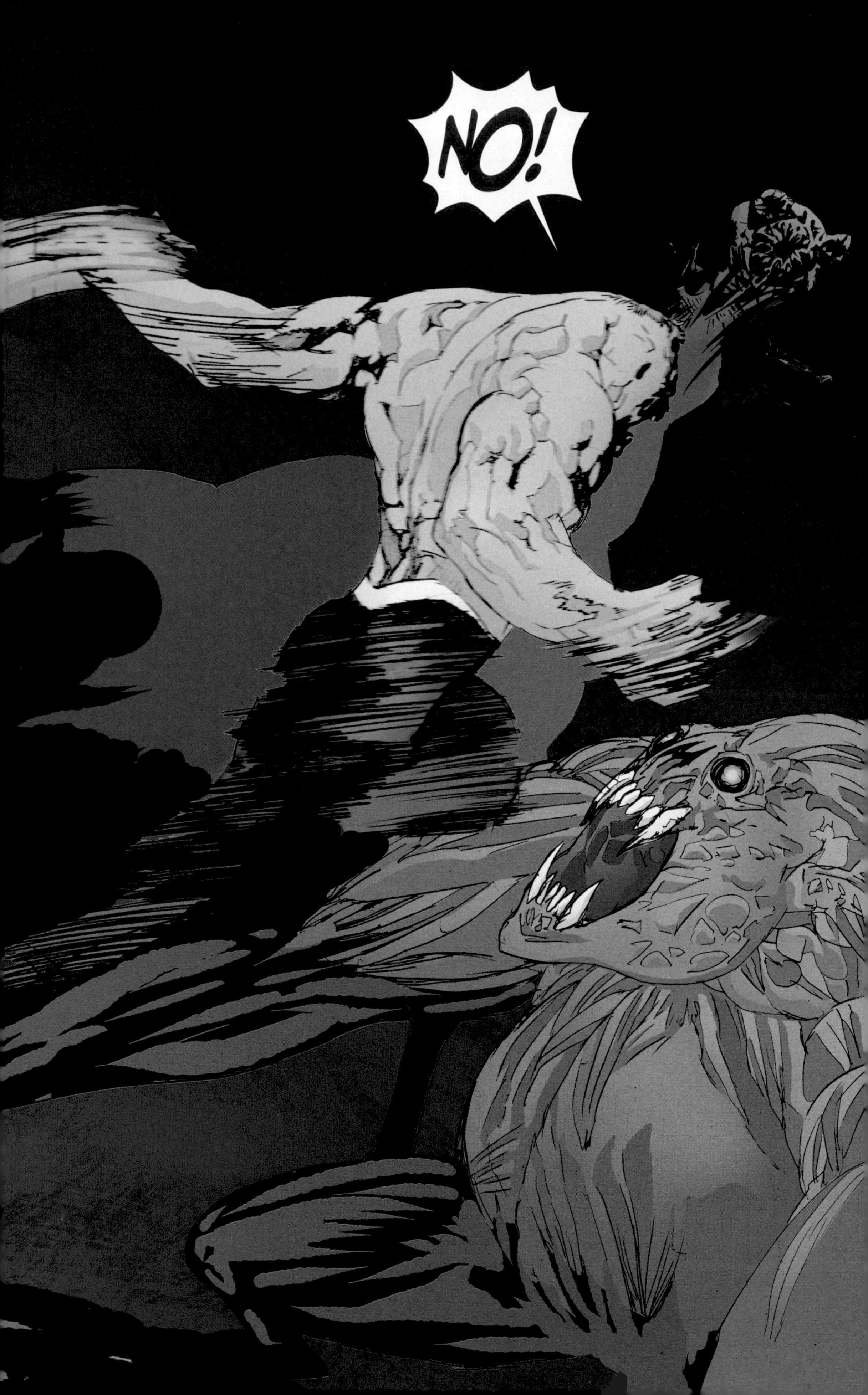
NO!

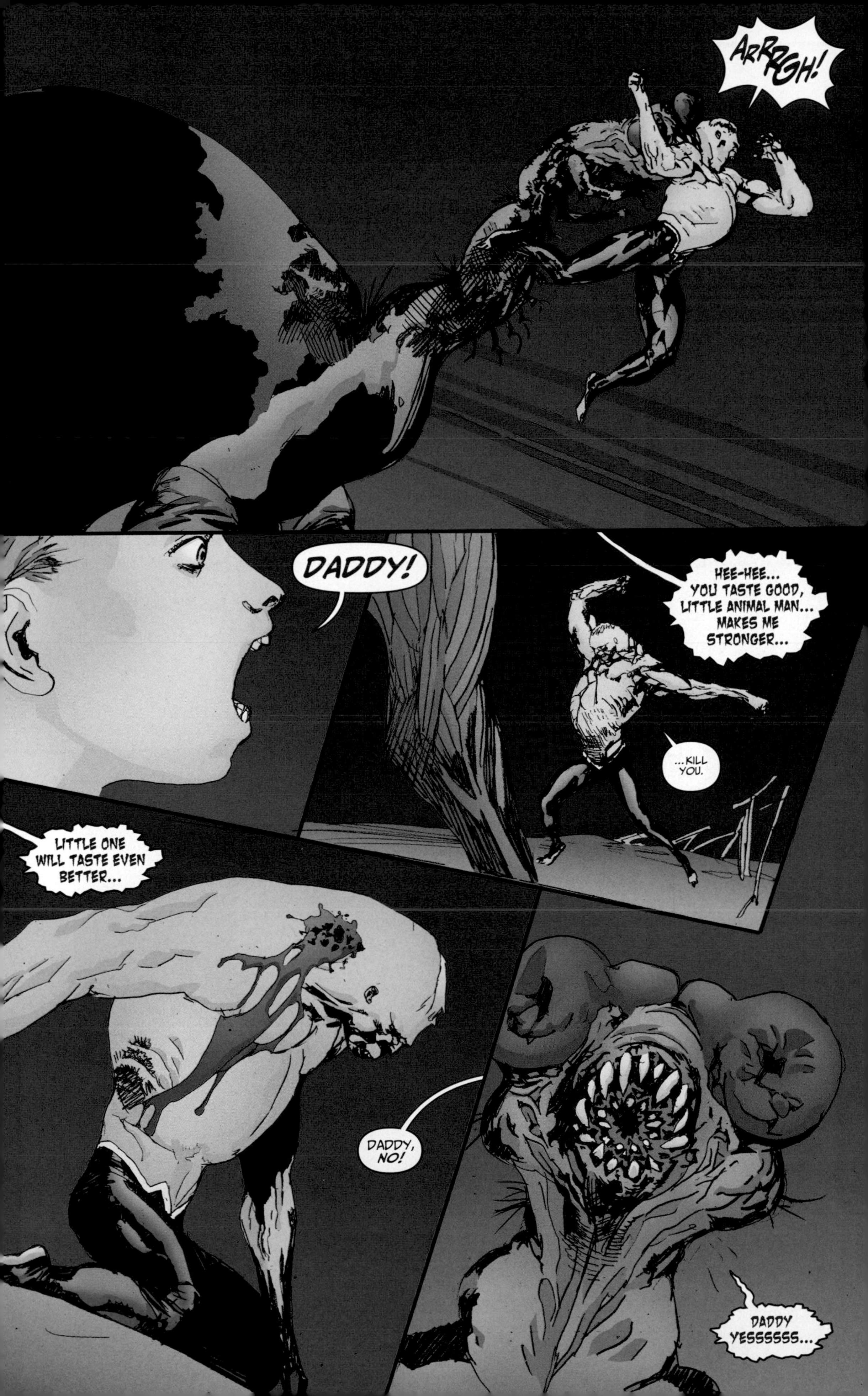
ARRRGH!
DADDY!
HEE-HEE... YOU TASTE GOOD, LITTLE ANIMAL MAN... MAKES ME STRONGER...
...KILL YOU.
LITTLE ONE WILL TASTE EVEN BETTER...
DADDY, NO!
DADDY YESSSSSS...

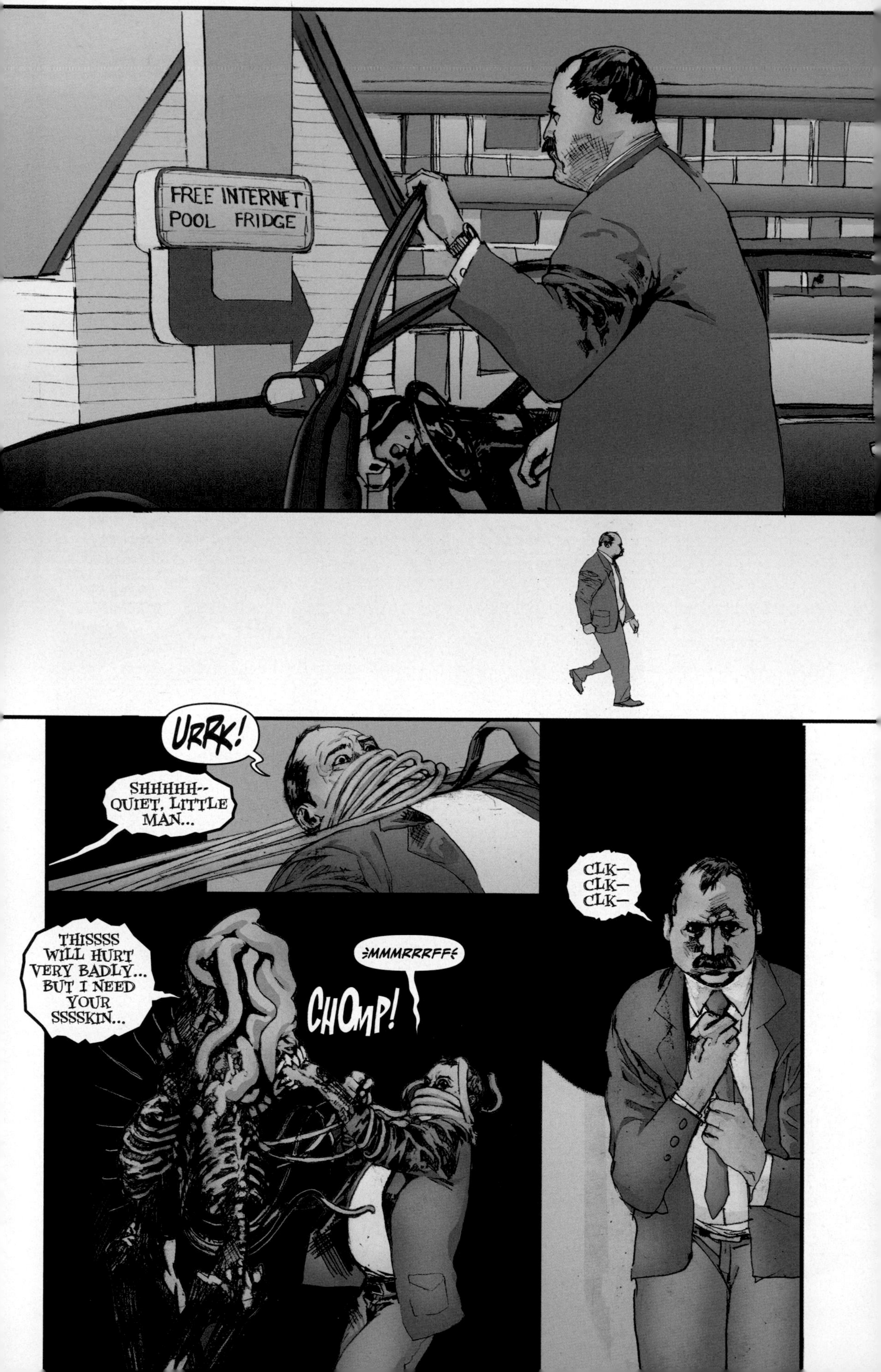
FREE INTERNET
POOL FRIDGE
URRK!
SHHHHH-- QUIET, LITTLE MAN...
THISSSS WILL HURT VERY BADLY... BUT I NEED YOUR SSSSKIN...
CHOMP!
MMMRRRFF
CLK— CLK— CLK—

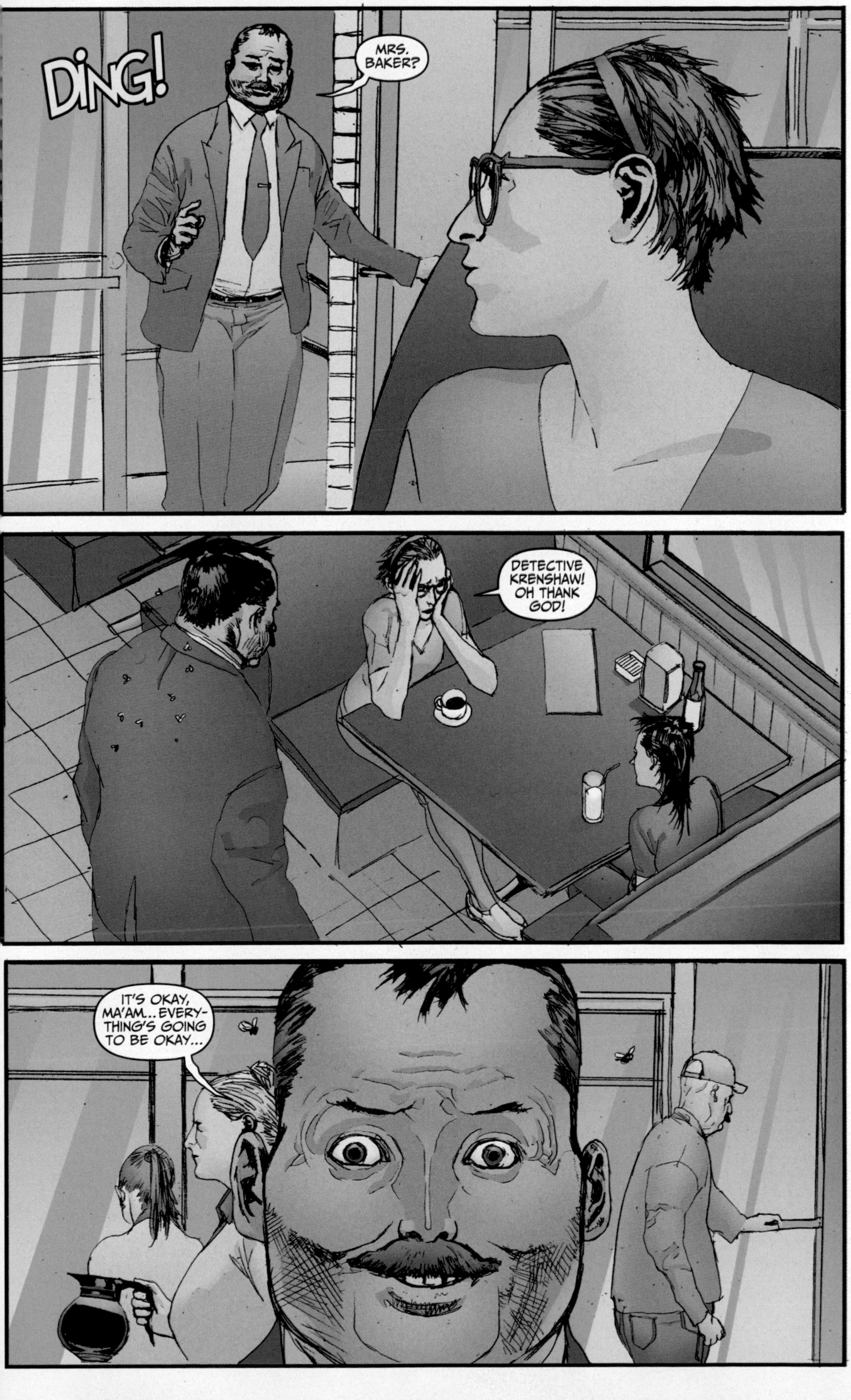
DING!
MRS. BAKER?
DETECTIVE KRENSHAW! OH THANK GOD!
IT'S OKAY, MA'AM... EVERYTHING'S GOING TO BE OKAY...

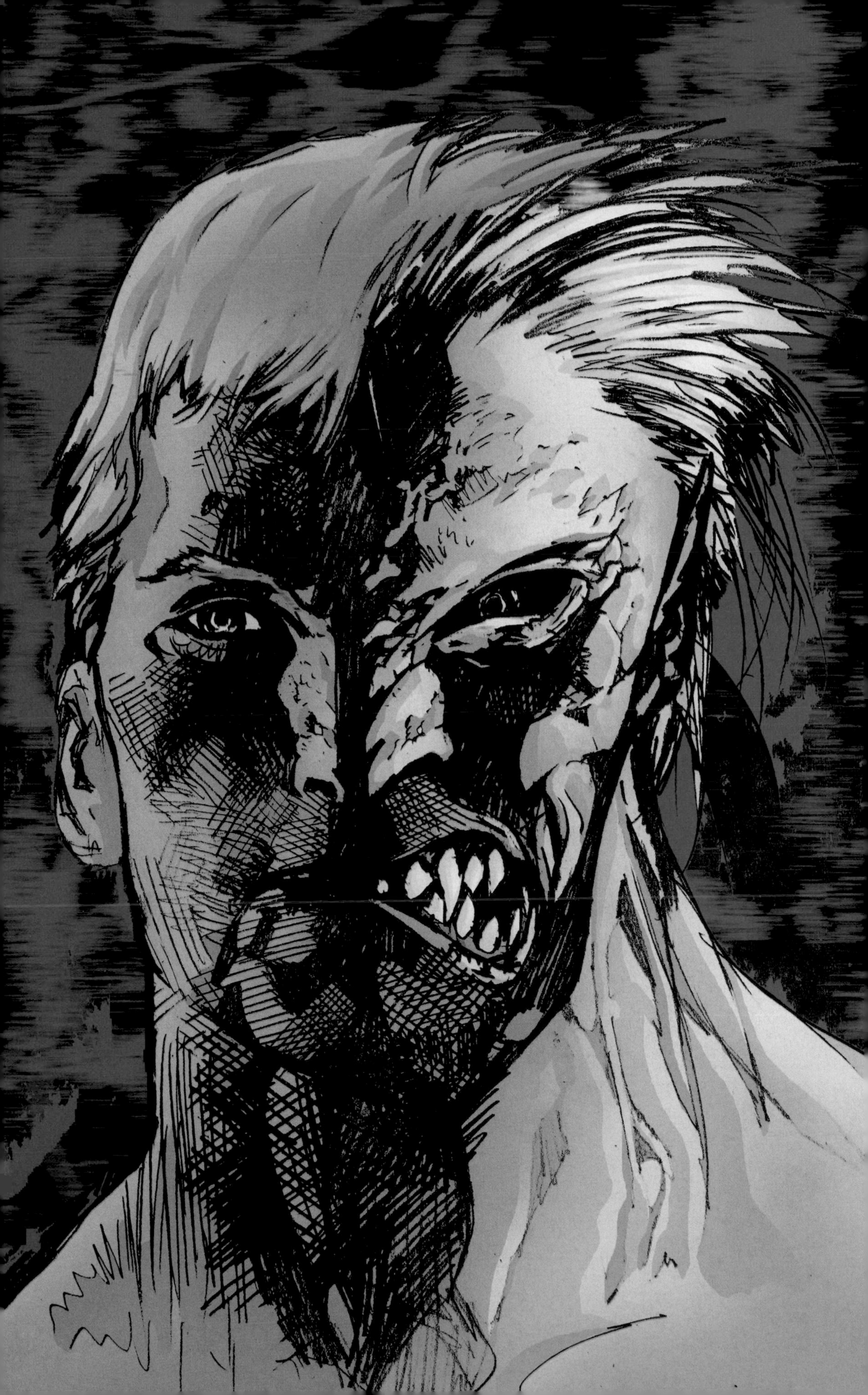

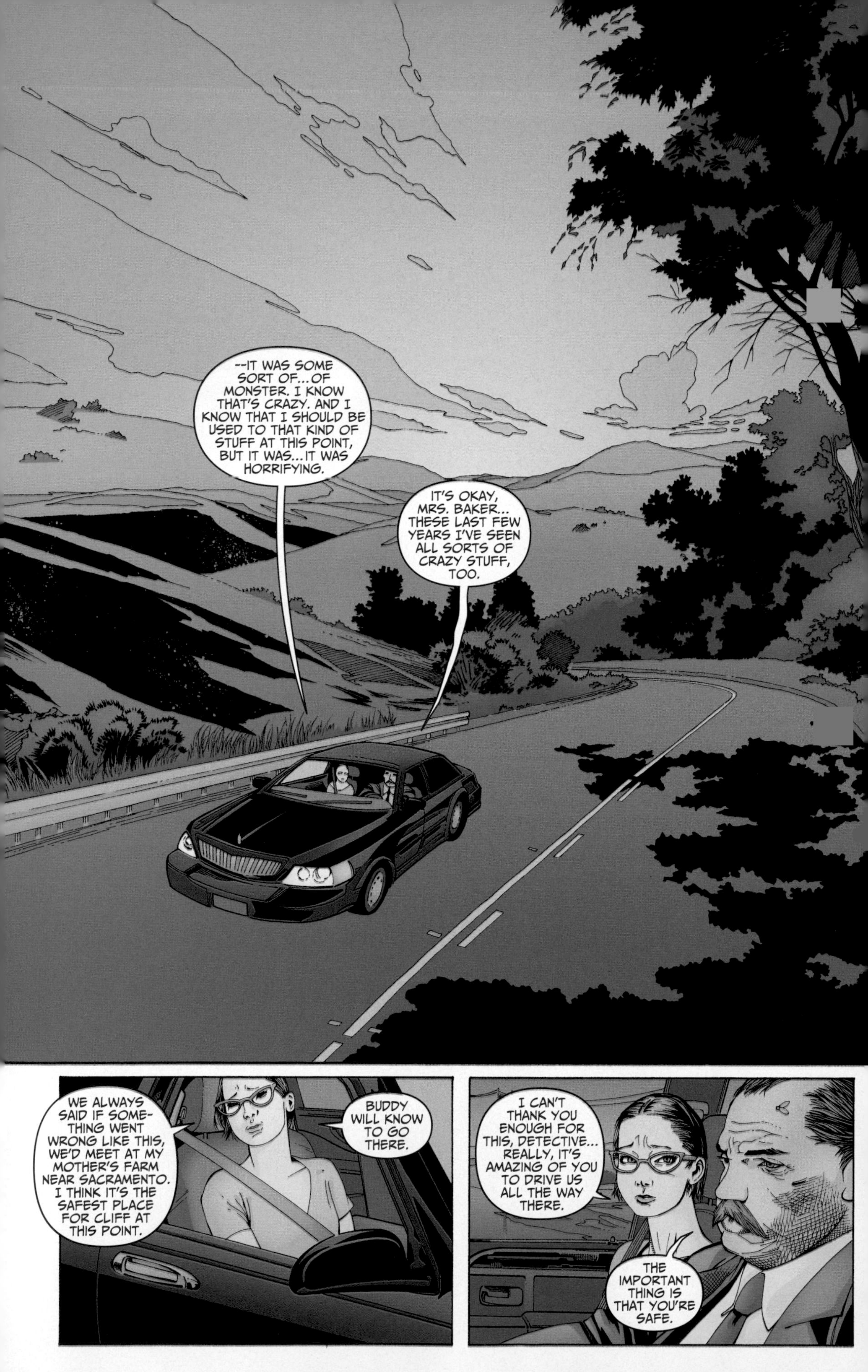
--IT WAS SOME SORT OF...OF MONSTER. I KNOW THAT'S CRAZY. AND I KNOW THAT I SHOULD BE USED TO THAT KIND OF STUFF AT THIS POINT, BUT IT WAS...IT WAS HORRIFYING.
IT'S OKAY, MRS. BAKER... THESE LAST FEW YEARS I'VE SEEN ALL SORTS OF CRAZY STUFF, TOO.
WE ALWAYS SAID IF SOME-THING WENT WRONG LIKE THIS, WE'D MEET AT MY MOTHER'S FARM NEAR SACRAMENTO. I THINK IT'S THE SAFEST PLACE FOR CLIFF AT THIS POINT.
BUDDY WILL KNOW TO GO THERE.
I CAN'T THANK YOU ENOUGH FOR THIS, DETECTIVE... REALLY, IT'S AMAZING OF YOU TO DRIVE US ALL THE WAY THERE.
THE IMPORTANT THING IS THAT YOU'RE SAFE.

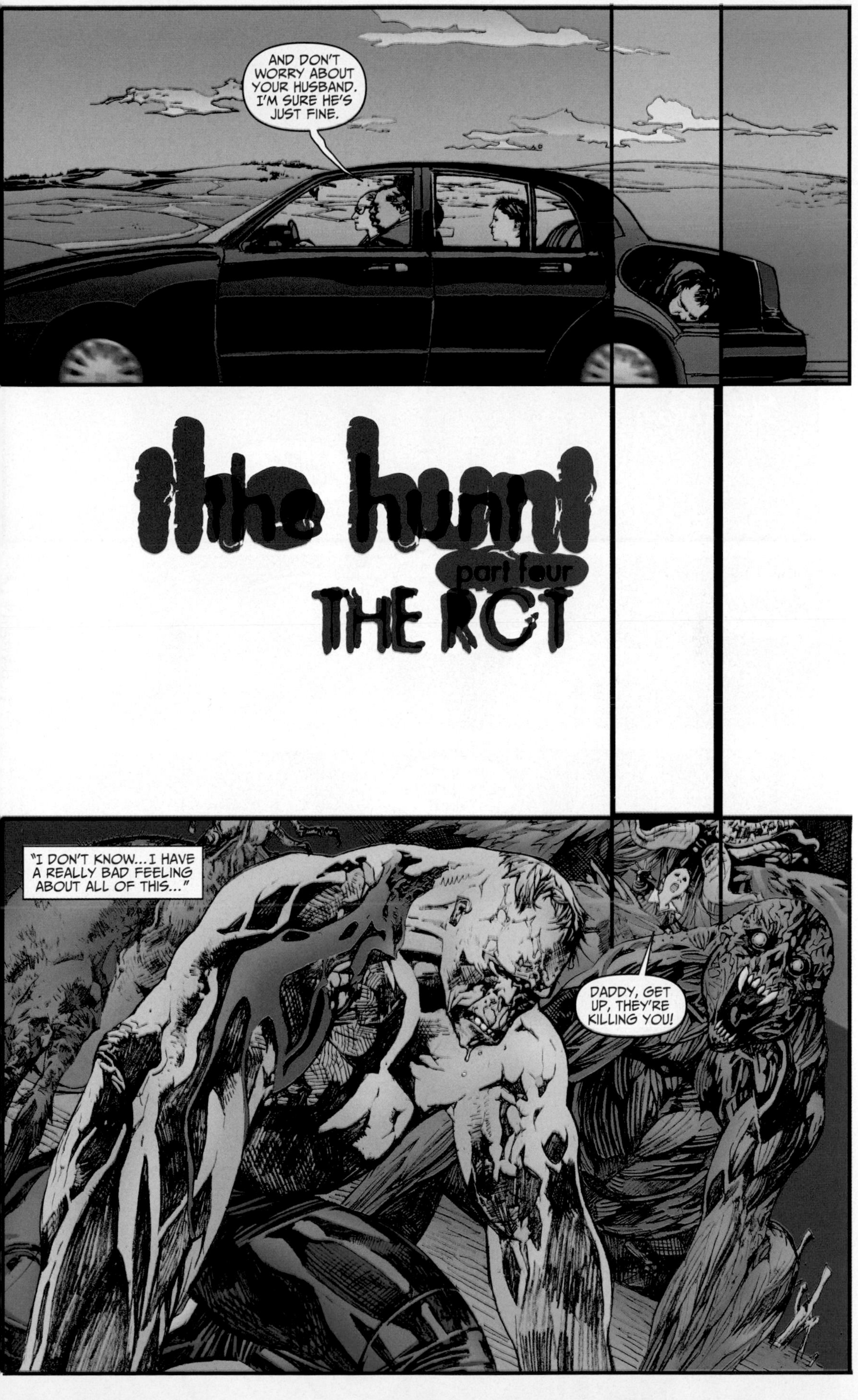
AND DON'T WORRY ABOUT YOUR HUSBAND. I'M SURE HE'S JUST FINE.
the hunt
part four
THE ROT
"I DON'T KNOW...I HAVE A REALLY BAD FEELING ABOUT ALL OF THIS..."
DADDY, GET UP, THEY'RE KILLING YOU!

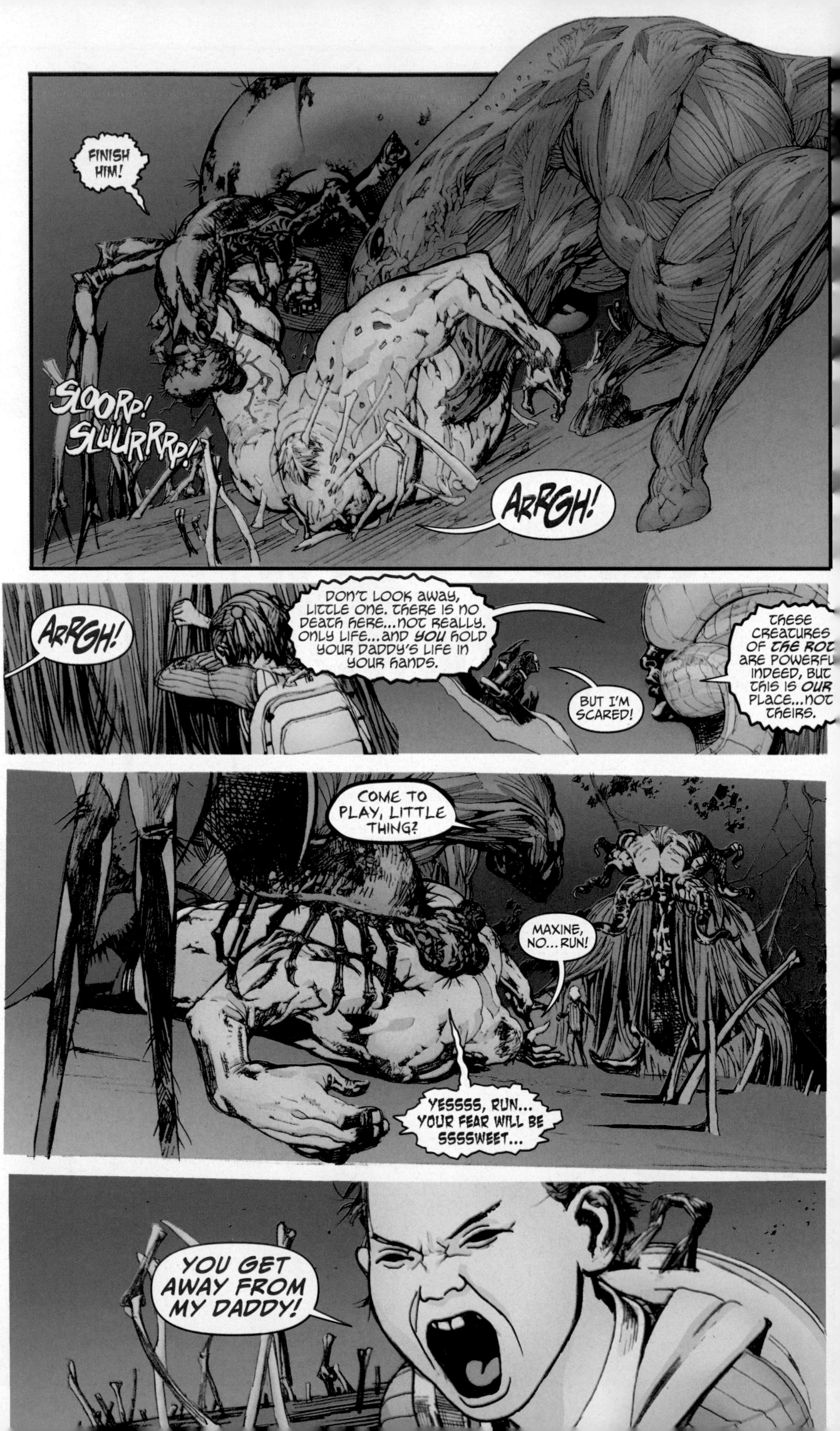
FINISH HIM!
SLOORP! SLUURRRP!
ARRGH!
ARRGH!
DON'T LOOK AWAY, LITTLE ONE. THERE IS NO DEATH HERE...NOT REALLY. ONLY LIFE...AND YOU HOLD YOUR DADDY'S LIFE IN YOUR HANDS.
BUT I'M SCARED!
THESE CREATURES OF THE ROT ARE POWERFU INDEED, BUT THIS IS OUR PLACE...NOT THEIRS.
COME TO PLAY, LITTLE THING?
MAXINE, NO... RUN!
YESSSS, RUN... YOUR FEAR WILL BE SSSSWEET...
YOU GET AWAY FROM MY DADDY!

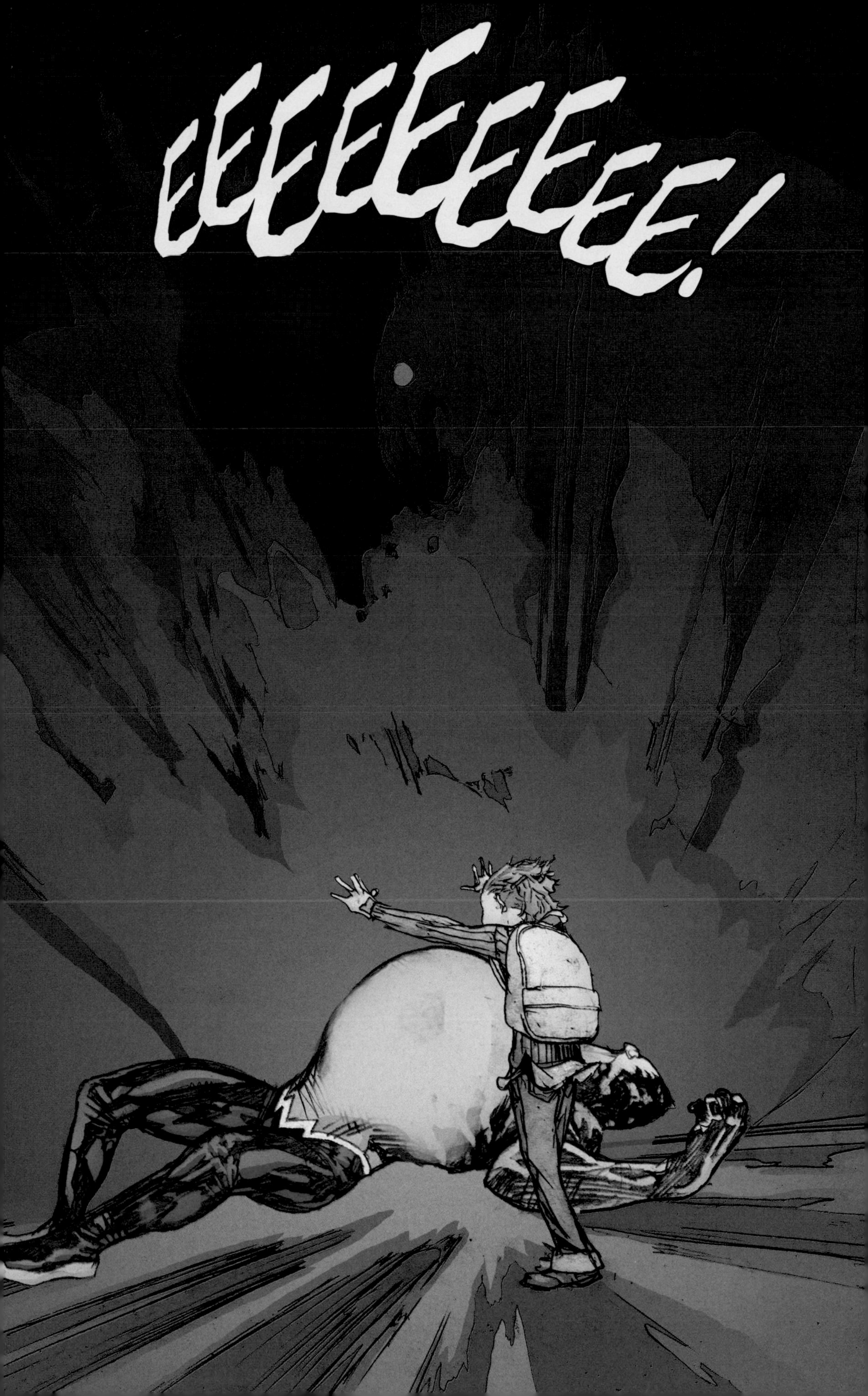
EEEEEEEEEE!

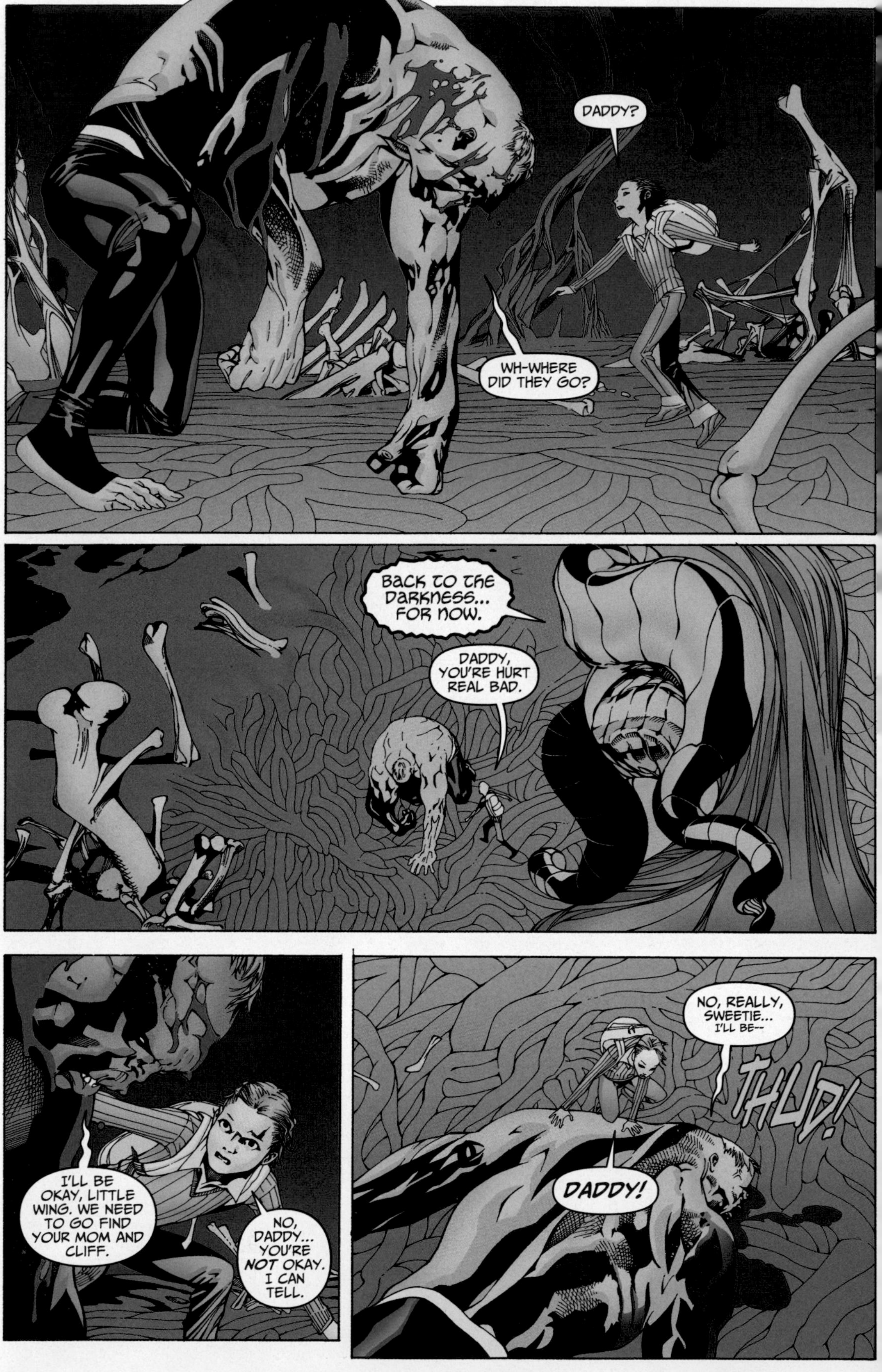
DADDY?
WH-WHERE DID THEY GO?
BACK TO THE DARKNESS... FOR NOW.
DADDY, YOU'RE HURT REAL BAD.
I'LL BE OKAY, LITTLE WING. WE NEED TO GO FIND YOUR MOM AND CLIFF.
NO, DADDY... YOU'RE NOT OKAY. I CAN TELL.
NO, REALLY, SWEETIE... I'LL BE--
THUD!
DADDY!

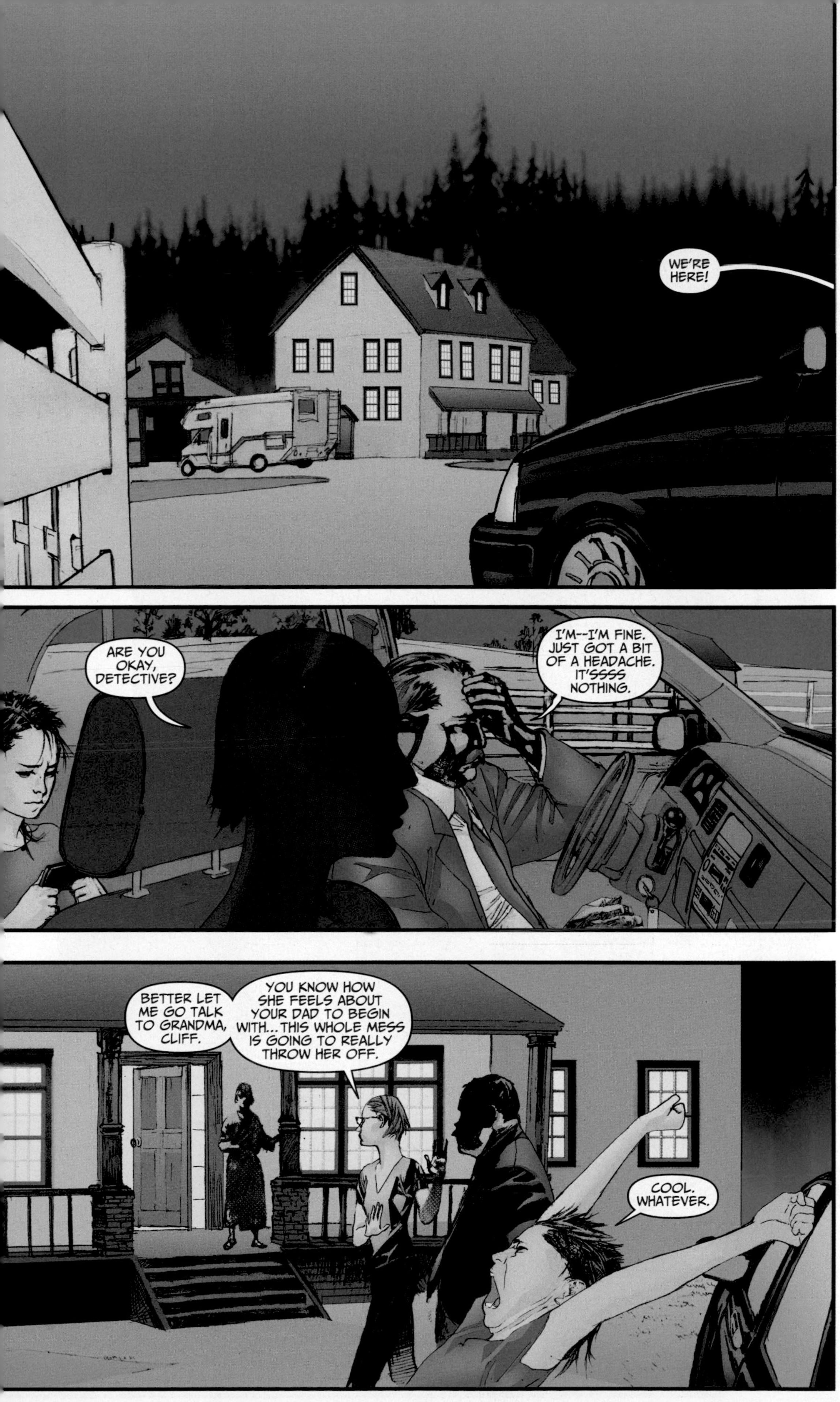
WE'RE HERE!
ARE YOU OKAY, DETECTIVE?
I'M--I'M FINE. JUST GOT A BIT OF A HEADACHE. IT'SSSS NOTHING.
BETTER LET ME GO TALK TO GRANDMA, CLIFF.
YOU KNOW HOW SHE FEELS ABOUT YOUR DAD TO BEGIN WITH...THIS WHOLE MESS IS GOING TO REALLY THROW HER OFF.
COOL. WHATEVER.

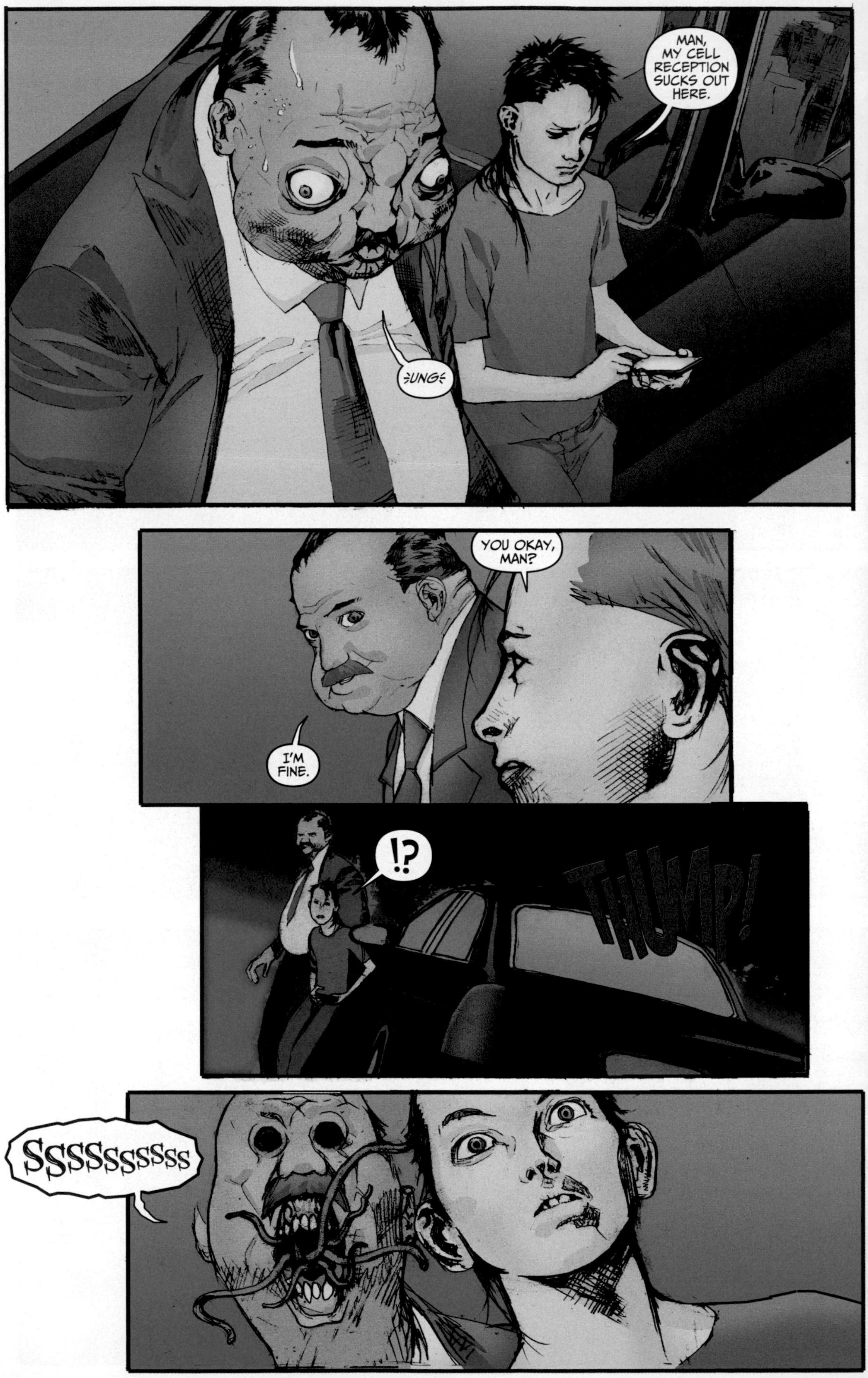
MAN, MY CELL RECEPTION SUCKS OUT HERE.
UNG
YOU OKAY, MAN?
I'M FINE.
!?
THUMP!
SSSSSSSSSS

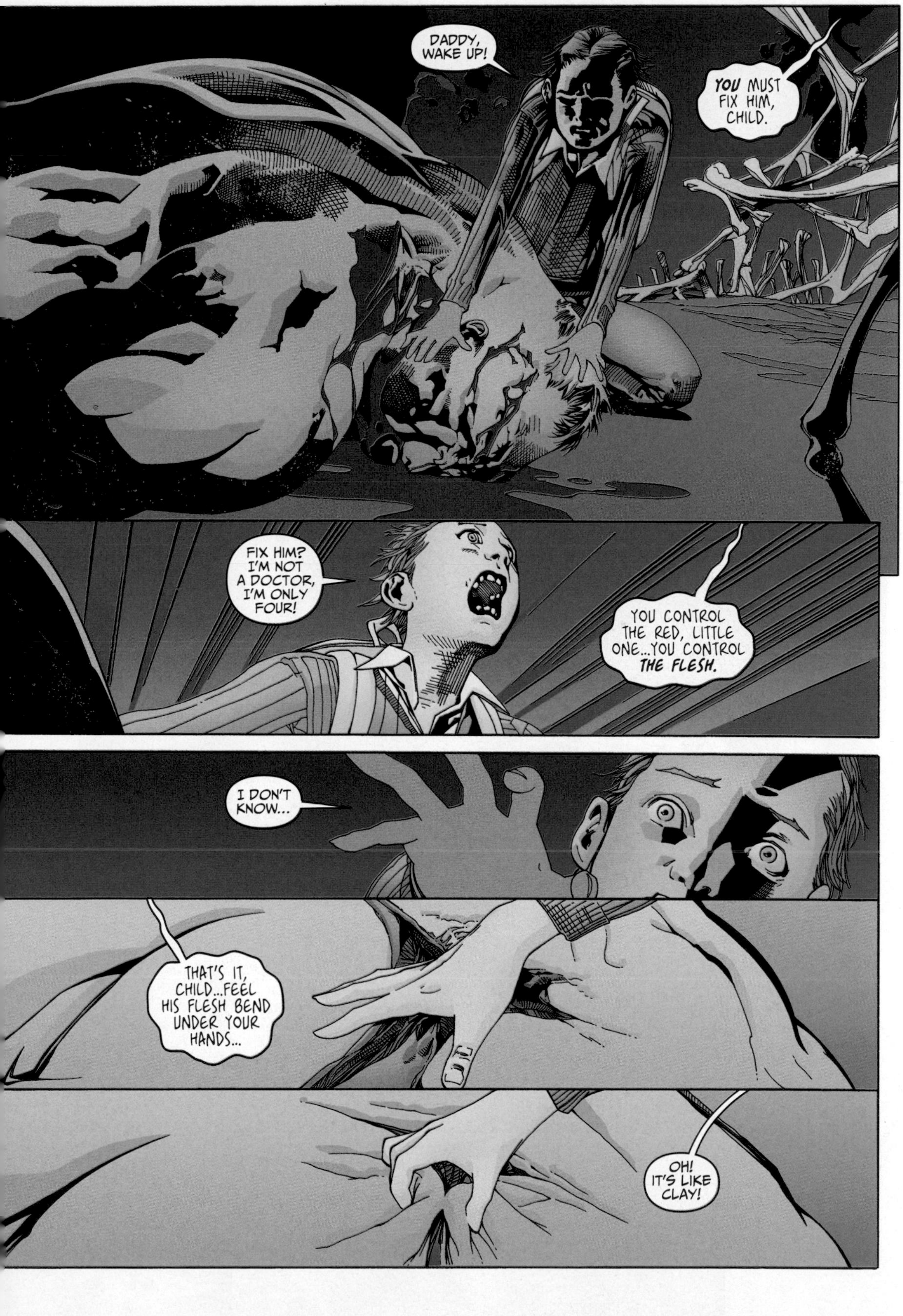
DADDY, WAKE UP!
YOU MUST FIX HIM, CHILD.
FIX HIM? I'M NOT A DOCTOR, I'M ONLY FOUR!
YOU CONTROL THE RED, LITTLE ONE...YOU CONTROL THE FLESH.
I DON'T KNOW...
THAT'S IT, CHILD...FEEL HIS FLESH BEND UNDER YOUR HANDS...
OH! IT'S LIKE CLAY!

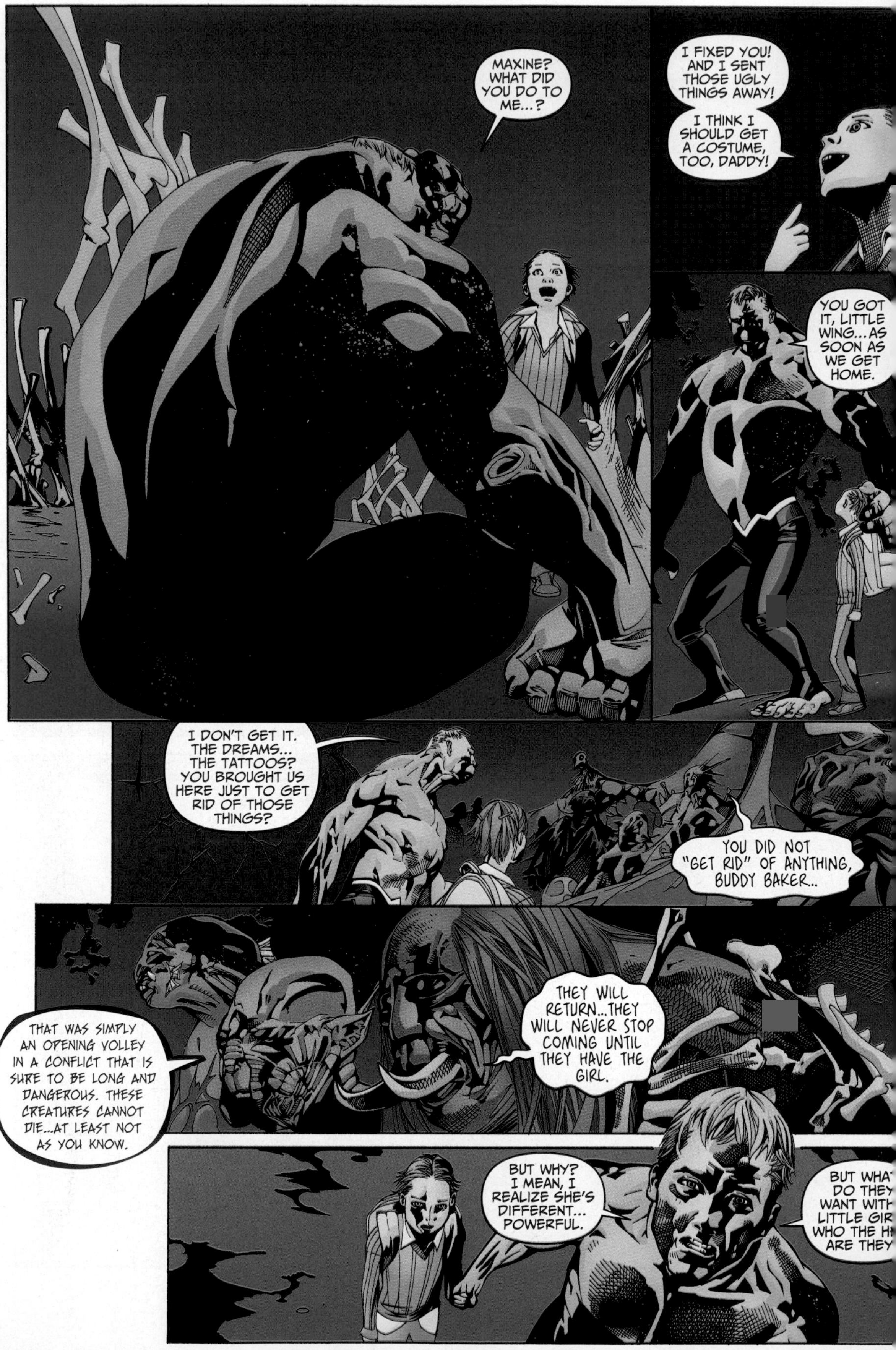
MAXINE? WHAT DID YOU DO TO ME...?
I FIXED YOU! AND I SENT THOSE UGLY THINGS AWAY!
I THINK I SHOULD GET A COSTUME, TOO, DADDY!
YOU GOT IT, LITTLE WING...AS SOON AS WE GET HOME.
I DON'T GET IT. THE DREAMS... THE TATTOOS? YOU BROUGHT US HERE JUST TO GET RID OF THOSE THINGS?
YOU DID NOT "GET RID" OF ANYTHING, BUDDY BAKER...
THAT WAS SIMPLY AN OPENING VOLLEY IN A CONFLICT THAT IS SURE TO BE LONG AND DANGEROUS. THESE CREATURES CANNOT DIE...AT LEAST NOT AS YOU KNOW.
THEY WILL RETURN...THEY WILL NEVER STOP COMING UNTIL THEY HAVE THE GIRL.
BUT WHY? I MEAN, I REALIZE SHE'S DIFFERENT... POWERFUL.

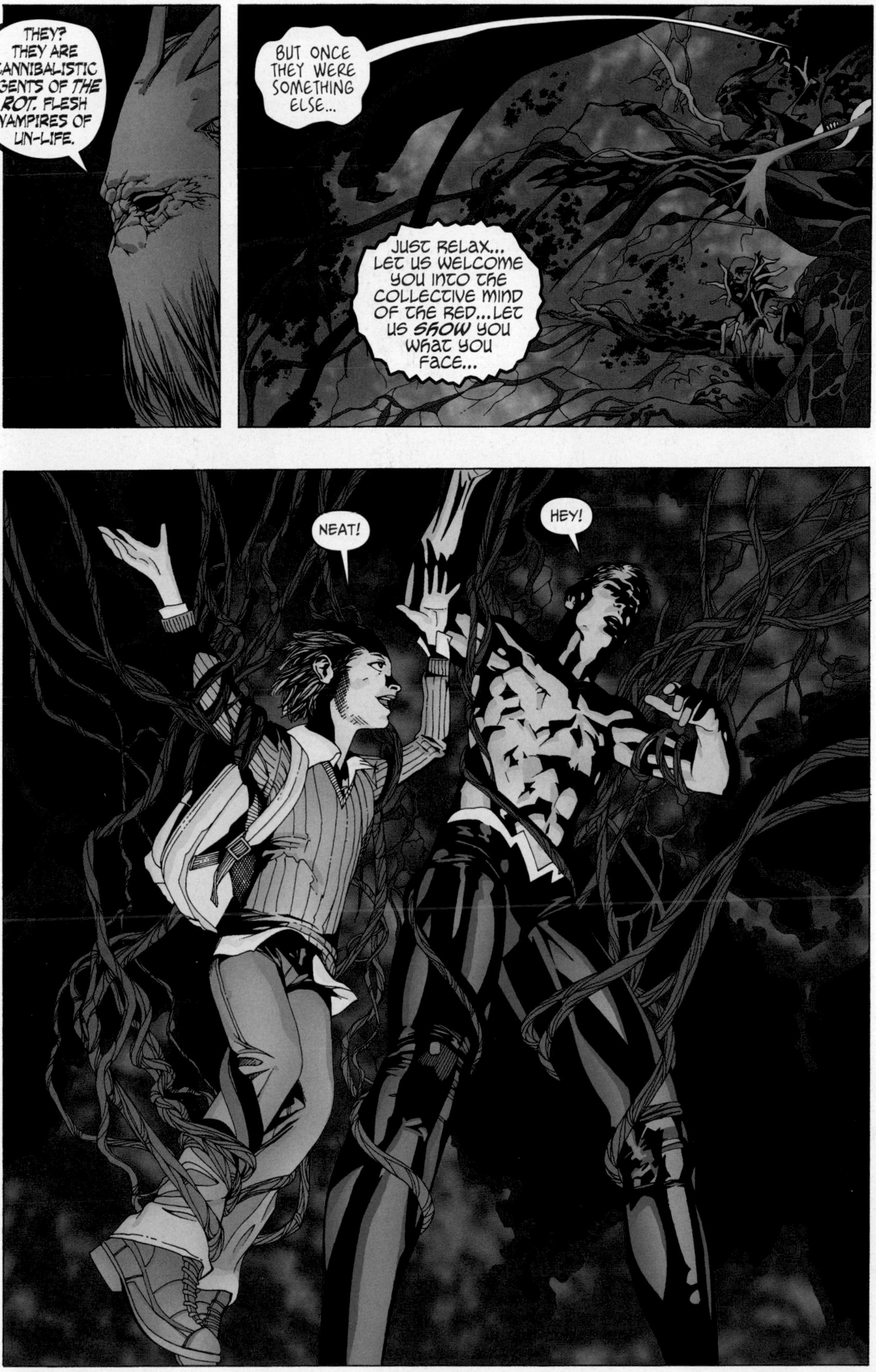
THEY? THEY ARE CANNIBALISTIC AGENTS OF THE ROT. FLESH VAMPIRES OF UN-LIFE.
BUT ONCE THEY WERE SOMETHING ELSE...
JUST RELAX... LET US WELCOME YOU INTO THE COLLECTIVE MIND OF THE RED...LET US SHOW YOU WHAT YOU FACE...
NEAT!
HEY!

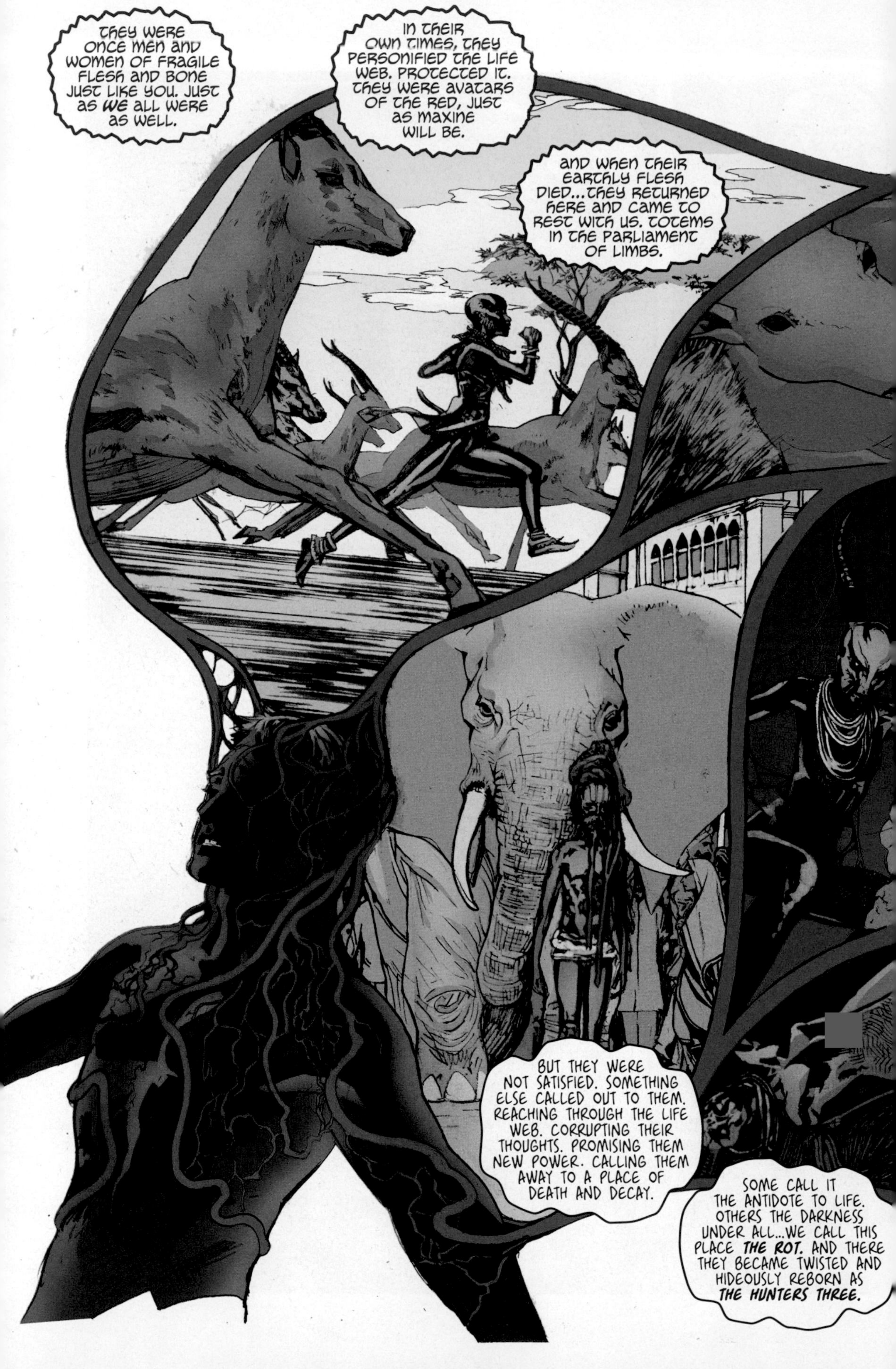
THEY WERE ONCE MEN AND WOMEN OF FRAGILE FLESH AND BONE JUST LIKE YOU. JUST AS WE ALL WERE AS WELL.
IN THEIR OWN TIMES, THEY PERSONIFIED THE LIFE WEB. PROTECTED IT. THEY WERE AVATARS OF THE RED, JUST AS MAXINE WILL BE.
AND WHEN THEIR EARTHLY FLESH DIED...THEY RETURNED HERE AND CAME TO REST WITH US. TOTEMS IN THE PARLIAMENT OF LIMBS.
BUT THEY WERE NOT SATISFIED. SOMETHING ELSE CALLED OUT TO THEM. REACHING THROUGH THE LIFE WEB. CORRUPTING THEIR THOUGHTS. PROMISING THEM NEW POWER. CALLING THEM AWAY TO A PLACE OF DEATH AND DECAY.
SOME CALL IT THE ANTIDOTE TO LIFE. OTHERS THE DARKNESS UNDER ALL...WE CALL THIS PLACE THE ROT. AND THERE THEY BECAME TWISTED AND HIDEOUSLY REBORN AS THE HUNTERS THREE.

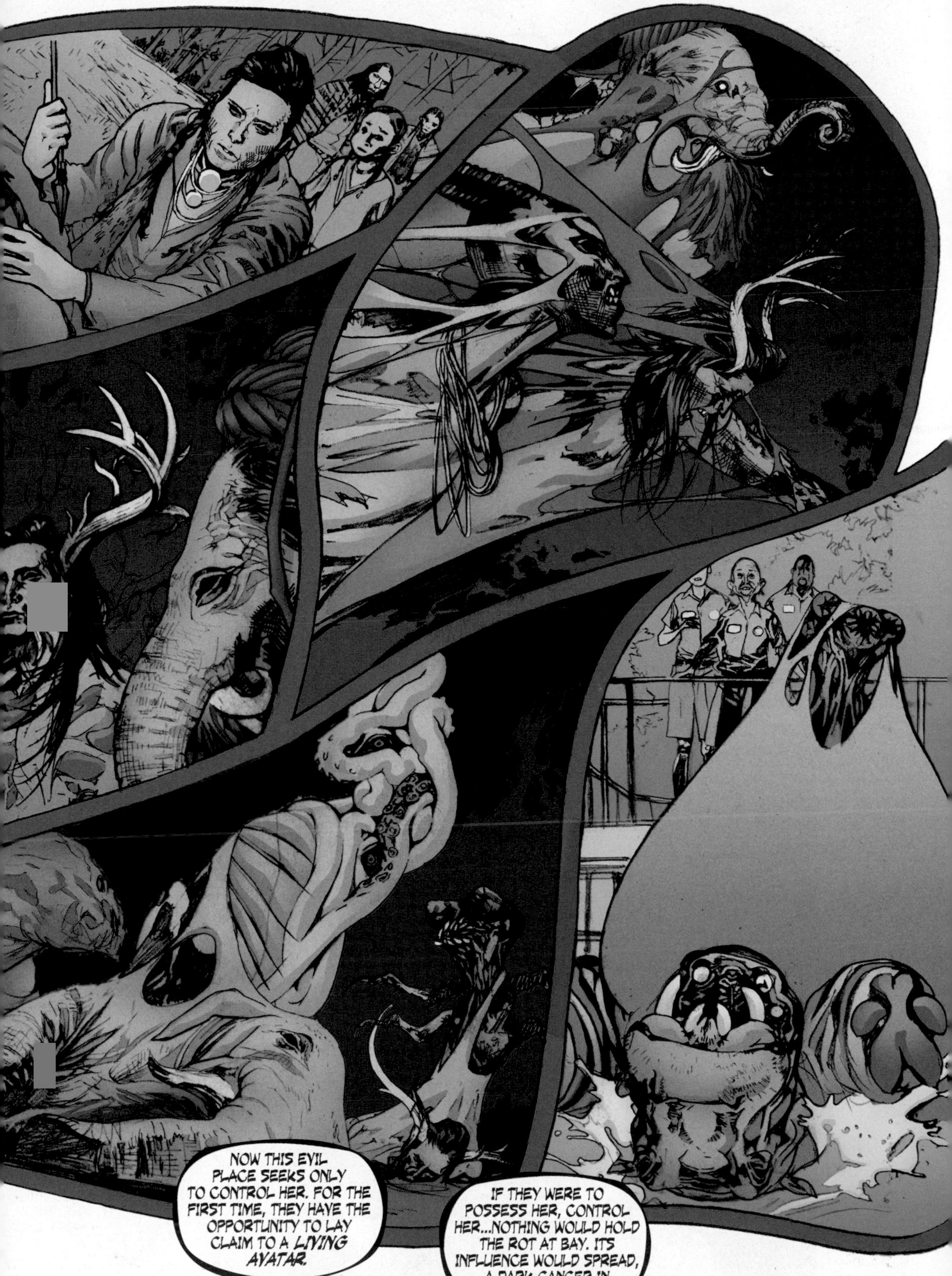
NOW THIS EVIL PLACE SEEKS ONLY TO CONTROL HER. FOR THE FIRST TIME, THEY HAVE THE OPPORTUNITY TO LAY CLAIM TO A *LIVING AVATAR*.
IF THEY WERE TO POSSESS HER, CONTROL HER...NOTHING WOULD HOLD THE ROT AT BAY. ITS INFLUENCE WOULD SPREAD, A DARK CANCER IN THE LIFE WEB.

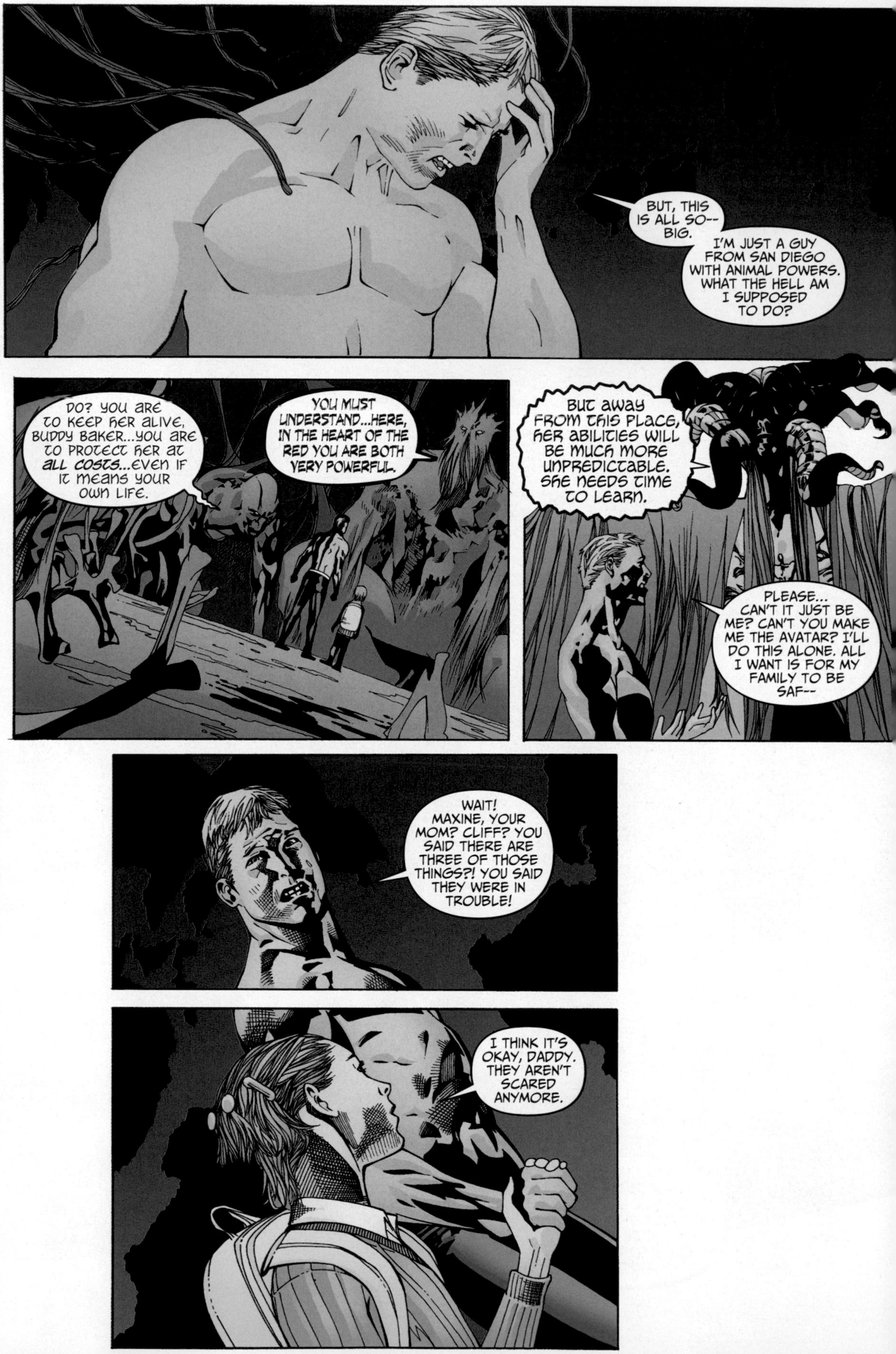
BUT, THIS IS ALL SO-- BIG.
I'M JUST A GUY FROM SAN DIEGO WITH ANIMAL POWERS. WHAT THE HELL AM I SUPPOSED TO DO?
DO? YOU ARE TO KEEP HER ALIVE, BUDDY BAKER...YOU ARE TO PROTECT HER AT ALL COSTS...EVEN IF IT MEANS YOUR OWN LIFE.
YOU MUST UNDERSTAND...HERE, IN THE HEART OF THE RED YOU ARE BOTH VERY POWERFUL.
BUT AWAY FROM THIS PLACE, HER ABILITIES WILL BE MUCH MORE UNPREDICTABLE. SHE NEEDS TIME TO LEARN.
PLEASE... CAN'T IT JUST BE ME? CAN'T YOU MAKE ME THE AVATAR? I'LL DO THIS ALONE. ALL I WANT IS FOR MY FAMILY TO BE SAF--
WAIT! MAXINE, YOUR MOM? CLIFF? YOU SAID THERE ARE THREE OF THOSE THINGS?! YOU SAID THEY WERE IN TROUBLE!
I THINK IT'S OKAY, DADDY. THEY AREN'T SCARED ANYMORE.

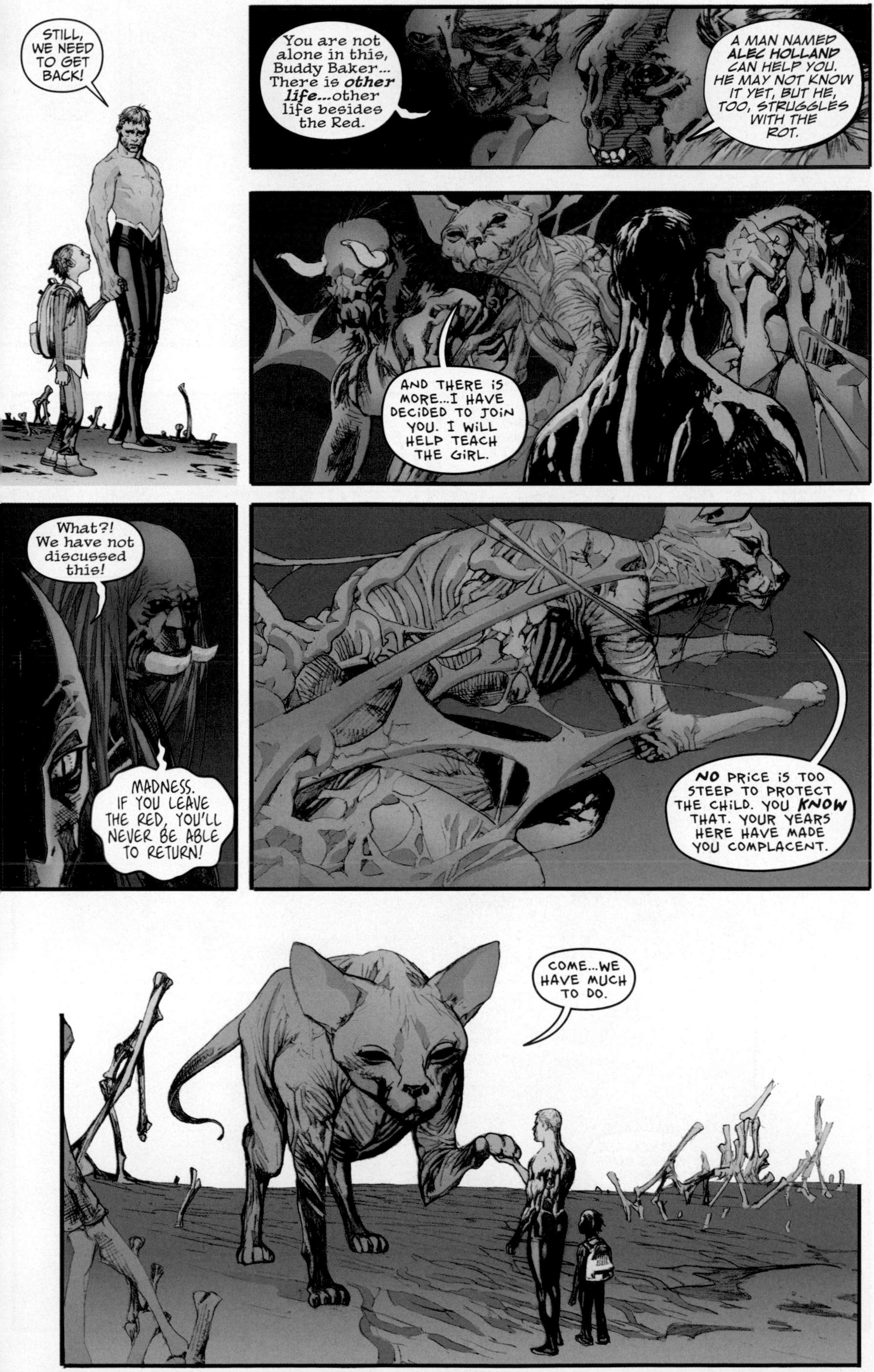
STILL, WE NEED TO GET BACK!
You are not alone in this, Buddy Baker... There is *other life...*other life besides the Red.
A MAN NAMED **ALEC HOLLAND** CAN HELP YOU. HE MAY NOT KNOW IT YET, BUT HE, TOO, STRUGGLES WITH THE ROT.
AND THERE IS MORE...I HAVE DECIDED TO JOIN YOU. I WILL HELP TEACH THE GIRL.
What?! We have not discussed this!
MADNESS. IF YOU LEAVE THE RED, YOU'LL NEVER BE ABLE TO RETURN!
NO PRICE IS TOO STEEP TO PROTECT THE CHILD. YOU **KNOW** THAT. YOUR YEARS HERE HAVE MADE YOU COMPLACENT.
COME...WE HAVE MUCH TO DO.

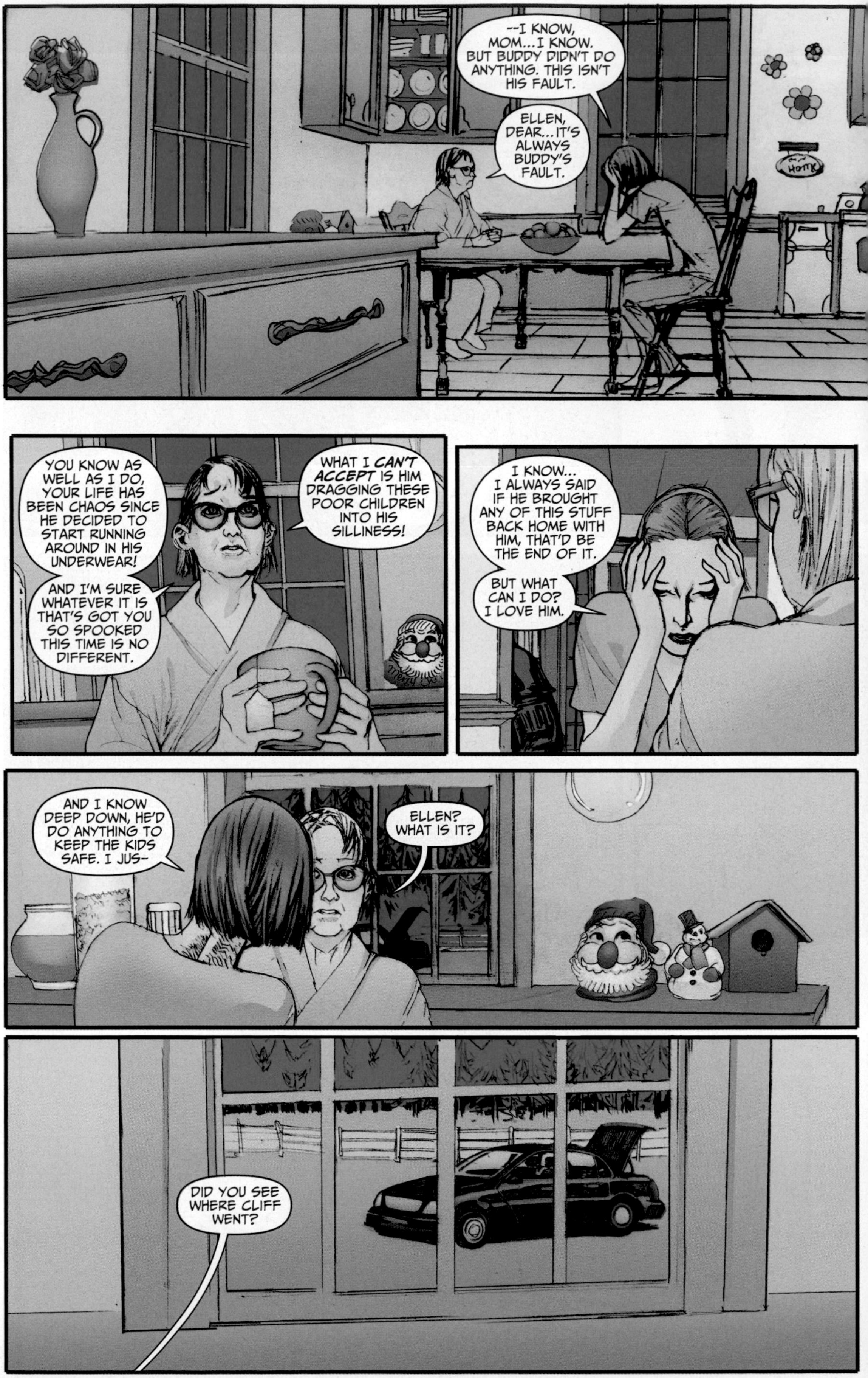
--I KNOW, MOM... I KNOW. BUT BUDDY DIDN'T DO ANYTHING. THIS ISN'T HIS FAULT.
ELLEN, DEAR... IT'S ALWAYS BUDDY'S FAULT.
YOU KNOW AS WELL AS I DO, YOUR LIFE HAS BEEN CHAOS SINCE HE DECIDED TO START RUNNING AROUND IN HIS UNDERWEAR!
AND I'M SURE WHATEVER IT IS THAT'S GOT YOU SO SPOOKED THIS TIME IS NO DIFFERENT.
WHAT I CAN'T ACCEPT IS HIM DRAGGING THESE POOR CHILDREN INTO HIS SILLINESS!
I KNOW... I ALWAYS SAID IF HE BROUGHT ANY OF THIS STUFF BACK HOME WITH HIM, THAT'D BE THE END OF IT.
BUT WHAT CAN I DO? I LOVE HIM.
AND I KNOW DEEP DOWN, HE'D DO ANYTHING TO KEEP THE KIDS SAFE. I JUS-
ELLEN? WHAT IS IT?
DID YOU SEE WHERE CLIFF WENT?

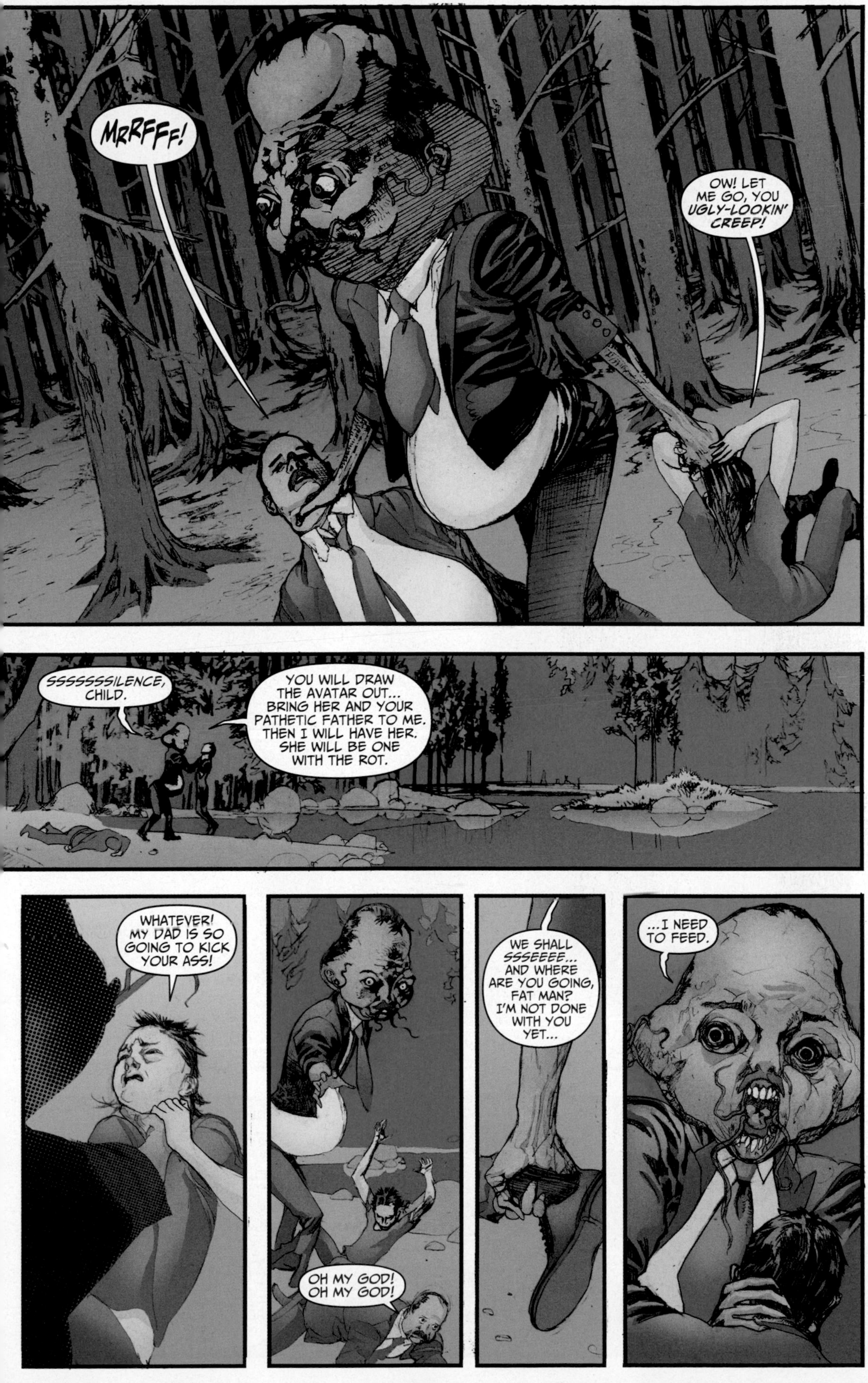
MRRFFF!
OW! LET ME GO, YOU UGLY-LOOKIN' CREEP!
SSSSSSSILENCE, CHILD.
YOU WILL DRAW THE AVATAR OUT... BRING HER AND YOUR PATHETIC FATHER TO ME. THEN I WILL HAVE HER. SHE WILL BE ONE WITH THE ROT.
WHATEVER! MY DAD IS SO GOING TO KICK YOUR ASS!
OH MY GOD! OH MY GOD!
WE SHALL SSSEEEE... AND WHERE ARE YOU GOING, FAT MAN? I'M NOT DONE WITH YOU YET...
...I NEED TO FEED.

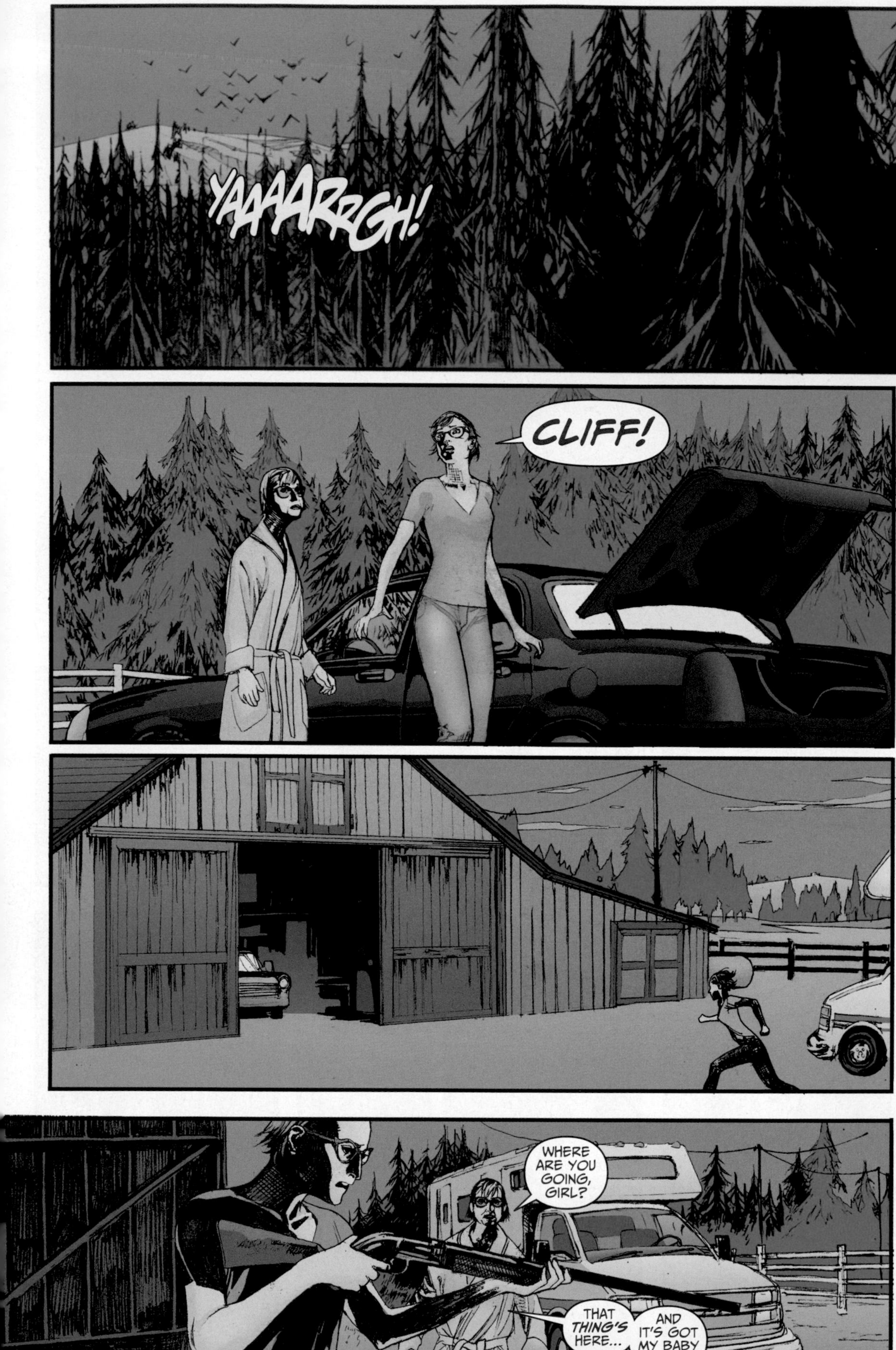

YAAAARRGH!
CLIFF!
WHERE ARE YOU GOING, GIRL?
THAT THING'S HERE...
AND IT'S GOT MY BABY BOY.

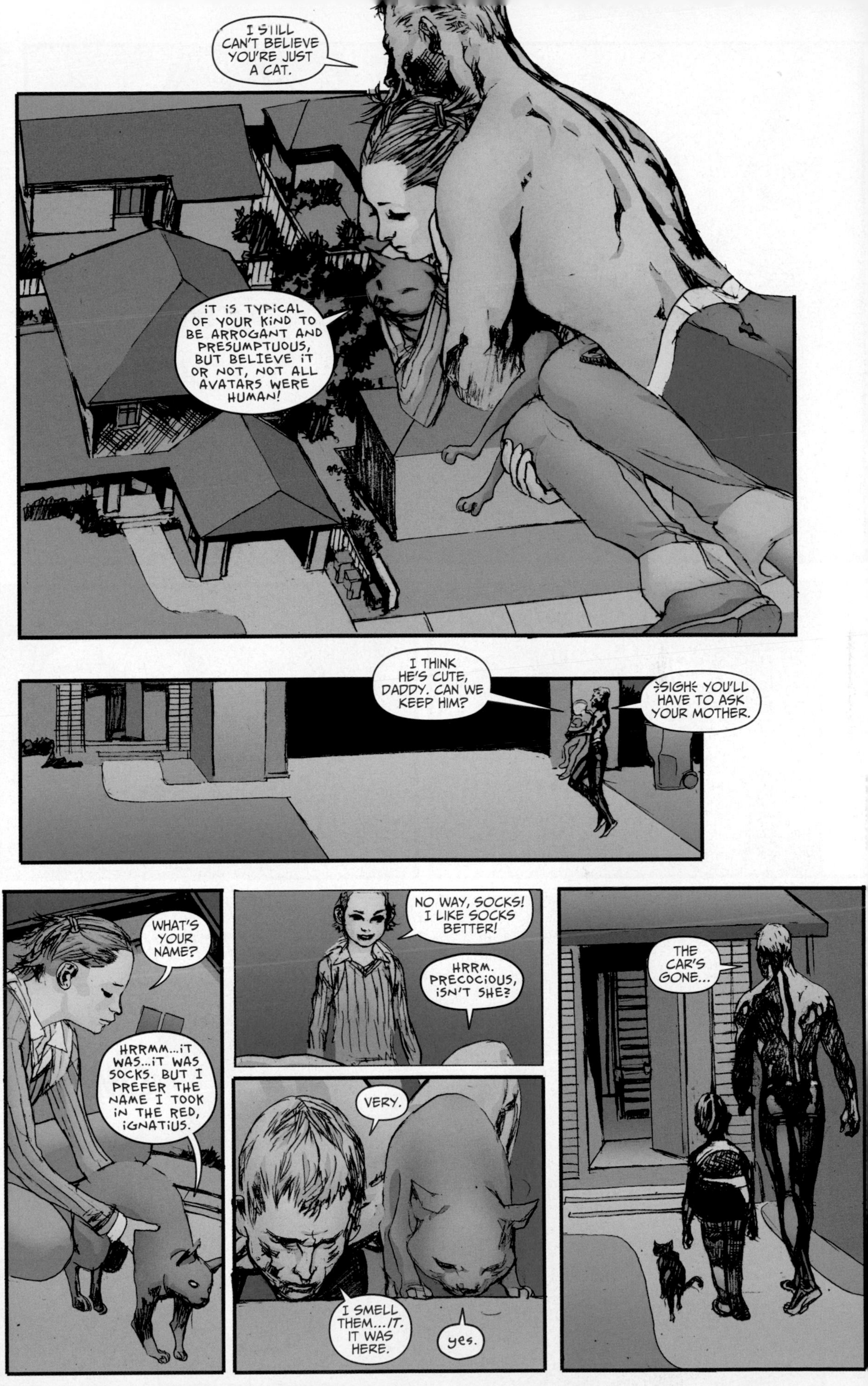
I STILL CAN'T BELIEVE YOU'RE JUST A CAT.
IT IS TYPICAL OF YOUR KIND TO BE ARROGANT AND PRESUMPTUOUS, BUT BELIEVE IT OR NOT, NOT ALL AVATARS WERE HUMAN!
I THINK HE'S CUTE, DADDY. CAN WE KEEP HIM?
SIGH YOU'LL HAVE TO ASK YOUR MOTHER.
WHAT'S YOUR NAME?
HRRMM...IT WAS...IT WAS SOCKS. BUT I PREFER THE NAME I TOOK IN THE RED, IGNATIUS.
NO WAY, SOCKS! I LIKE SOCKS BETTER!
HRRM. PRECOCIOUS, ISN'T SHE?
VERY.
I SMELL THEM...IT. IT WAS HERE.
yes.
THE CAR'S GONE...

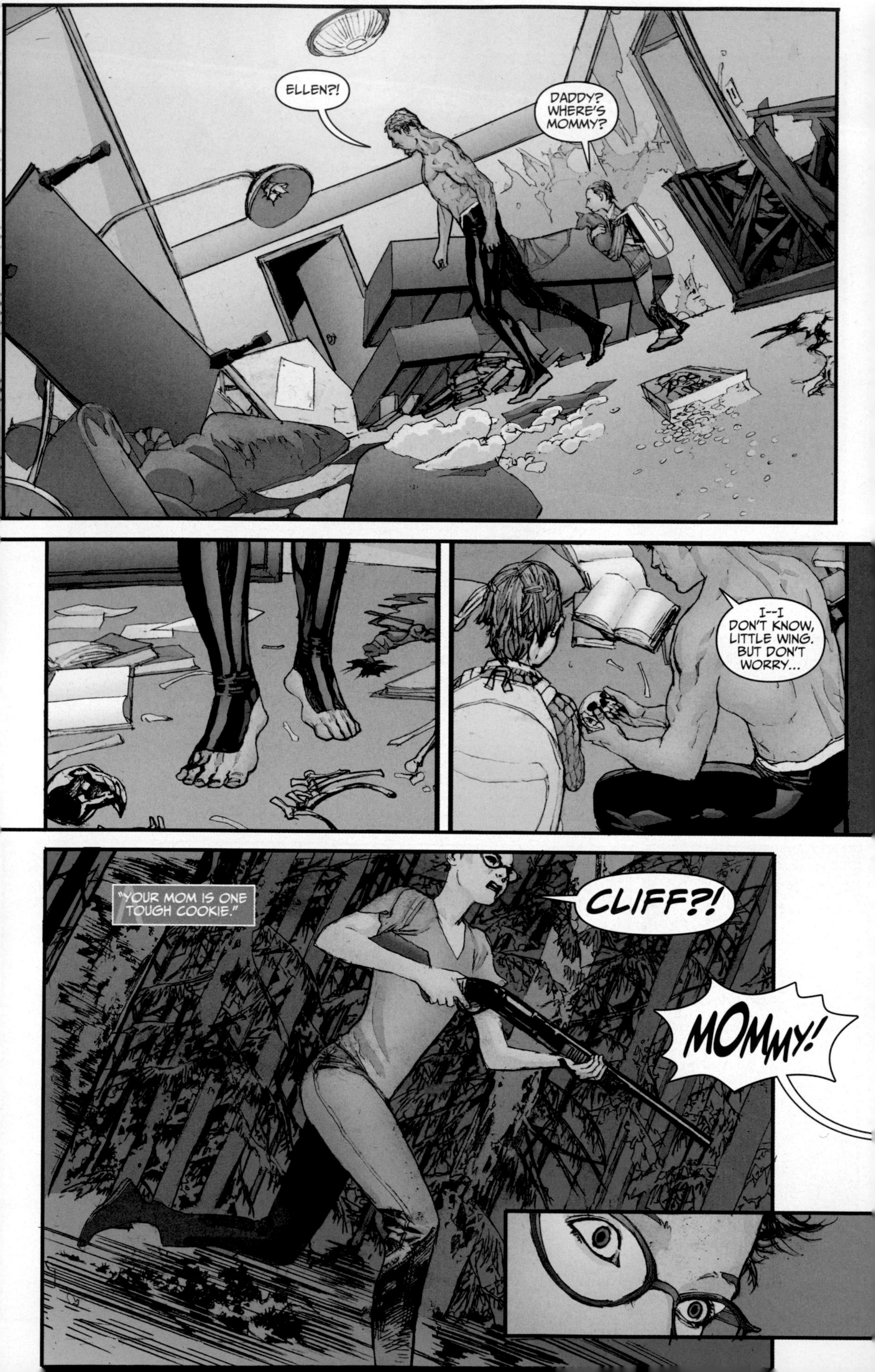
ELLEN?!
DADDY? WHERE'S MOMMY?
I--I DON'T KNOW, LITTLE WING. BUT DON'T WORRY...
"YOUR MOM IS ONE TOUGH COOKIE."
CLIFF?!
MOMMY!

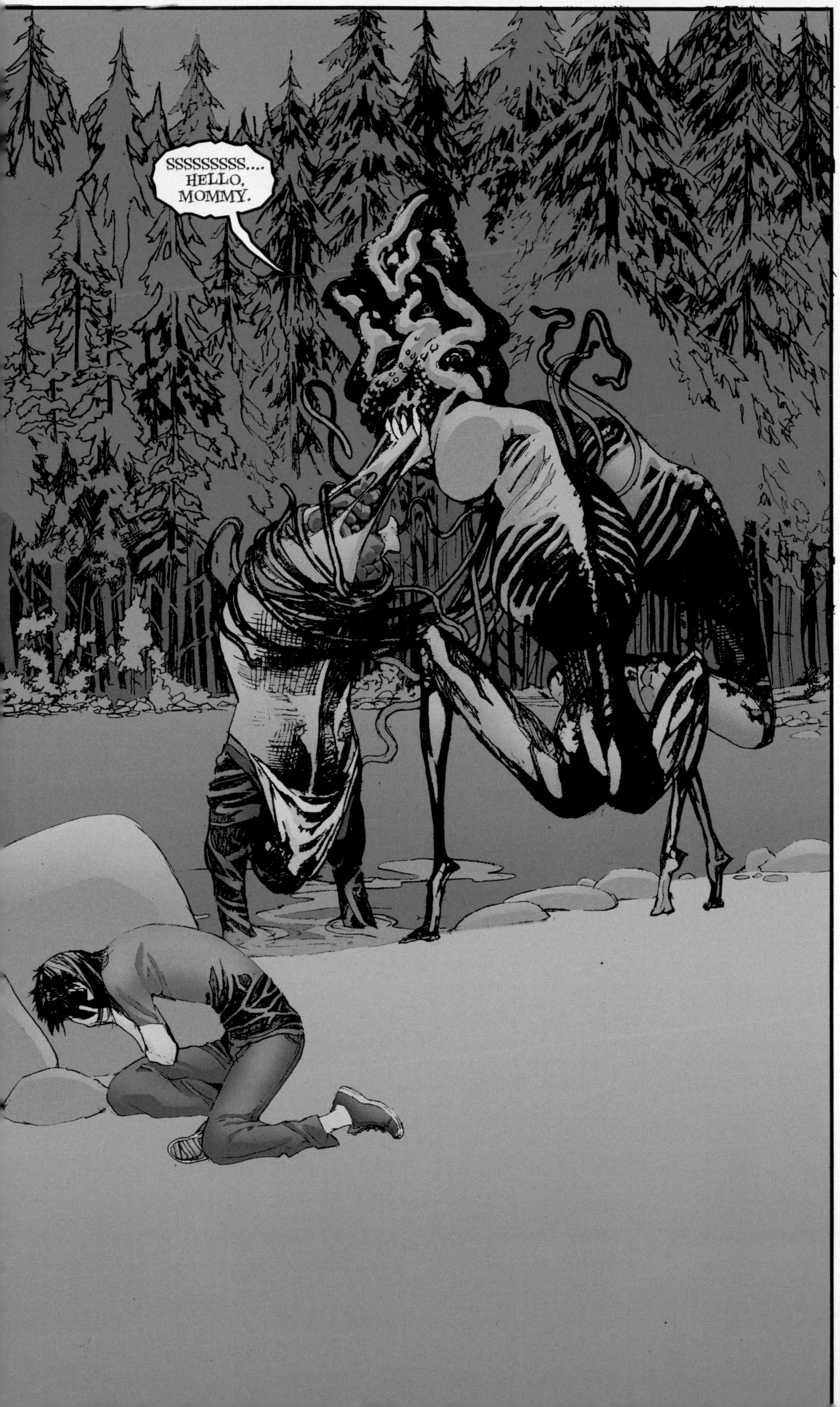
SSSSSSSS.... HELLO, MOMMY.

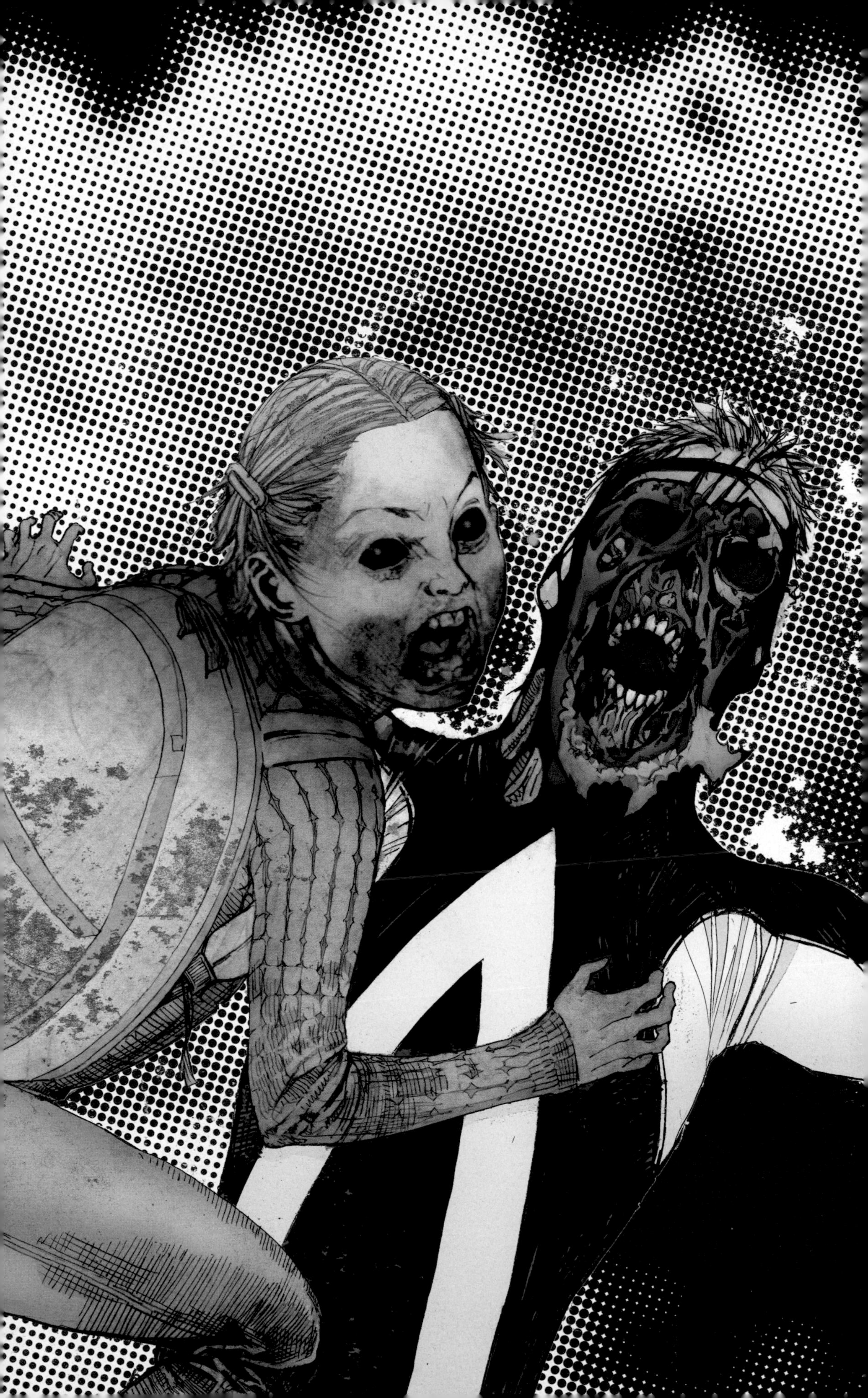

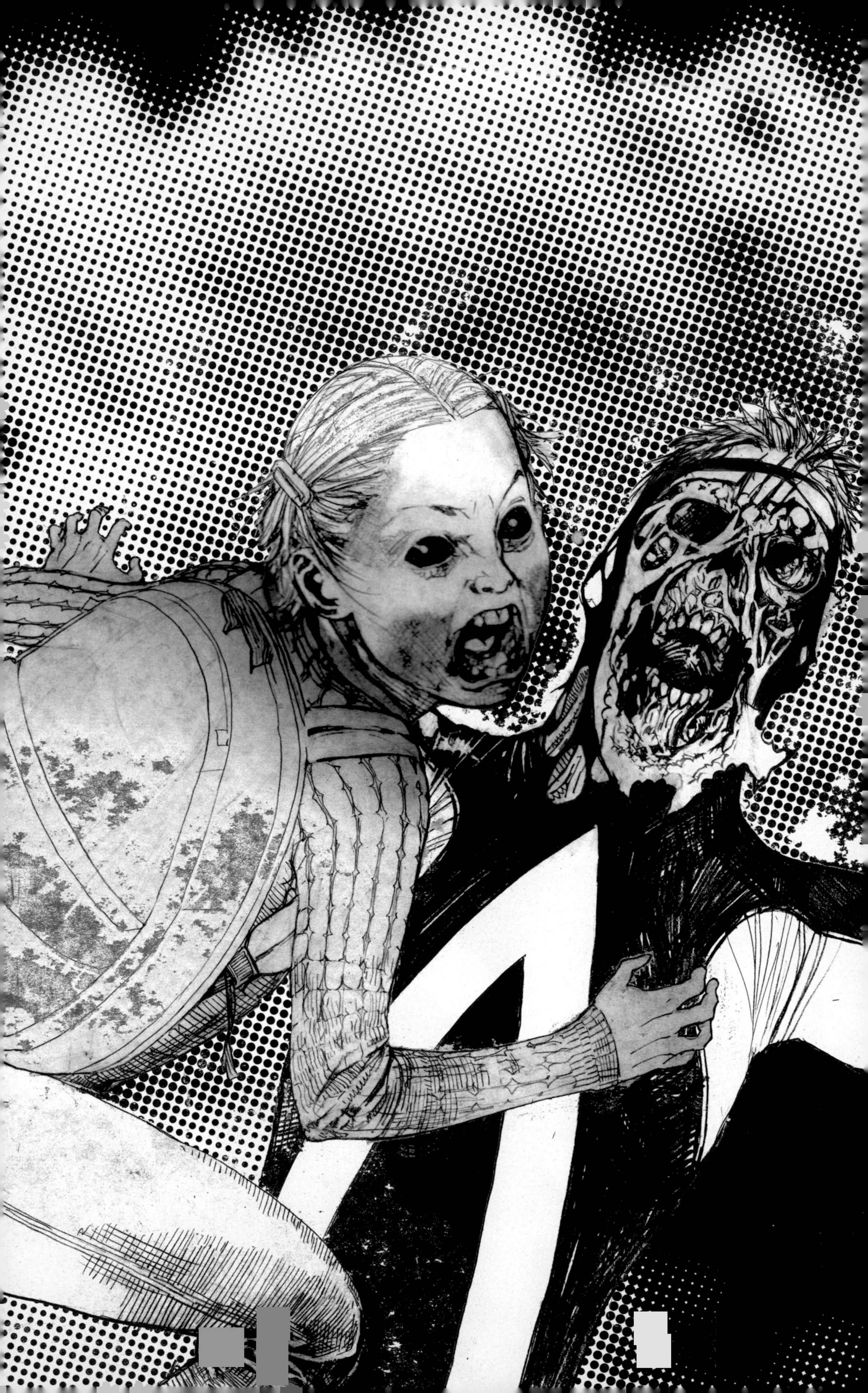

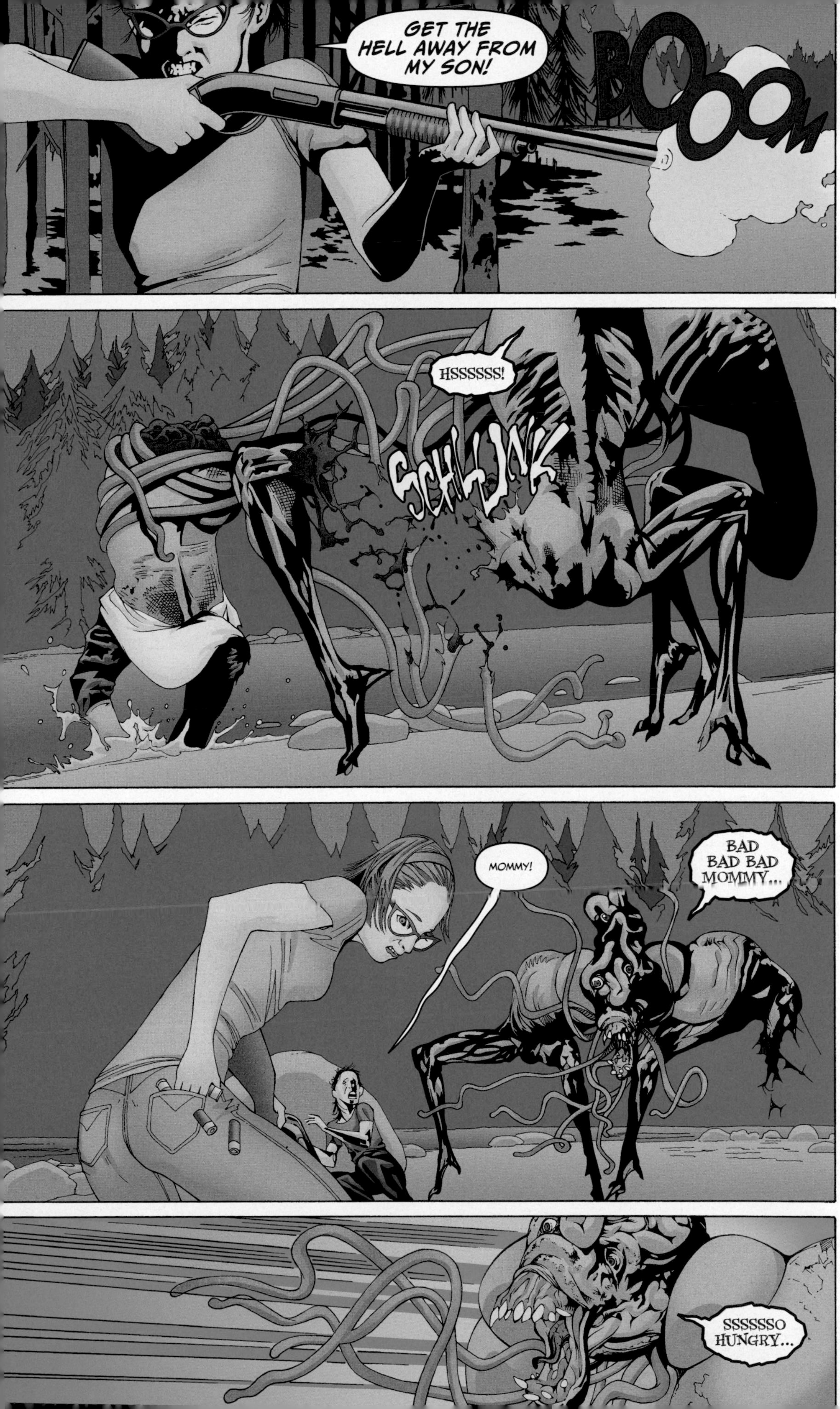
GET THE HELL AWAY FROM MY SON!
BOOOOM
HSSSSSS!
SCHLUNK
MOMMY!
BAD BAD BAD MOMMY...
SSSSSSO HUNGRY...

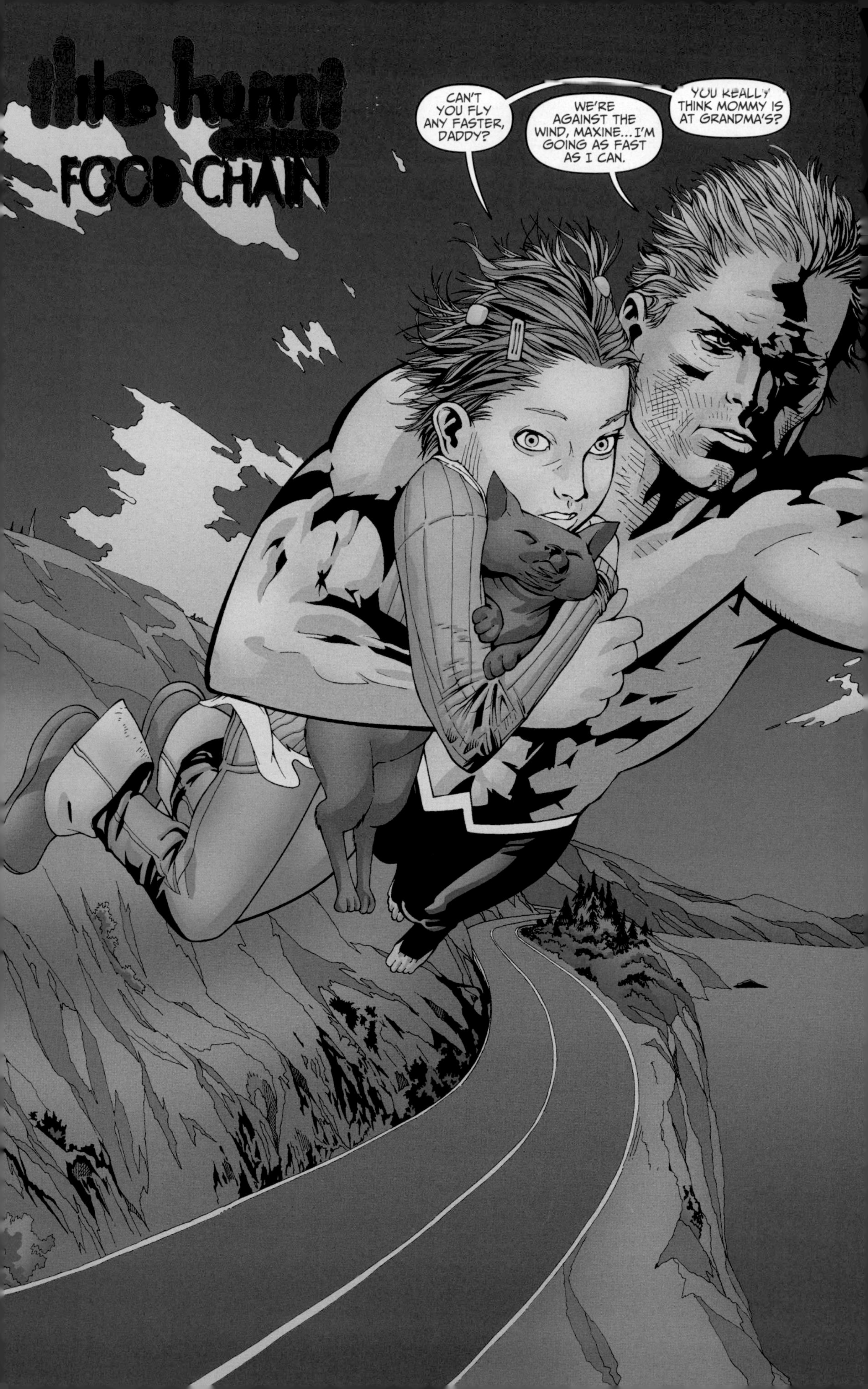
the hunt
FOOD CHAIN
CAN'T YOU FLY ANY FASTER, DADDY?
WE'RE AGAINST THE WIND, MAXINE... I'M GOING AS FAST AS I CAN.
YOU REALLY THINK MOMMY IS AT GRANDMA'S?

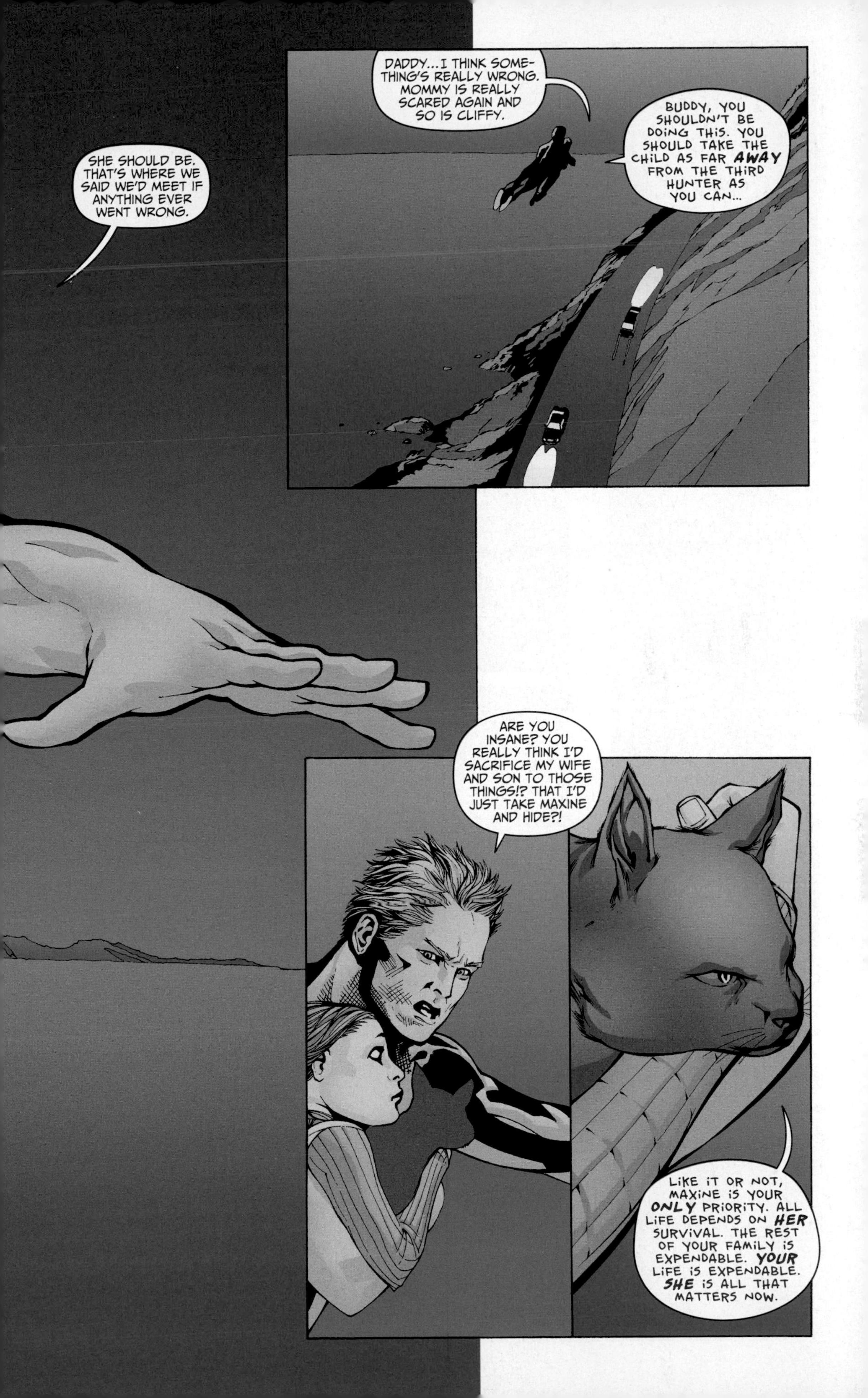
DADDY... I THINK SOMETHING'S REALLY WRONG. MOMMY IS REALLY SCARED AGAIN AND SO IS CLIFFY.
SHE SHOULD BE. THAT'S WHERE WE SAID WE'D MEET IF ANYTHING EVER WENT WRONG.
BUDDY, YOU SHOULDN'T BE DOING THIS. YOU SHOULD TAKE THE CHILD AS FAR AWAY FROM THE THIRD HUNTER AS YOU CAN...
ARE YOU INSANE? YOU REALLY THINK I'D SACRIFICE MY WIFE AND SON TO THOSE THINGS!? THAT I'D JUST TAKE MAXINE AND HIDE?!
LIKE IT OR NOT, MAXINE IS YOUR ONLY PRIORITY. ALL LIFE DEPENDS ON HER SURVIVAL. THE REST OF YOUR FAMILY IS EXPENDABLE. YOUR LIFE IS EXPENDABLE. SHE IS ALL THAT MATTERS NOW.

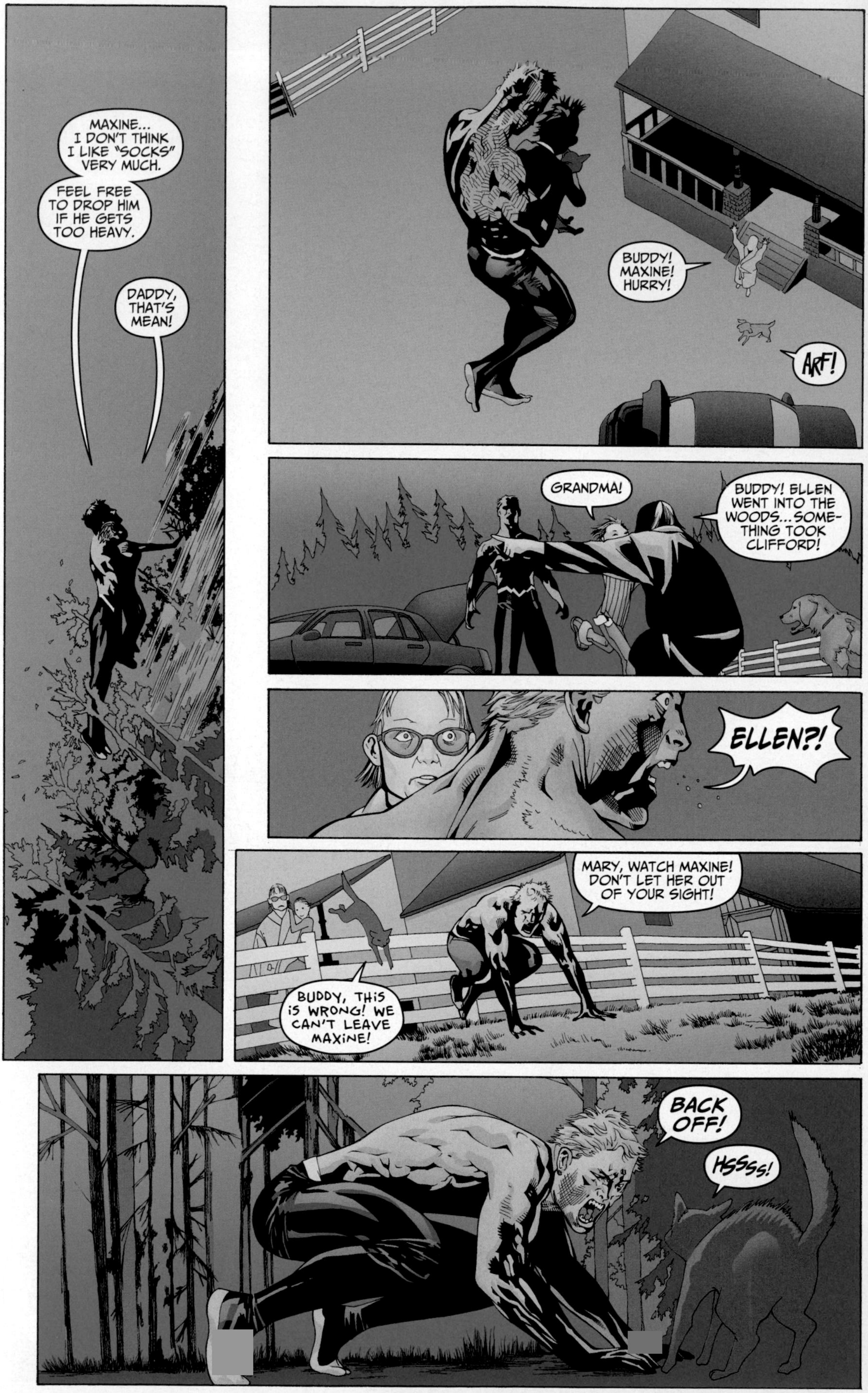

MAXINE... I DON'T THINK I LIKE "SOCKS" VERY MUCH.
FEEL FREE TO DROP HIM IF HE GETS TOO HEAVY.
DADDY, THAT'S MEAN!
BUDDY! MAXINE! HURRY!
ARF!
GRANDMA!
BUDDY! ELLEN WENT INTO THE WOODS...SOMETHING TOOK CLIFFORD!
ELLEN?!
MARY, WATCH MAXINE! DON'T LET HER OUT OF YOUR SIGHT!
BUDDY, THIS IS WRONG! WE CAN'T LEAVE MAXINE!
BACK OFF!
HSSss!

UNGH!

SSSLLLURRR

SSSOOOO TASTY.

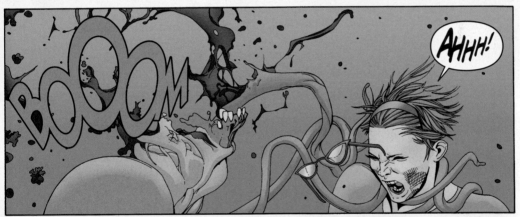

BOOOM

AHHH!

CLIFF!

BLAAAARRRR! GET YOU NEXT, BOY!

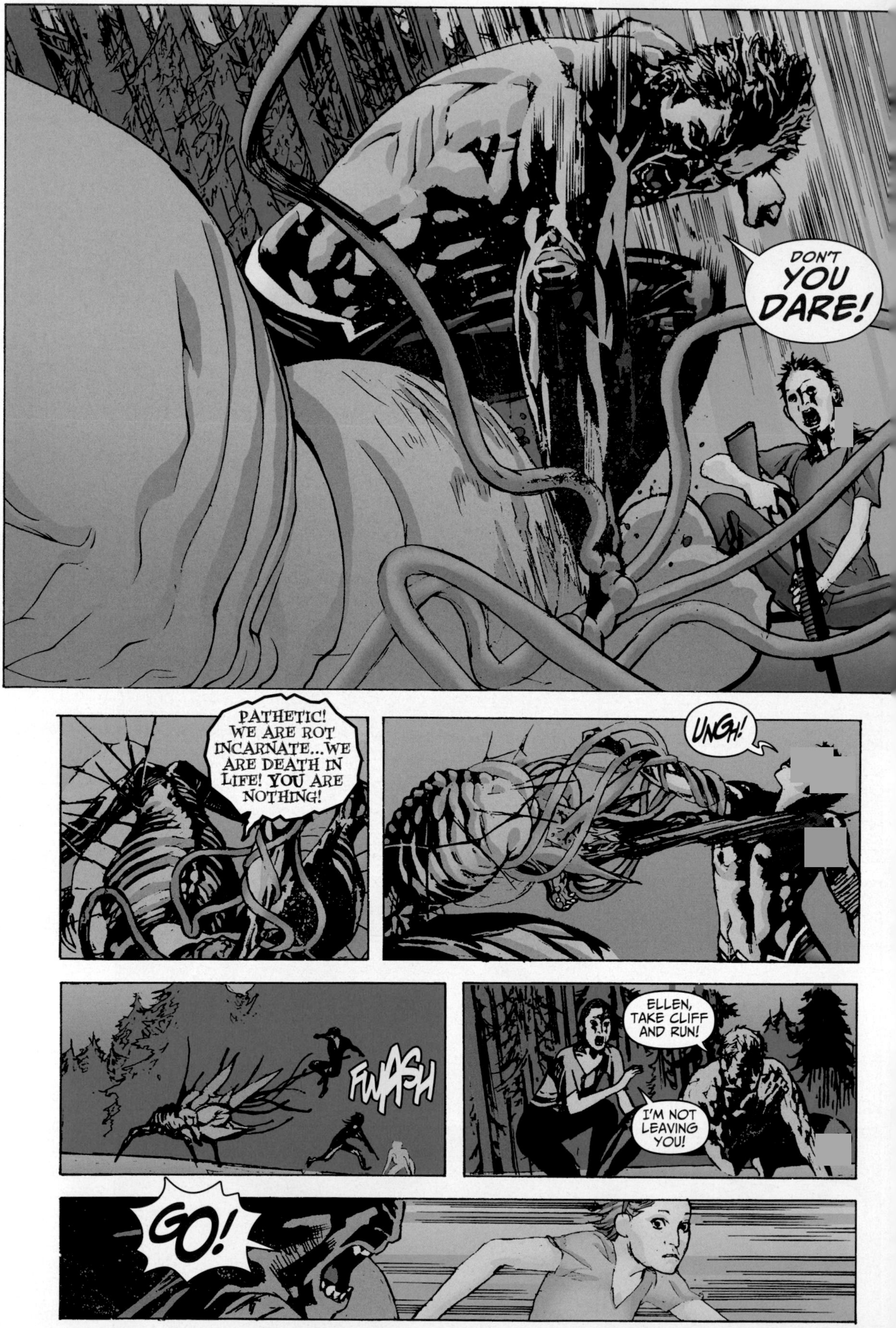
DON'T YOU DARE!
PATHETIC! WE ARE ROT INCARNATE...WE ARE DEATH IN LIFE! YOU ARE NOTHING!
UNGH!
FWASH
ELLEN, TAKE CLIFF AND RUN!
I'M NOT LEAVING YOU!
GO!

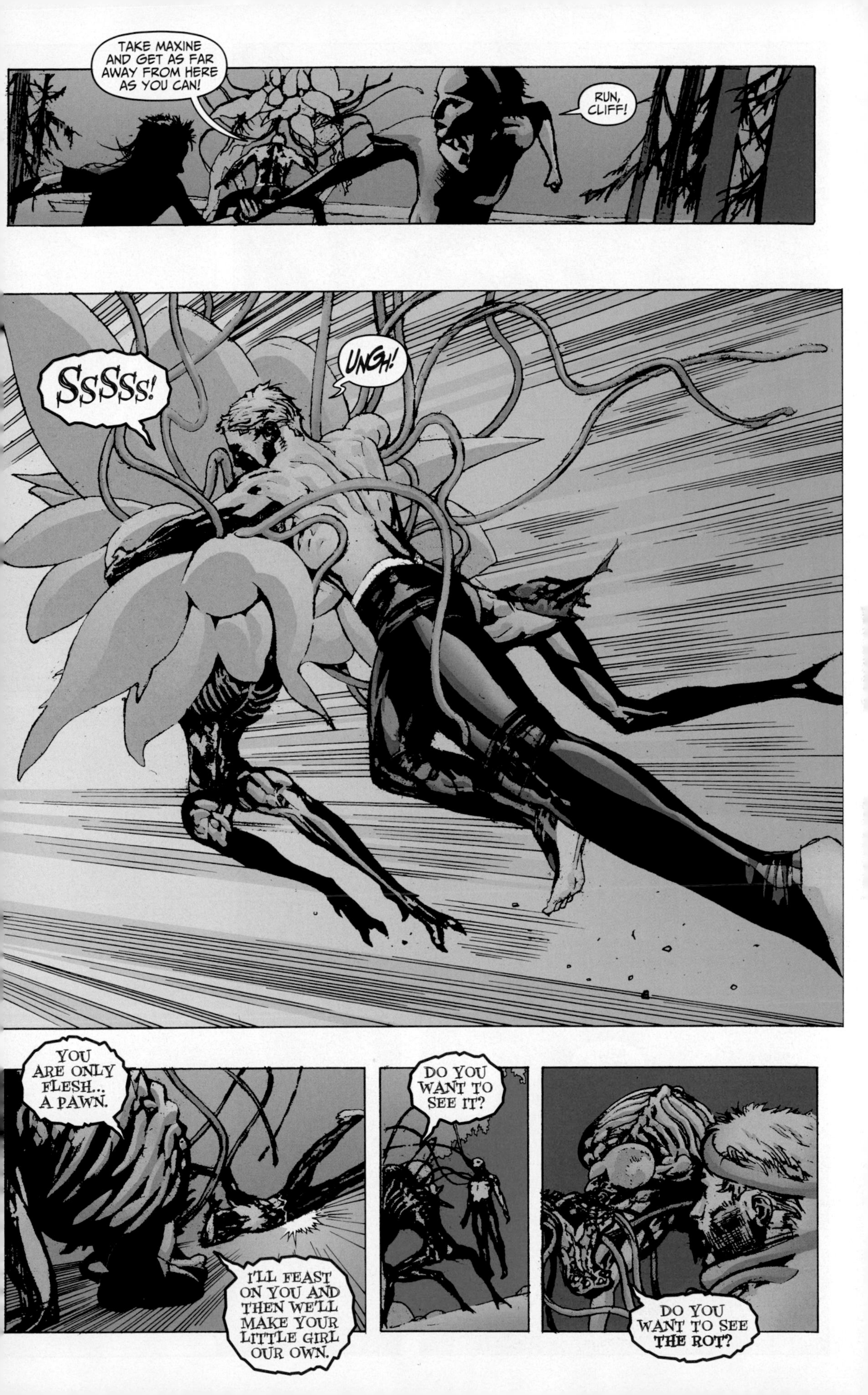
TAKE MAXINE AND GET AS FAR AWAY FROM HERE AS YOU CAN!
RUN, CLIFF!
SSSSS!
UNGH!
YOU ARE ONLY FLESH... A PAWN.
I'LL FEAST ON YOU AND THEN WE'LL MAKE YOUR LITTLE GIRL OUR OWN.
DO YOU WANT TO SEE IT?
DO YOU WANT TO SEE THE ROT?

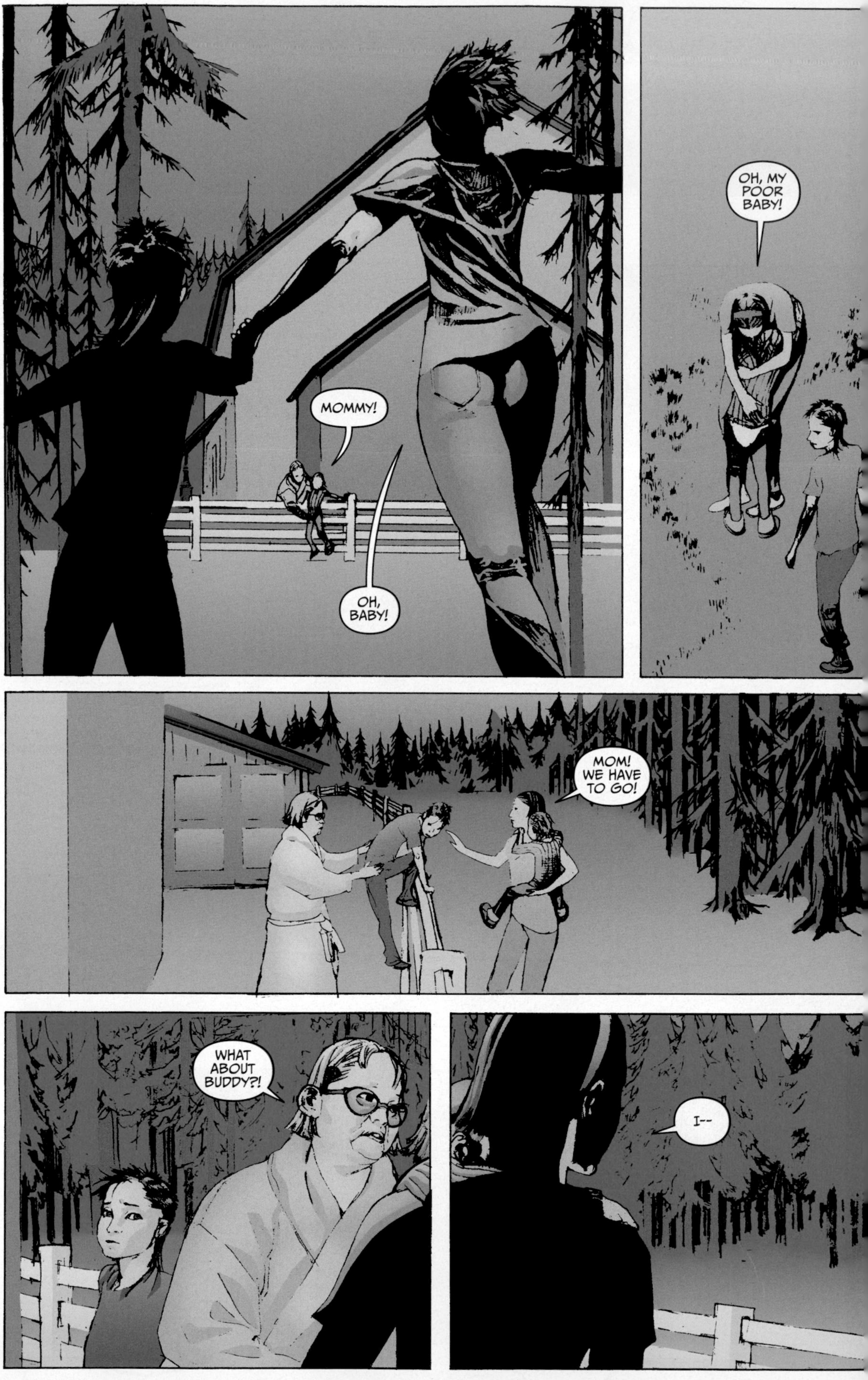
MOMMY!
OH, BABY!
OH, MY POOR BABY!
MOM! WE HAVE TO GO!
WHAT ABOUT BUDDY?!
I--

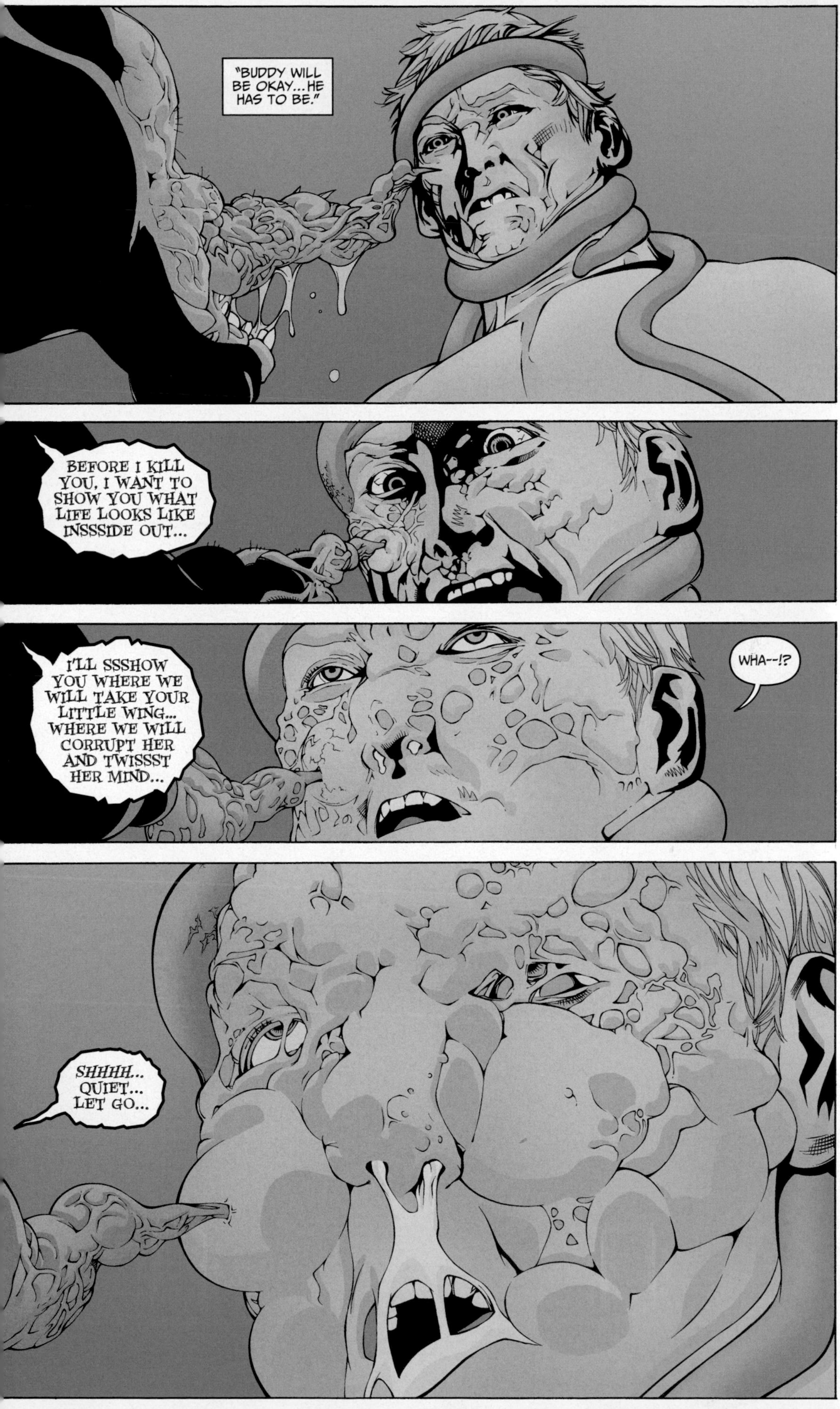
"BUDDY WILL BE OKAY...HE HAS TO BE."
BEFORE I KILL YOU, I WANT TO SHOW YOU WHAT LIFE LOOKS LIKE INSSSIDE OUT...
I'LL SSSHOW YOU WHERE WE WILL TAKE YOUR LITTLE WING... WHERE WE WILL CORRUPT HER AND TWISSST HER MIND...
WHA--!?
SHHHH... QUIET... LET GO...

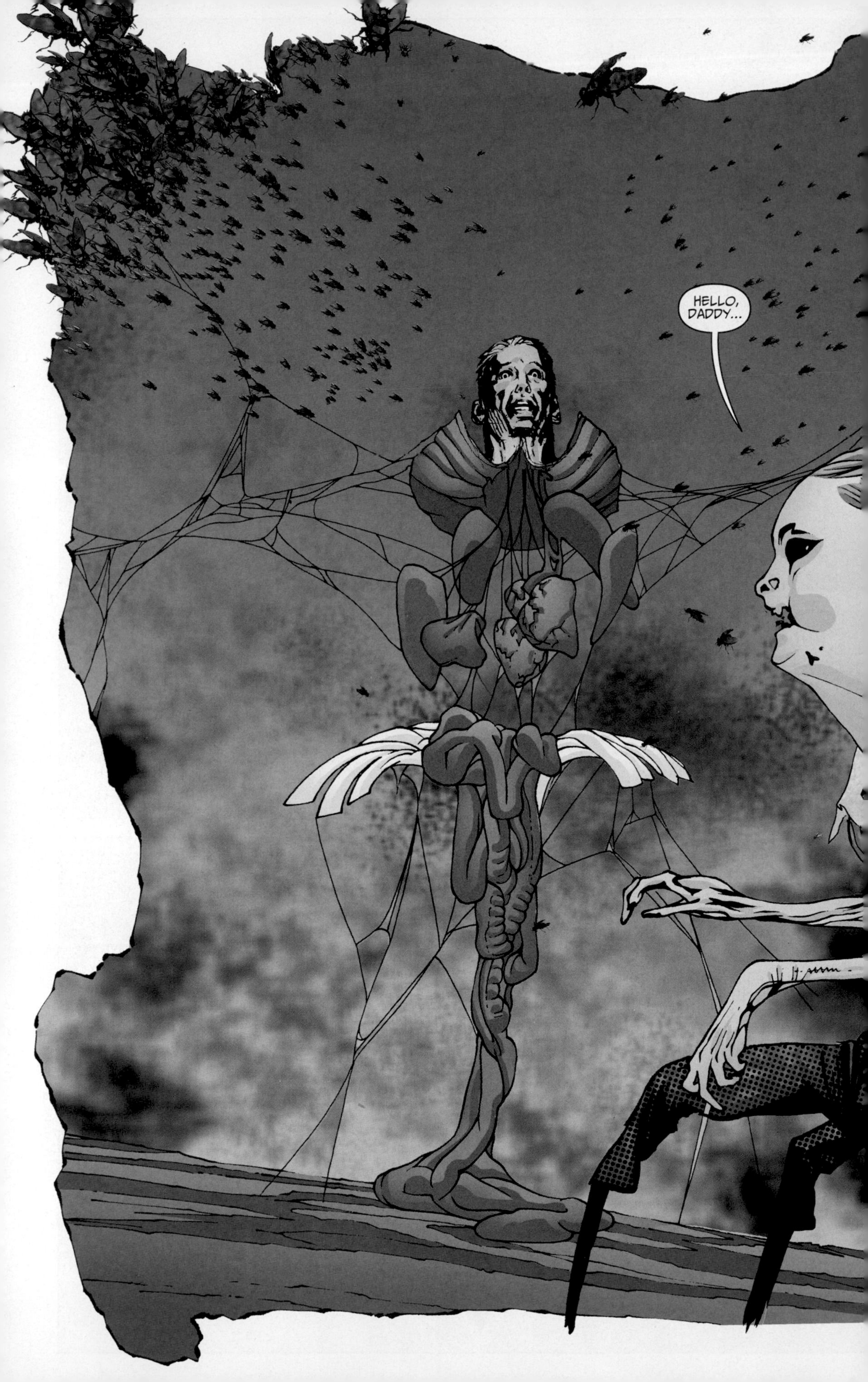
HELLO, DADDY...

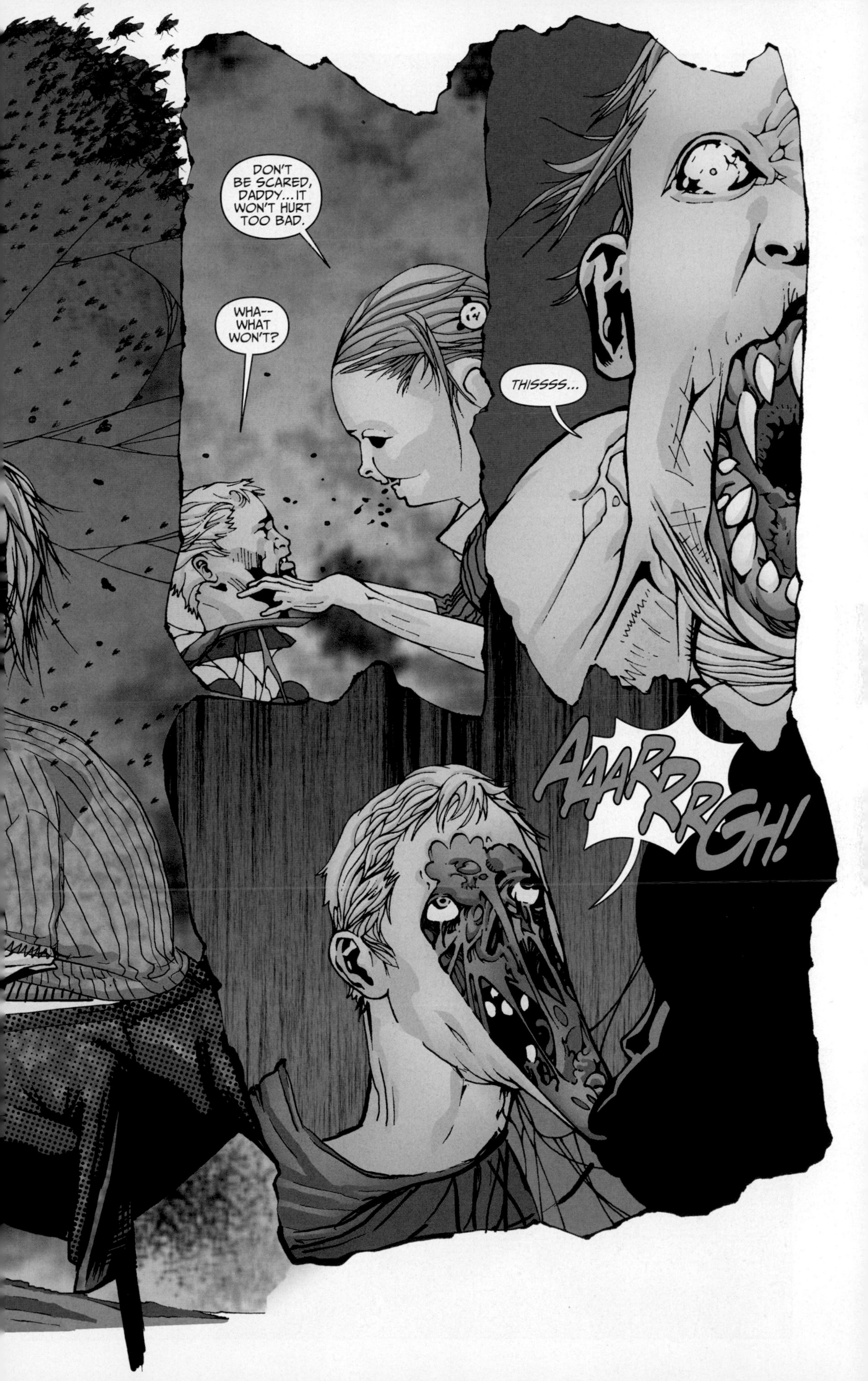
DON'T BE SCARED, DADDY... IT WON'T HURT TOO BAD.
WHA-- WHAT WON'T?
THISSSS...
AAARRRGH!

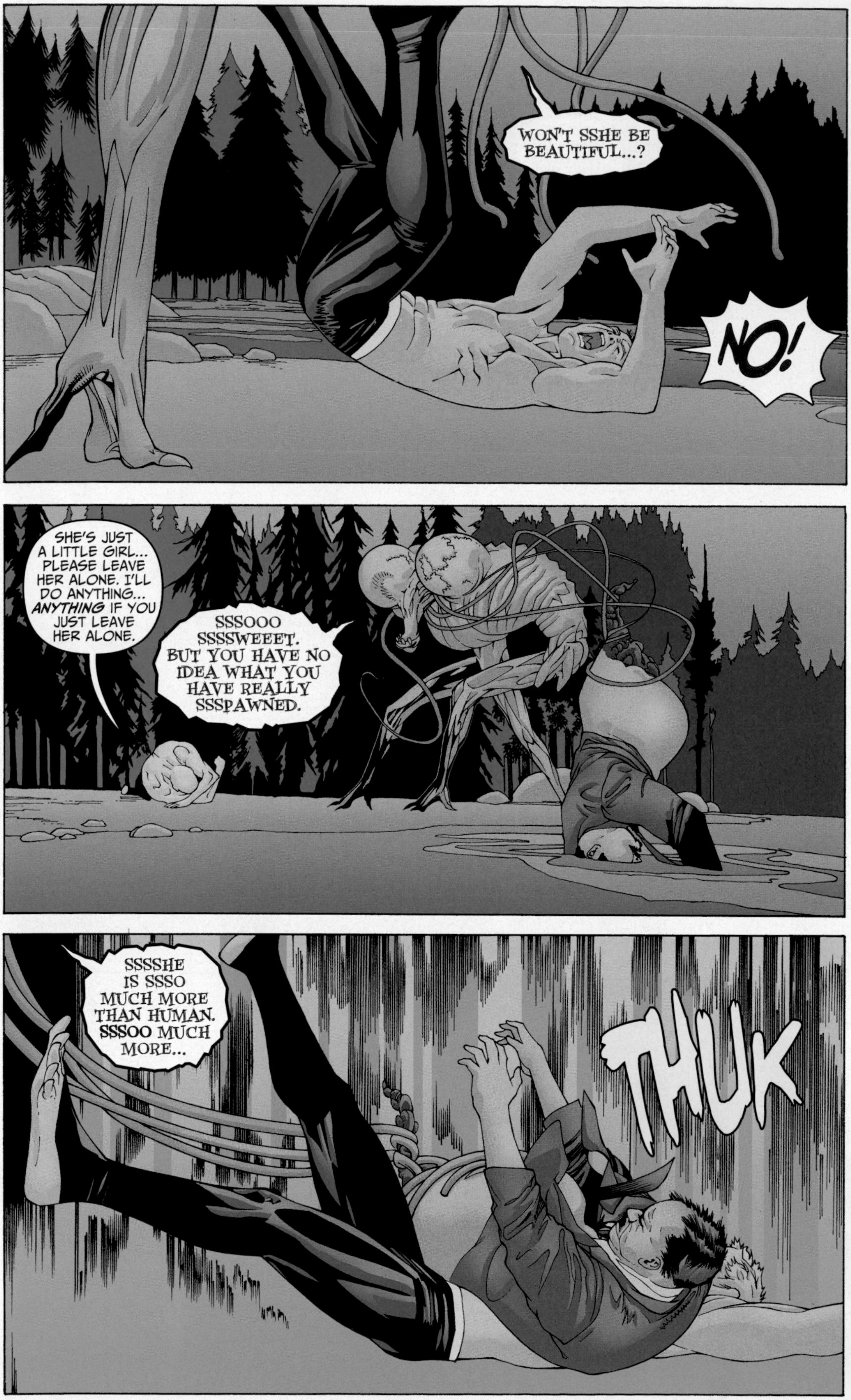
WON'T SSHE BE BEAUTIFUL...?
NO!
SHE'S JUST A LITTLE GIRL... PLEASE LEAVE HER ALONE. I'LL DO ANYTHING... ANYTHING IF YOU JUST LEAVE HER ALONE.
SSSOOO SSSSWEEET. BUT YOU HAVE NO IDEA WHAT YOU HAVE REALLY SSSPAWNED.
SSSSHE IS SSSO MUCH MORE THAN HUMAN. SSSOO MUCH MORE...
THUK

DADDY'S IN TROUBLE... I NEED TO HELP HIM, MOMMY.

HONEY, YOUR DADDY IS FIGHTING THAT THING OUT THERE. HE'S REALLY STRONG. HE'LL BE OKAY. WE NEED TO STAY HERE!

NO, YOU DON'T GET IT, MOM... I DON'T HAVE TO GO ANYWHERE...

WHAT ARE YOU DOING, CHILD?

THE CAT TALKS!

THAT YOU'RE SURPRISED BY?

I CAN HELP DADDY FROM HERE...

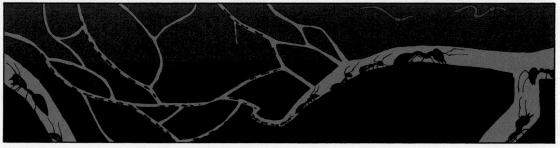

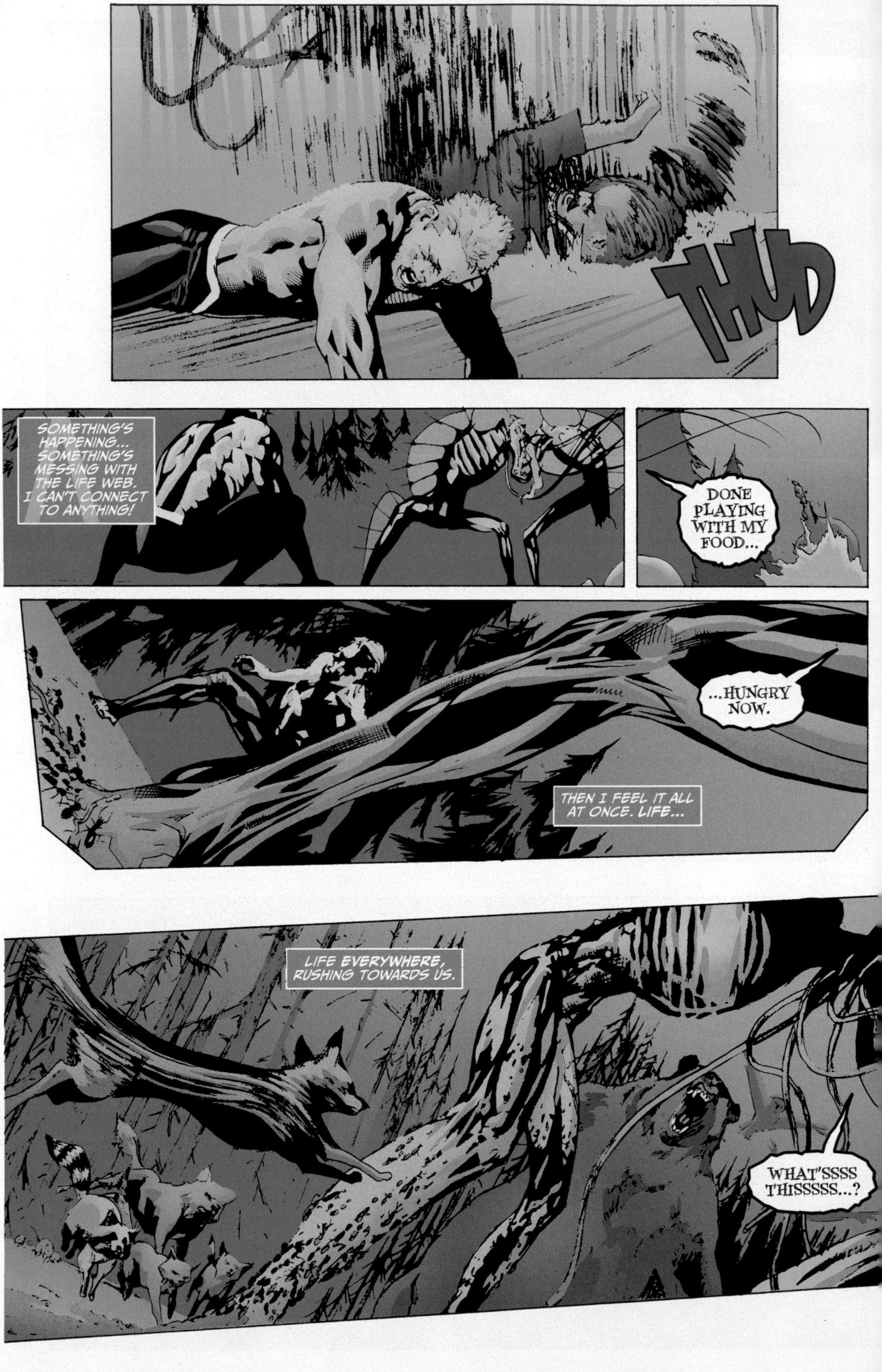
THUD
SOMETHING'S HAPPENING... SOMETHING'S MESSING WITH THE LIFE WEB. I CAN'T CONNECT TO ANYTHING!
DONE PLAYING WITH MY FOOD...
...HUNGRY NOW.
THEN I FEEL IT ALL AT ONCE. LIFE...
LIFE EVERYWHERE, RUSHING TOWARDS US.
WHAT'SSSS THISSSSS...?

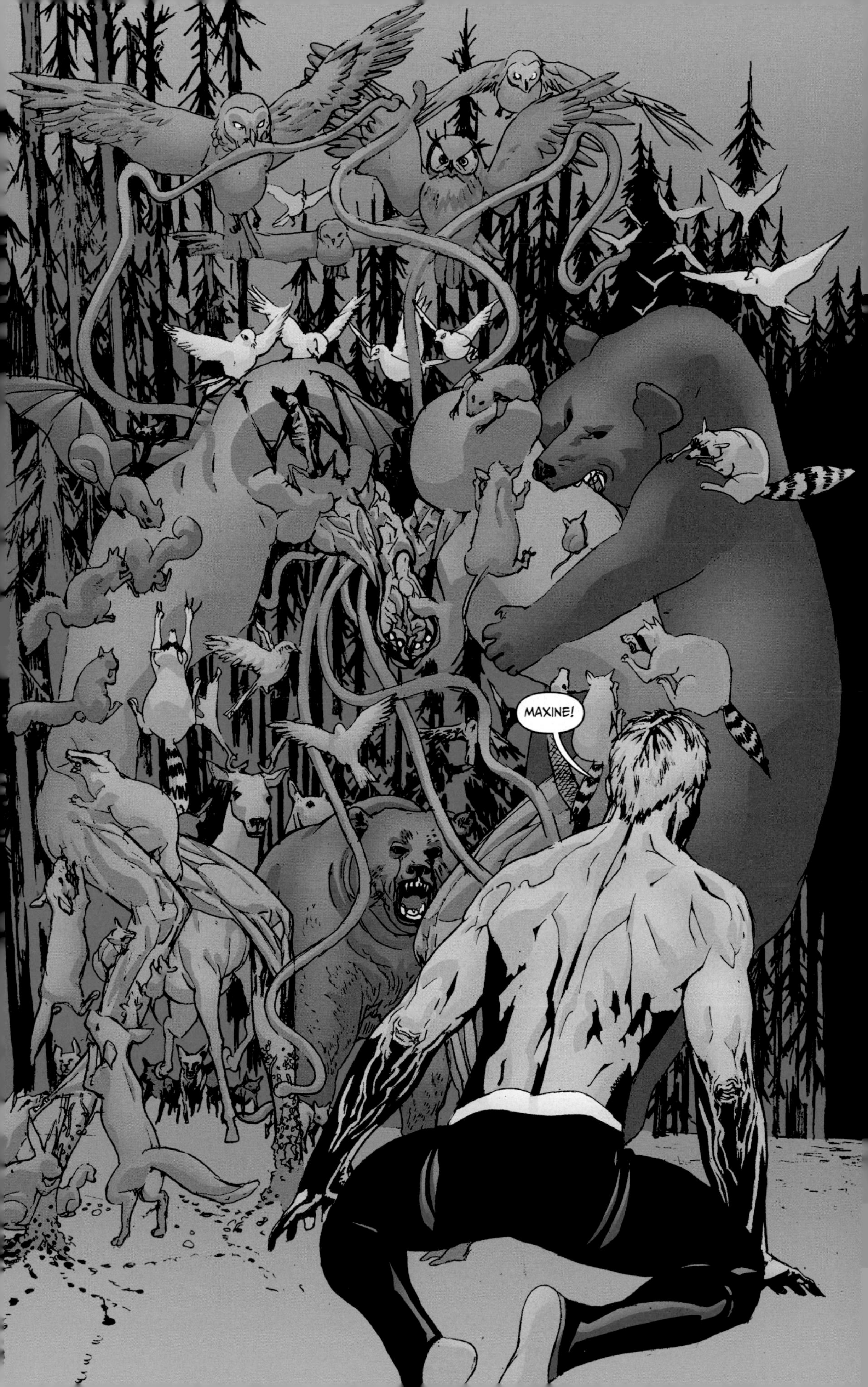
MAXINE!

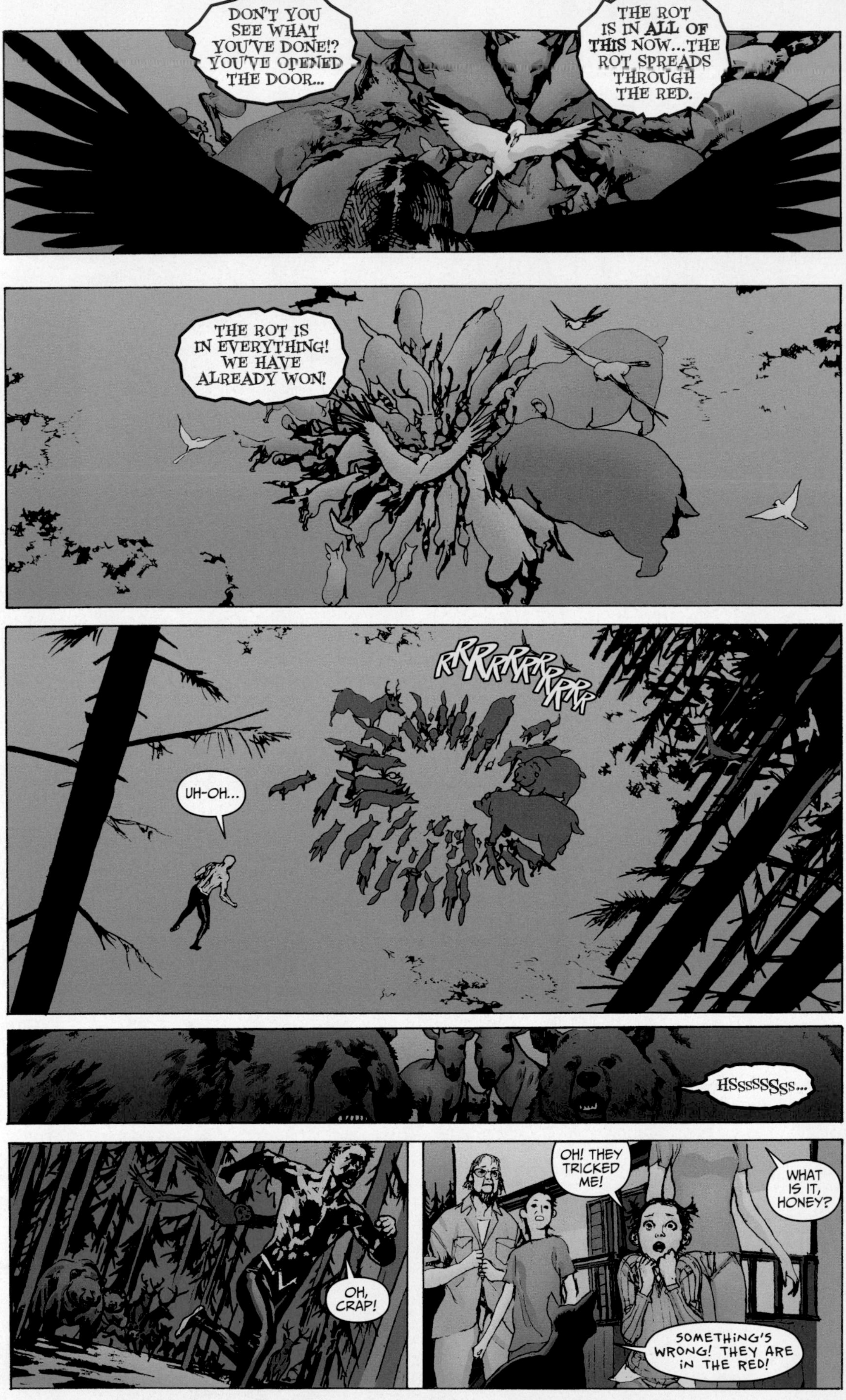
DON'T YOU SEE WHAT YOU'VE DONE!? YOU'VE OPENED THE DOOR...
THE ROT IS IN ALL OF THIS NOW...THE ROT SPREADS THROUGH THE RED.
THE ROT IS IN EVERYTHING! WE HAVE ALREADY WON!
RRRRRRRRRRRR
UH-OH...
HSSSSSSS...
OH, CRAP!
OH! THEY TRICKED ME!
WHAT IS IT, HONEY?
SOMETHING'S WRONG! THEY ARE IN THE RED!

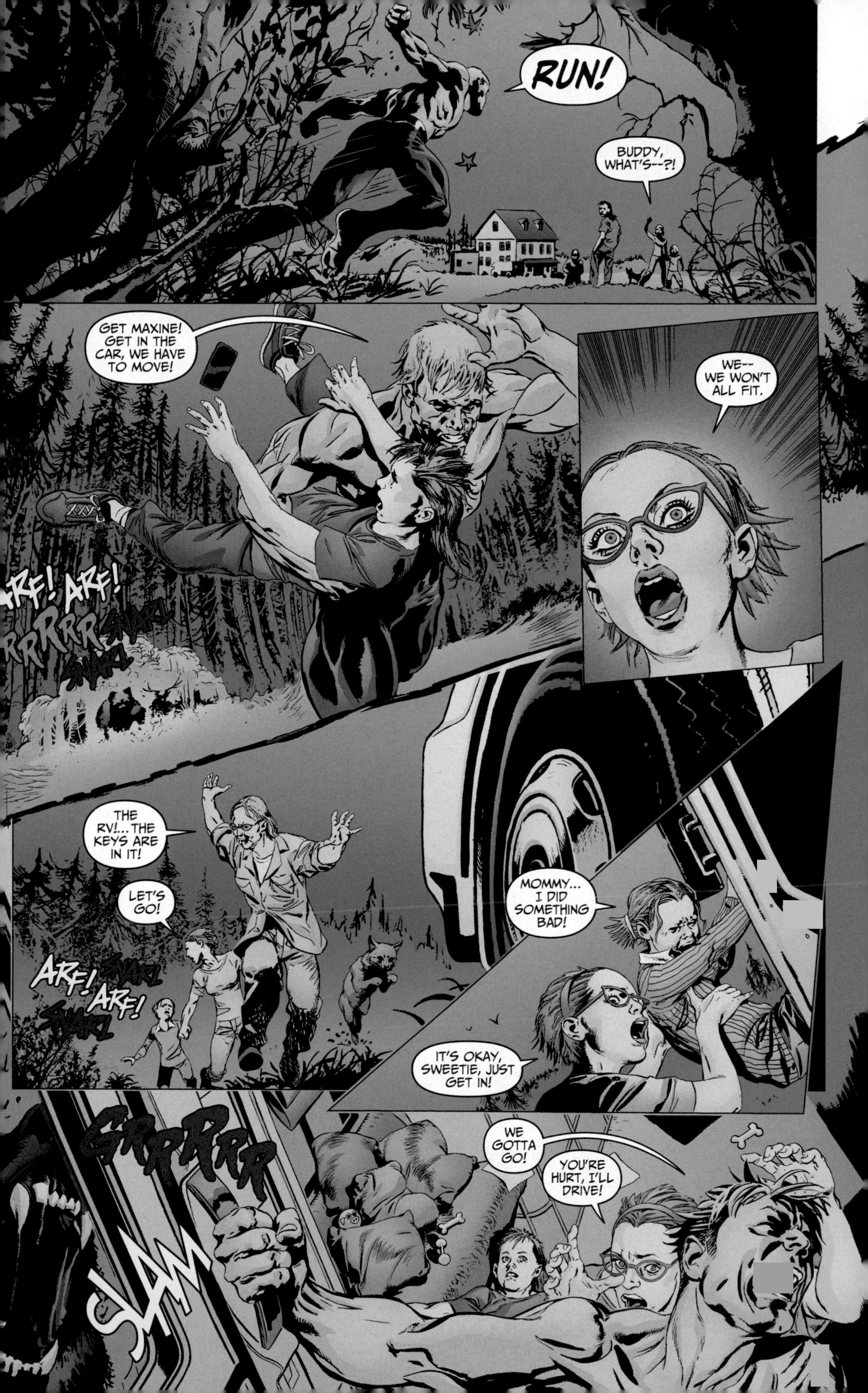
RUN!
BUDDY, WHAT'S--?!
GET MAXINE! GET IN THE CAR, WE HAVE TO MOVE!
WE-- WE WON'T ALL FIT.
ARF! ARF!
RRRRR
SNARL
THE RV!... THE KEYS ARE IN IT!
LET'S GO!
ARF! ARF!
SNARL
SNARL
MOMMY... I DID SOMETHING BAD!
IT'S OKAY, SWEETIE, JUST GET IN!
GRRRRR
WE GOTTA GO!
YOU'RE HURT, I'LL DRIVE!
SLAM

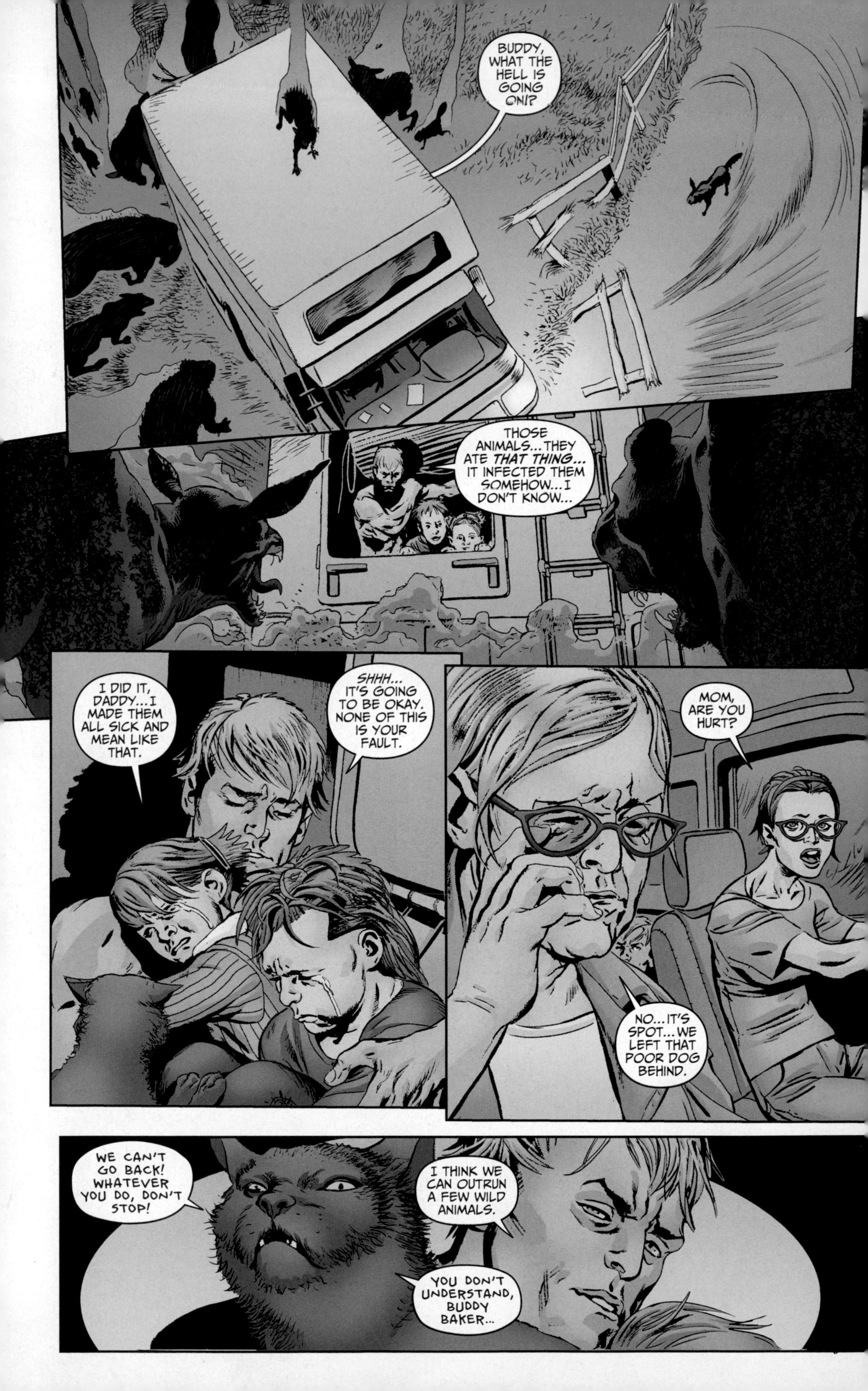
BUDDY, WHAT THE HELL IS GOING ON!?
THOSE ANIMALS... THEY ATE *THAT THING*... IT INFECTED THEM SOMEHOW... I DON'T KNOW...
I DID IT, DADDY... I MADE THEM ALL SICK AND MEAN LIKE THAT.
SHHH... IT'S GOING TO BE OKAY. NONE OF THIS IS YOUR FAULT.
MOM, ARE YOU HURT?
NO... IT'S SPOT... WE LEFT THAT POOR DOG BEHIND.
WE CAN'T GO BACK! WHATEVER YOU DO, DON'T STOP!
I THINK WE CAN OUTRUN A FEW WILD ANIMALS.
YOU DON'T UNDERSTAND, BUDDY BAKER...

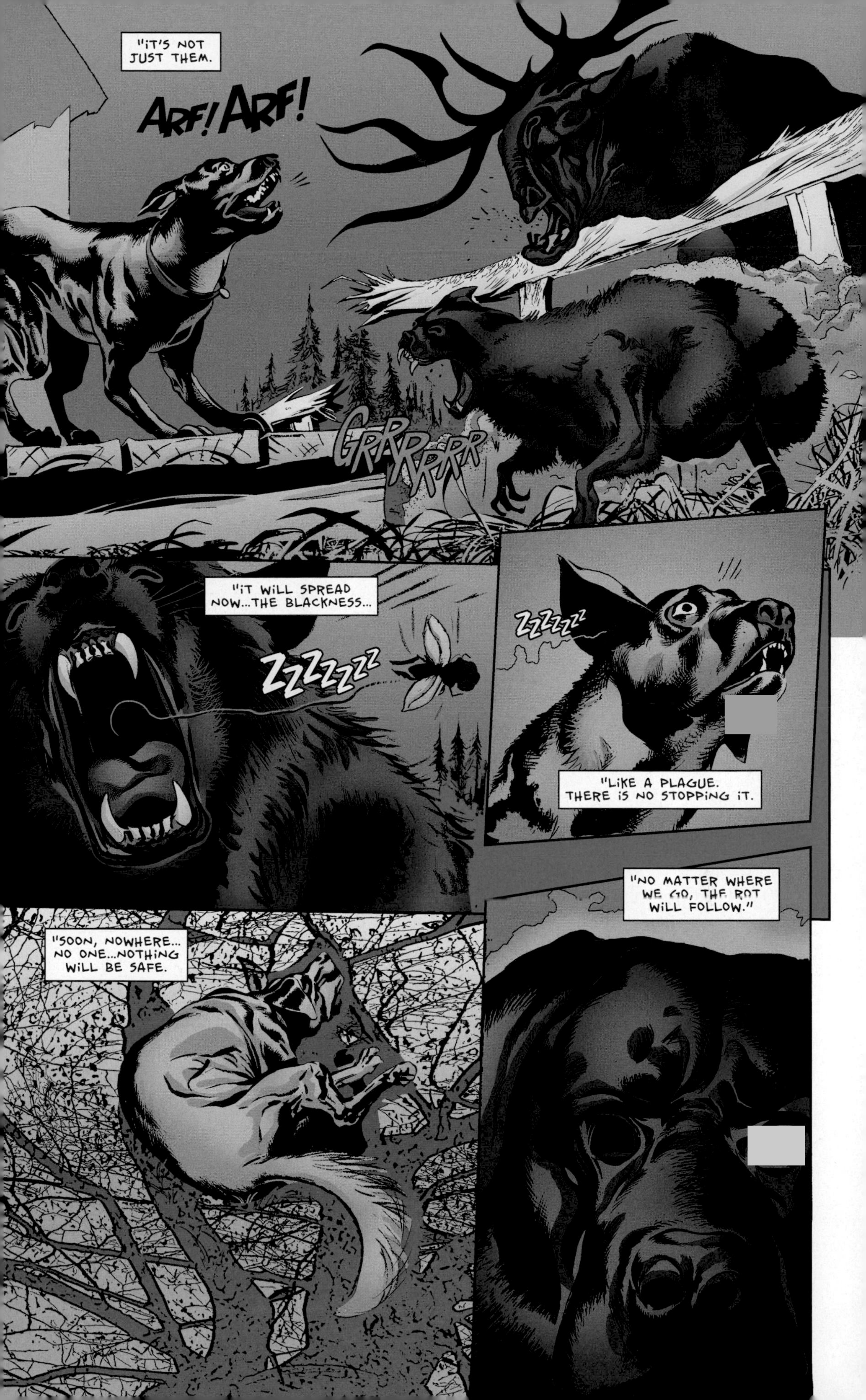
"IT'S NOT JUST THEM.
ARF! ARF!
GRRRRRRR
"IT WILL SPREAD NOW...THE BLACKNESS...
ZZZZZZZ
ZZZZZZZ
"LIKE A PLAGUE. THERE IS NO STOPPING IT.
"NO MATTER WHERE WE GO, THE ROT WILL FOLLOW."
"SOON, NOWHERE... NO ONE...NOTHING WILL BE SAFE.

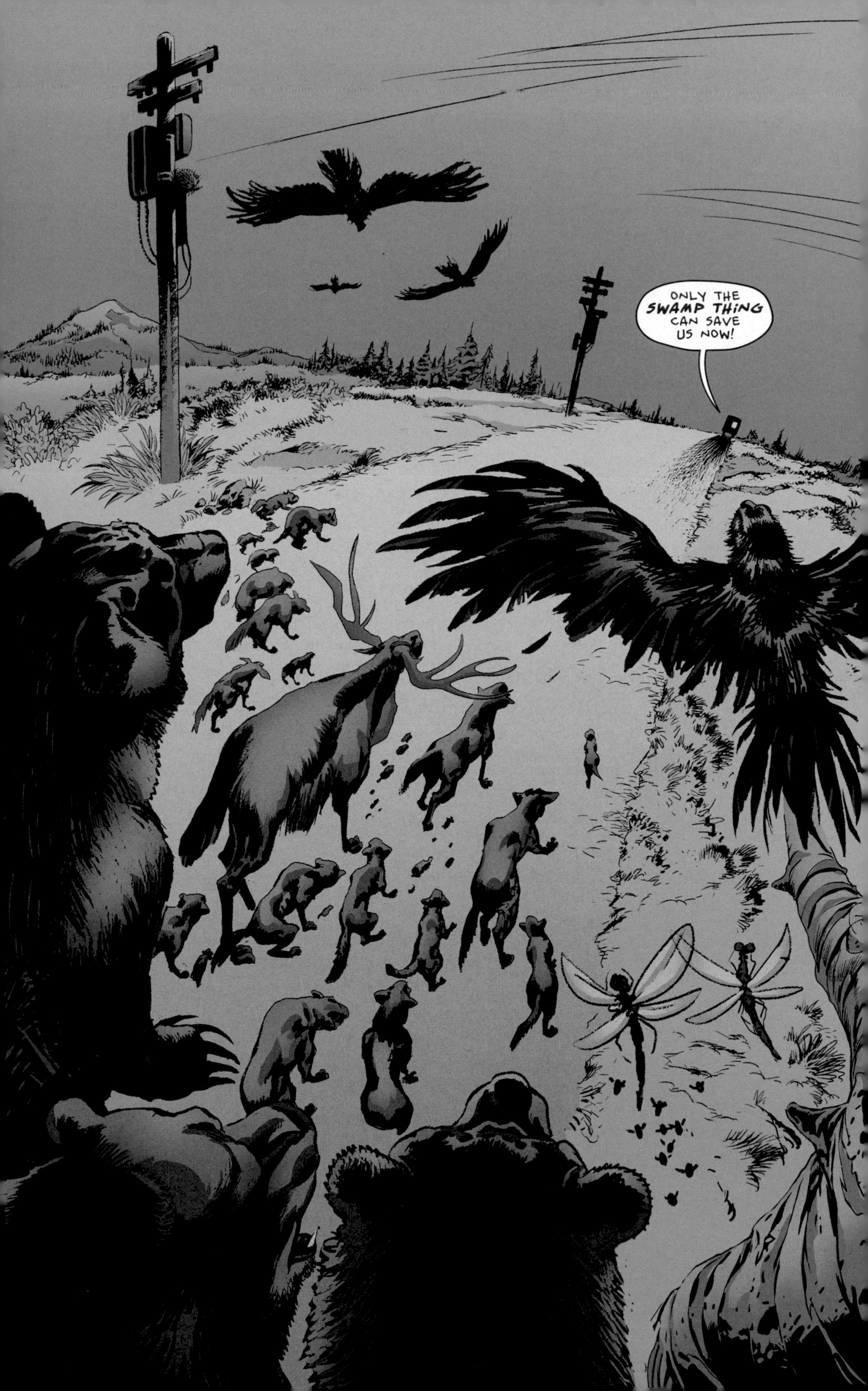
ONLY THE SWAMP THING CAN SAVE US NOW!

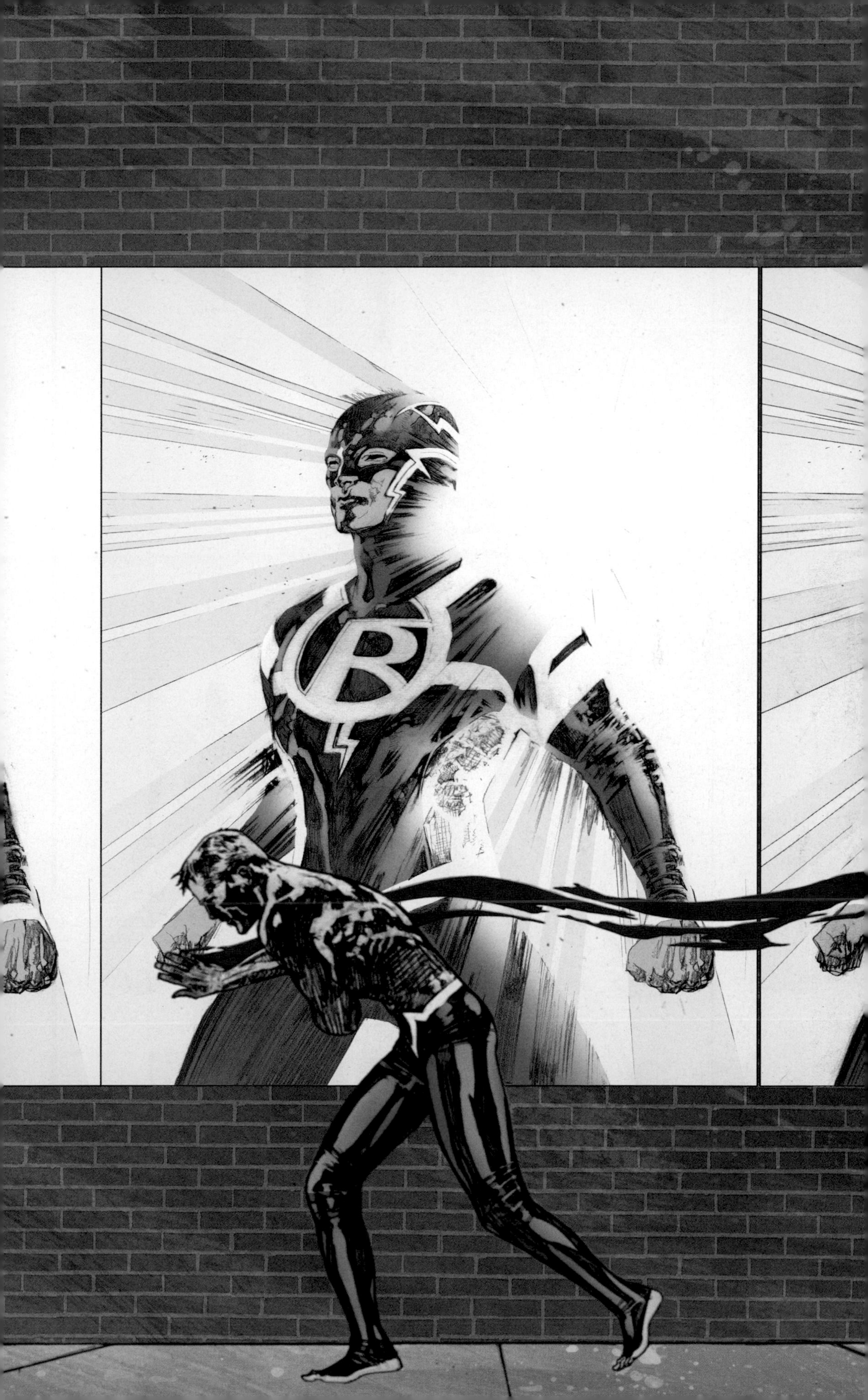

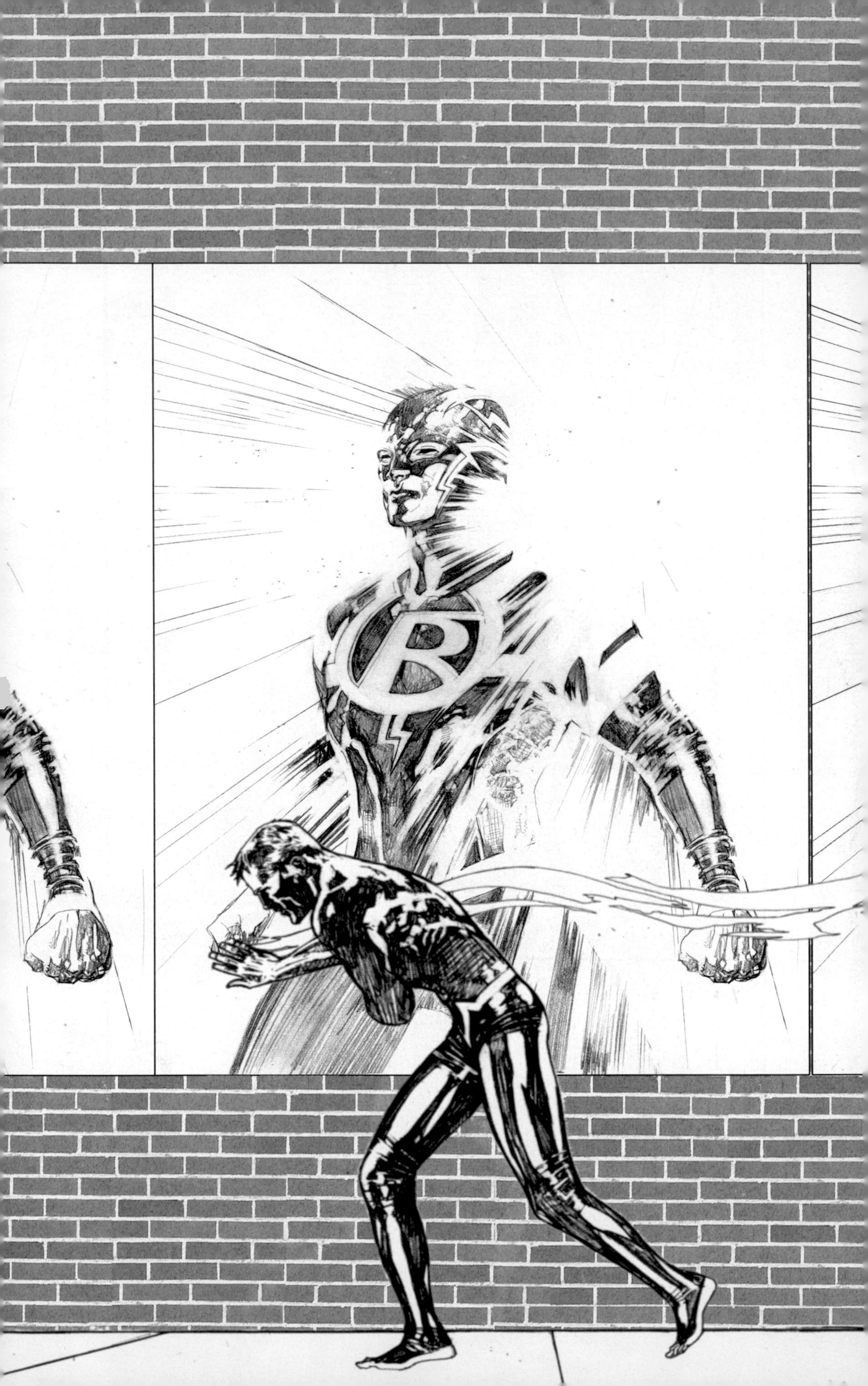

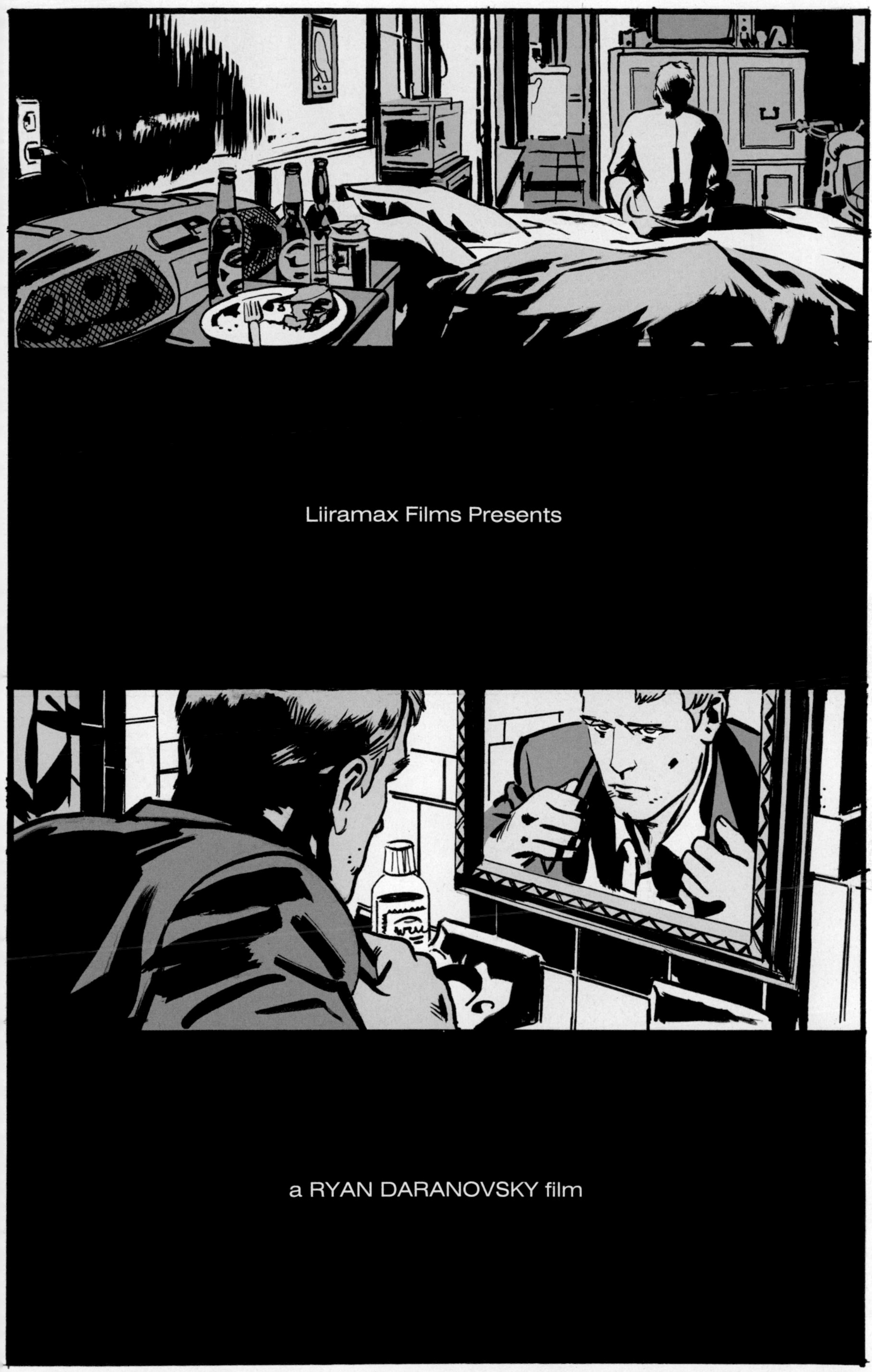
Liiramax Films Presents
a RYAN DARANOVSKY film

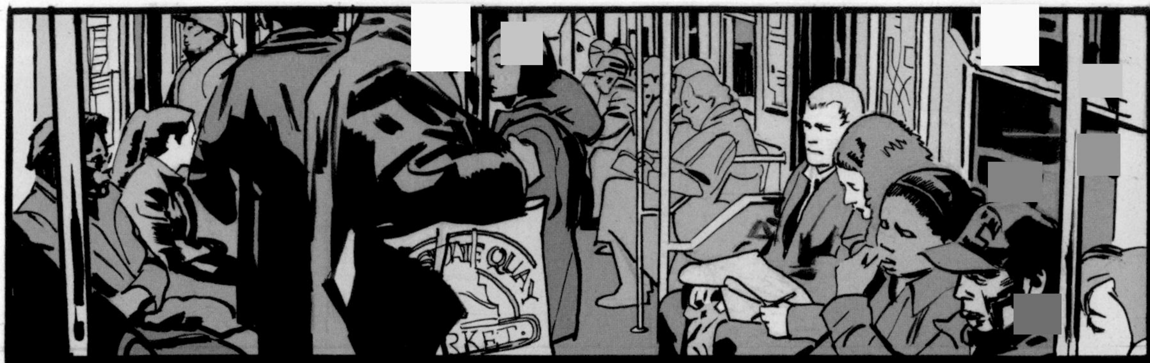

BUDDY BAKER in

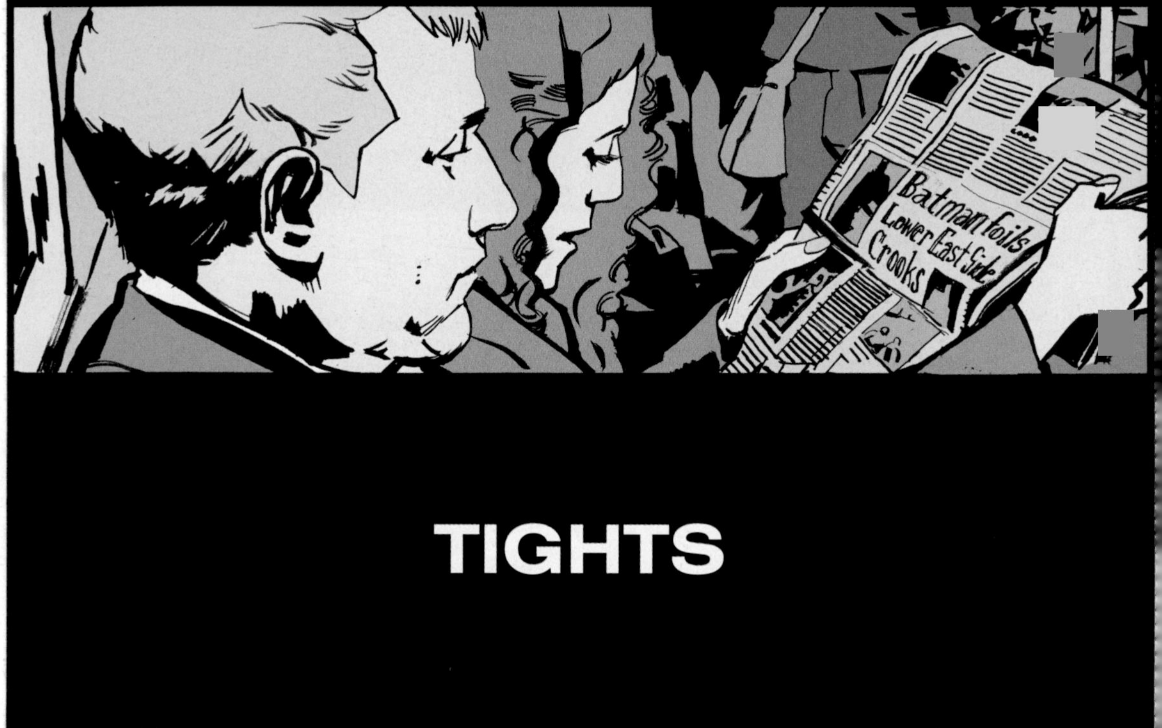
Batman foils
Lower East Side
Crooks

TIGHTS

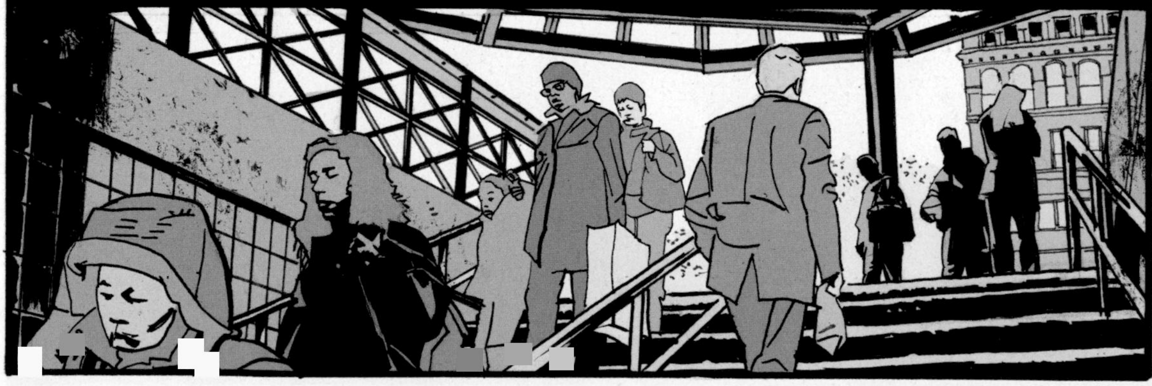

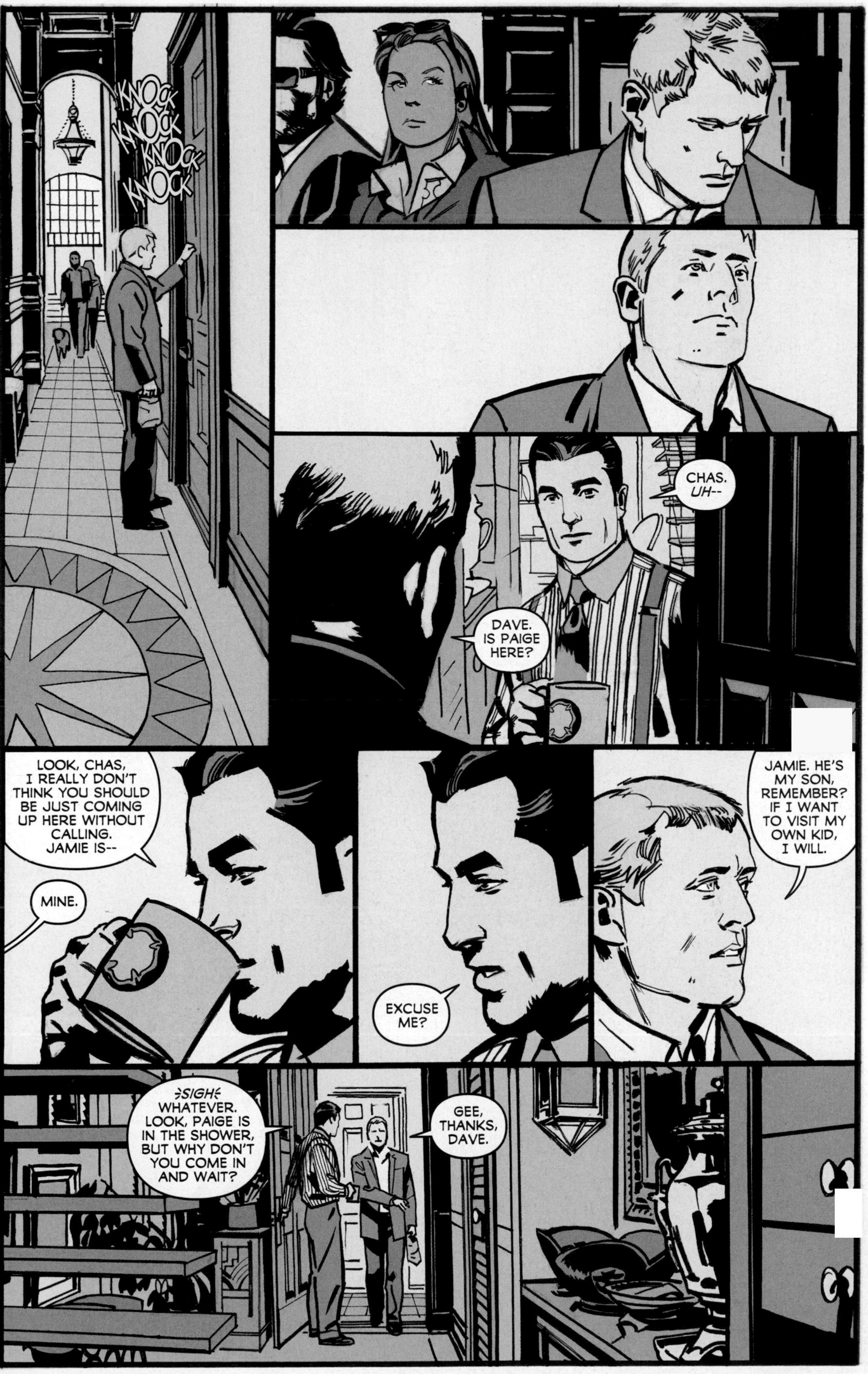
KNOCK KNOCK KNOCK KNOCK
CHAS. UH--
DAVE. IS PAIGE HERE?
LOOK, CHAS, I REALLY DON'T THINK YOU SHOULD BE JUST COMING UP HERE WITHOUT CALLING. JAMIE IS--
MINE.
EXCUSE ME?
JAMIE. HE'S MY SON, REMEMBER? IF I WANT TO VISIT MY OWN KID, I WILL.
SIGH WHATEVER. LOOK, PAIGE IS IN THE SHOWER, BUT WHY DON'T YOU COME IN AND WAIT?
GEE, THANKS, DAVE.

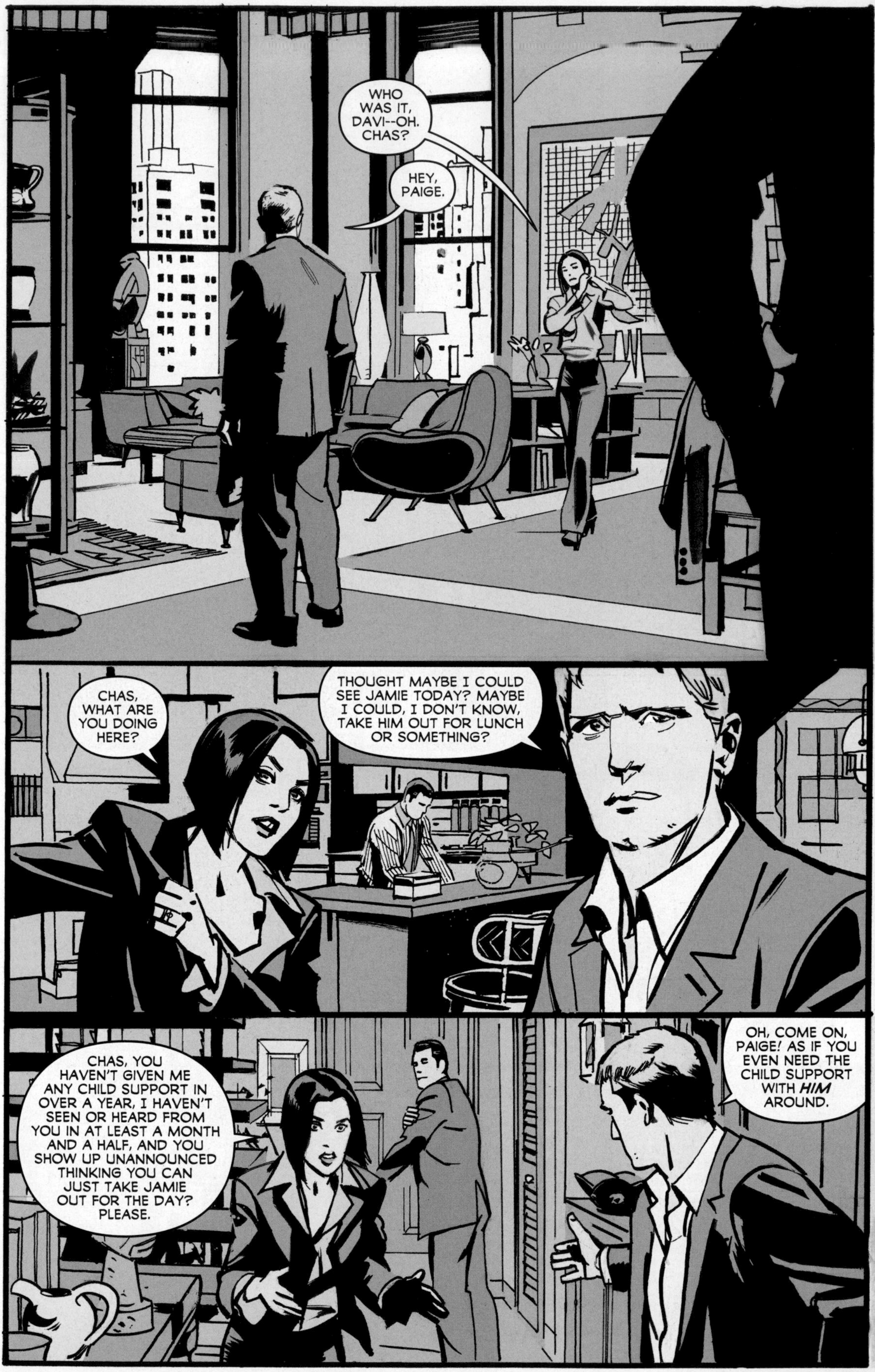
WHO WAS IT, DAVI--OH. CHAS?
HEY, PAIGE.
CHAS, WHAT ARE YOU DOING HERE?
THOUGHT MAYBE I COULD SEE JAMIE TODAY? MAYBE I COULD, I DON'T KNOW, TAKE HIM OUT FOR LUNCH OR SOMETHING?
CHAS, YOU HAVEN'T GIVEN ME ANY CHILD SUPPORT IN OVER A YEAR, I HAVEN'T SEEN OR HEARD FROM YOU IN AT LEAST A MONTH AND A HALF, AND YOU SHOW UP UNANNOUNCED THINKING YOU CAN JUST TAKE JAMIE OUT FOR THE DAY? PLEASE.
OH, COME ON, PAIGE! AS IF YOU EVEN NEED THE CHILD SUPPORT WITH *HIM* AROUND.

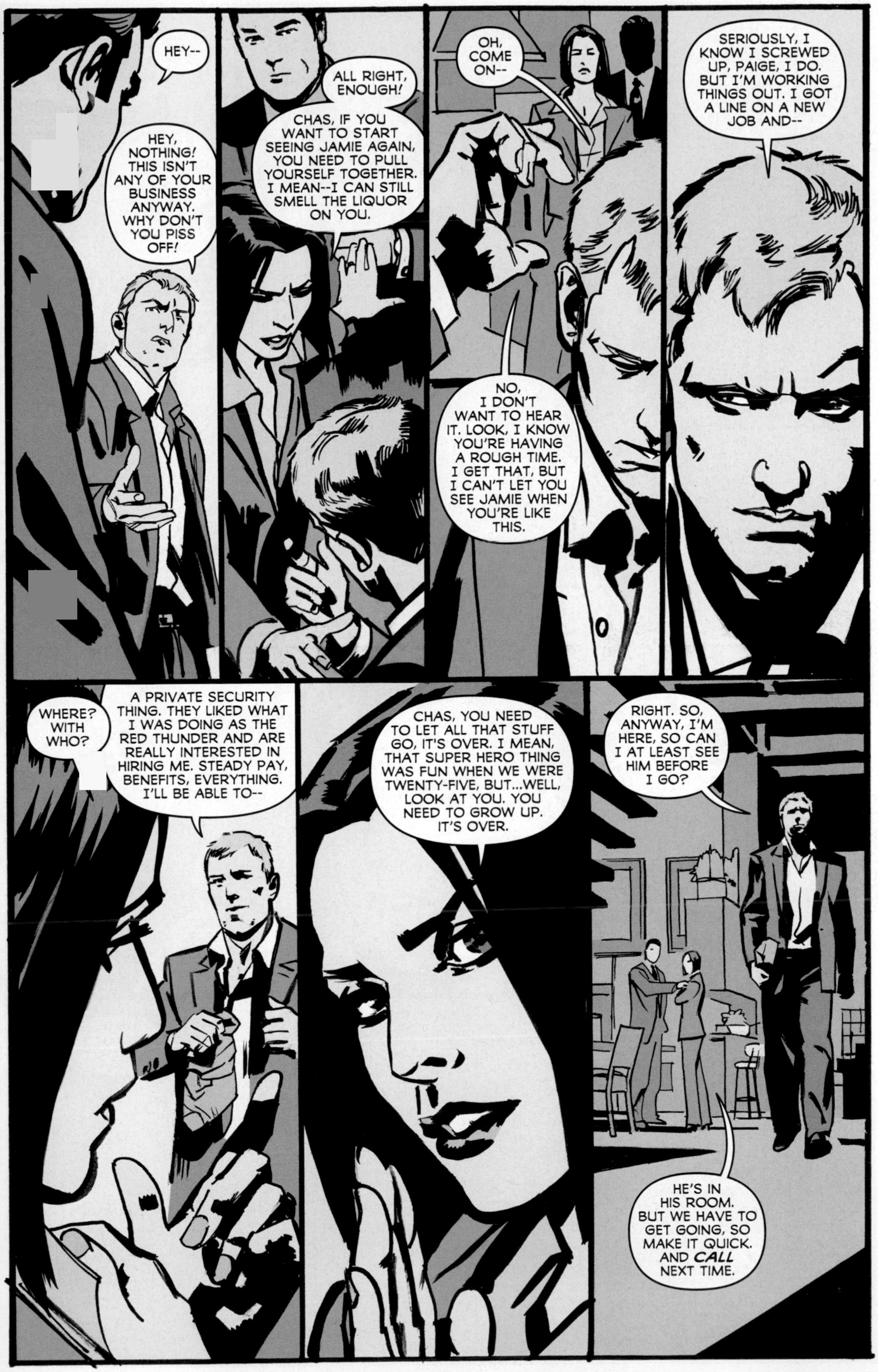
HEY--
HEY, NOTHING! THIS ISN'T ANY OF YOUR BUSINESS ANYWAY. WHY DON'T YOU PISS OFF!
ALL RIGHT, ENOUGH!
CHAS, IF YOU WANT TO START SEEING JAMIE AGAIN, YOU NEED TO PULL YOURSELF TOGETHER. I MEAN--I CAN STILL SMELL THE LIQUOR ON YOU.
OH, COME ON--
NO, I DON'T WANT TO HEAR IT. LOOK, I KNOW YOU'RE HAVING A ROUGH TIME. I GET THAT, BUT I CAN'T LET YOU SEE JAMIE WHEN YOU'RE LIKE THIS.
SERIOUSLY, I KNOW I SCREWED UP, PAIGE, I DO. BUT I'M WORKING THINGS OUT. I GOT A LINE ON A NEW JOB AND--
WHERE? WITH WHO?
A PRIVATE SECURITY THING. THEY LIKED WHAT I WAS DOING AS THE RED THUNDER AND ARE REALLY INTERESTED IN HIRING ME. STEADY PAY, BENEFITS, EVERYTHING. I'LL BE ABLE TO--
CHAS, YOU NEED TO LET ALL THAT STUFF GO, IT'S OVER. I MEAN, THAT SUPER HERO THING WAS FUN WHEN WE WERE TWENTY-FIVE, BUT...WELL, LOOK AT YOU. YOU NEED TO GROW UP. IT'S OVER.
RIGHT. SO, ANYWAY, I'M HERE, SO CAN I AT LEAST SEE HIM BEFORE I GO?
HE'S IN HIS ROOM. BUT WE HAVE TO GET GOING, SO MAKE IT QUICK. AND CALL NEXT TIME.

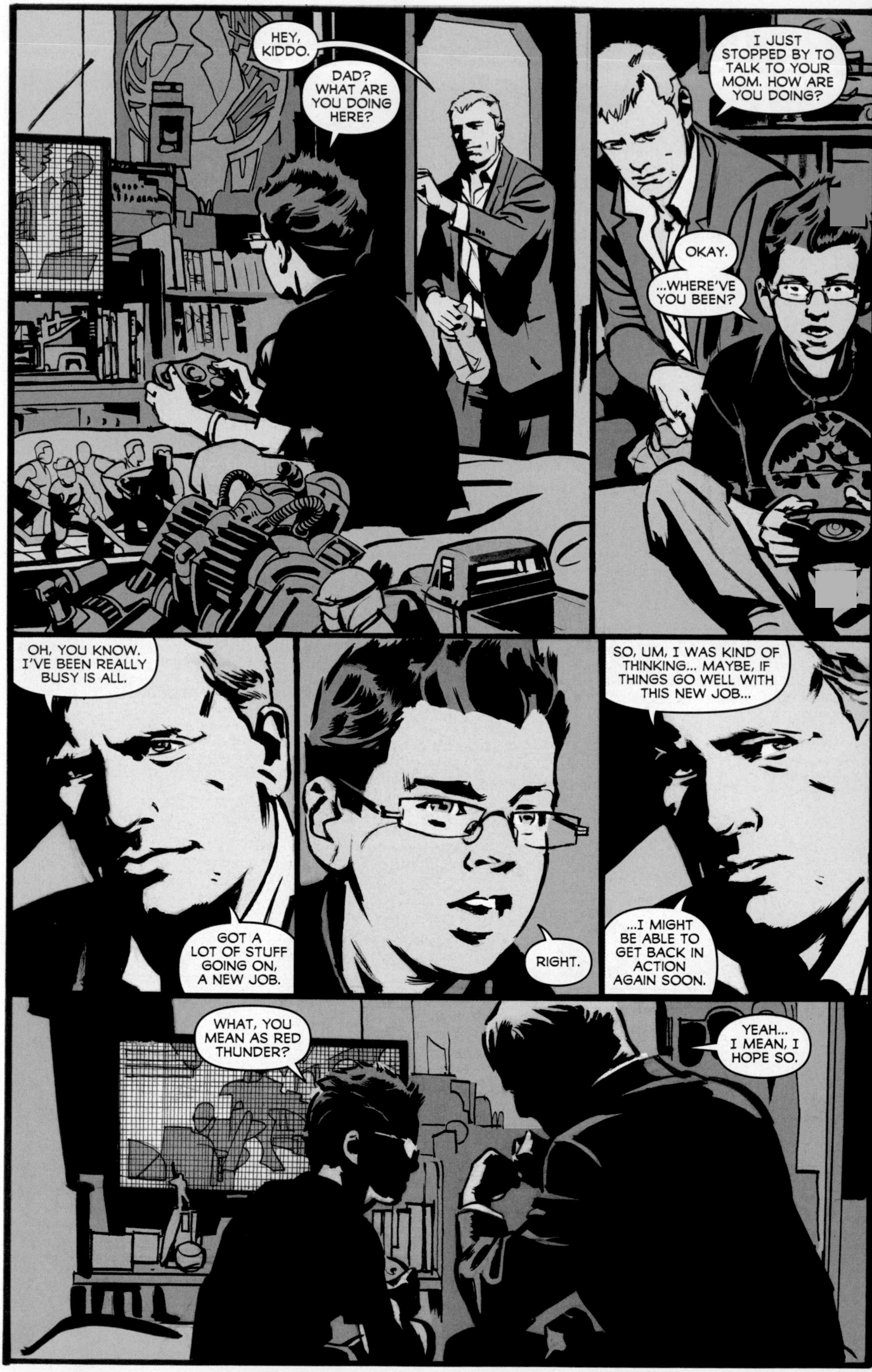
HEY, KIDDO.
DAD? WHAT ARE YOU DOING HERE?
I JUST STOPPED BY TO TALK TO YOUR MOM. HOW ARE YOU DOING?
OKAY.
...WHERE'VE YOU BEEN?
OH, YOU KNOW. I'VE BEEN REALLY BUSY IS ALL.
GOT A LOT OF STUFF GOING ON, A NEW JOB.
RIGHT.
SO, UM, I WAS KIND OF THINKING... MAYBE, IF THINGS GO WELL WITH THIS NEW JOB...
...I MIGHT BE ABLE TO GET BACK IN ACTION AGAIN SOON.
WHAT, YOU MEAN AS RED THUNDER?
YEAH... I MEAN, I HOPE SO.

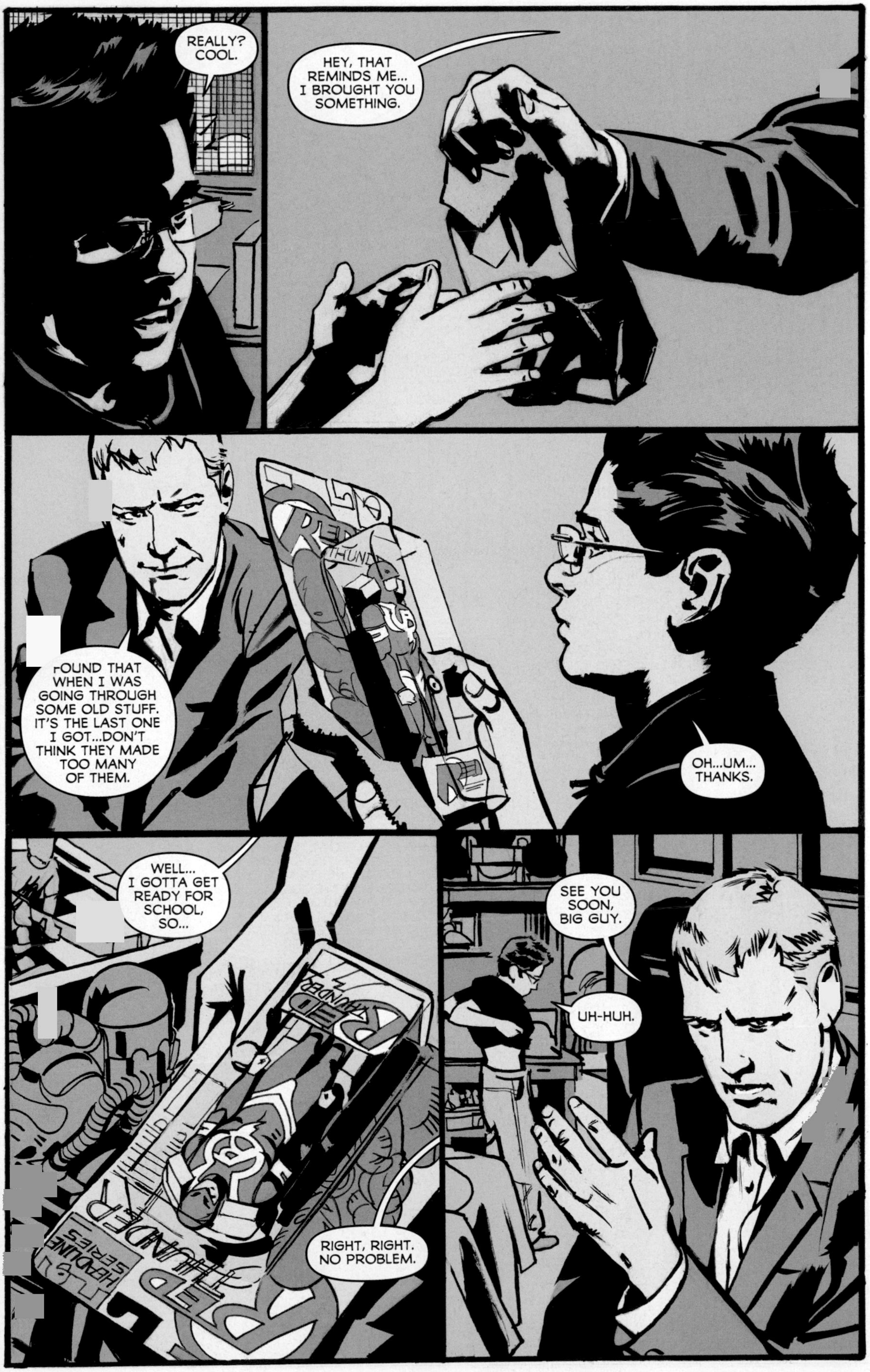
REALLY? COOL.
HEY, THAT REMINDS ME... I BROUGHT YOU SOMETHING.
FOUND THAT WHEN I WAS GOING THROUGH SOME OLD STUFF. IT'S THE LAST ONE I GOT...DON'T THINK THEY MADE TOO MANY OF THEM.
OH...UM... THANKS.
WELL... I GOTTA GET READY FOR SCHOOL, SO...
RIGHT, RIGHT. NO PROBLEM.
SEE YOU SOON, BIG GUY.
UH-HUH.

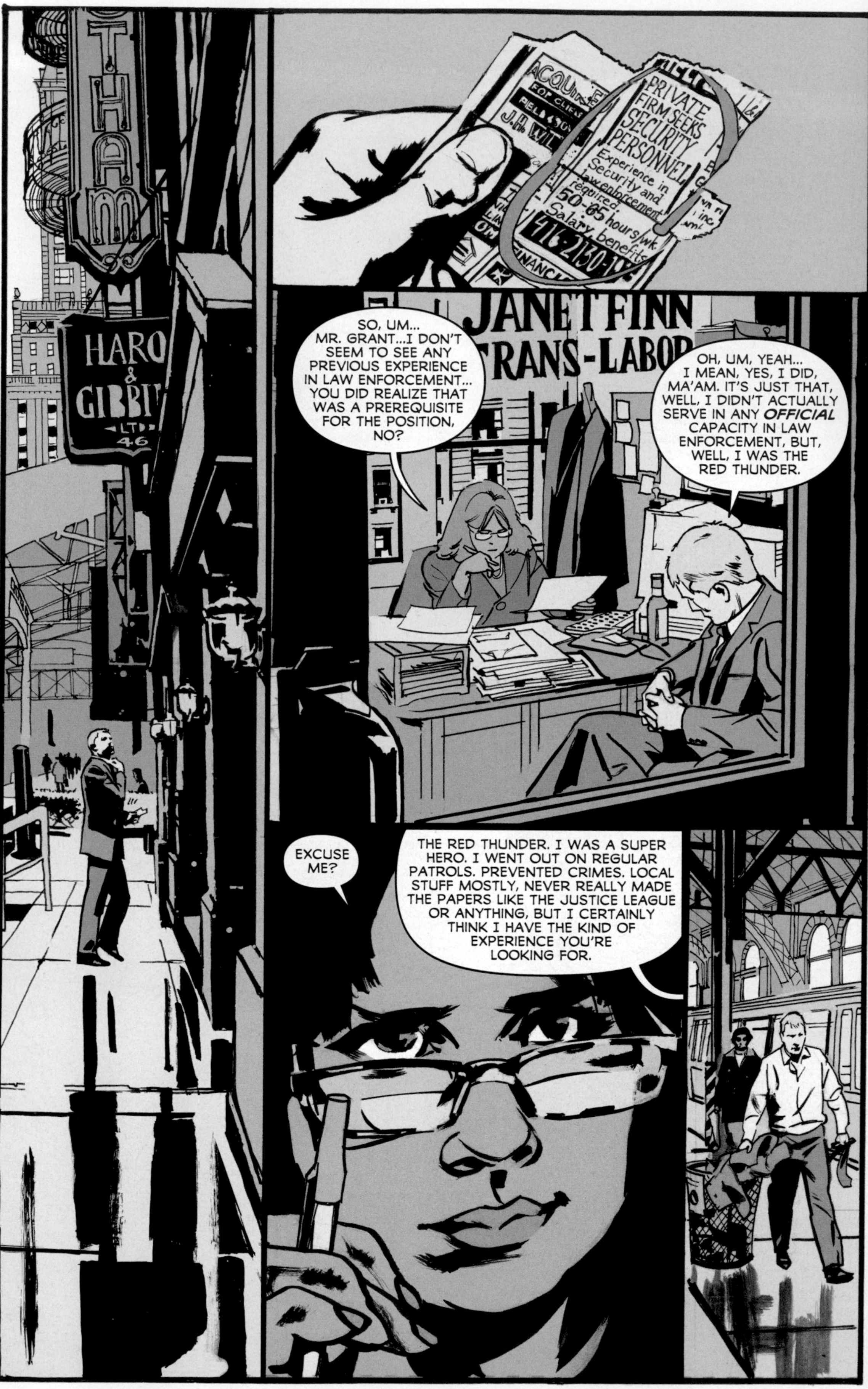

GOTHAM
HARO & GIBBI LTD 46
ACQUIRE FOR CLIENT
PRIVATE FIRM SEEKS SECURITY PERSONNEL Experience in Security and lawenforcement required. 50-65 hours/wk. Salary, benefits.
JANET FINN TRANS-LABOR
SO, UM... MR. GRANT...I DON'T SEEM TO SEE ANY PREVIOUS EXPERIENCE IN LAW ENFORCEMENT... YOU DID REALIZE THAT WAS A PREREQUISITE FOR THE POSITION, NO?
OH, UM, YEAH... I MEAN, YES, I DID, MA'AM. IT'S JUST THAT, WELL, I DIDN'T ACTUALLY SERVE IN ANY *OFFICIAL* CAPACITY IN LAW ENFORCEMENT, BUT, WELL, I WAS THE RED THUNDER.
EXCUSE ME?
THE RED THUNDER. I WAS A SUPER HERO. I WENT OUT ON REGULAR PATROLS. PREVENTED CRIMES. LOCAL STUFF MOSTLY, NEVER REALLY MADE THE PAPERS LIKE THE JUSTICE LEAGUE OR ANYTHING, BUT I CERTAINLY THINK I HAVE THE KIND OF EXPERIENCE YOU'RE LOOKING FOR.

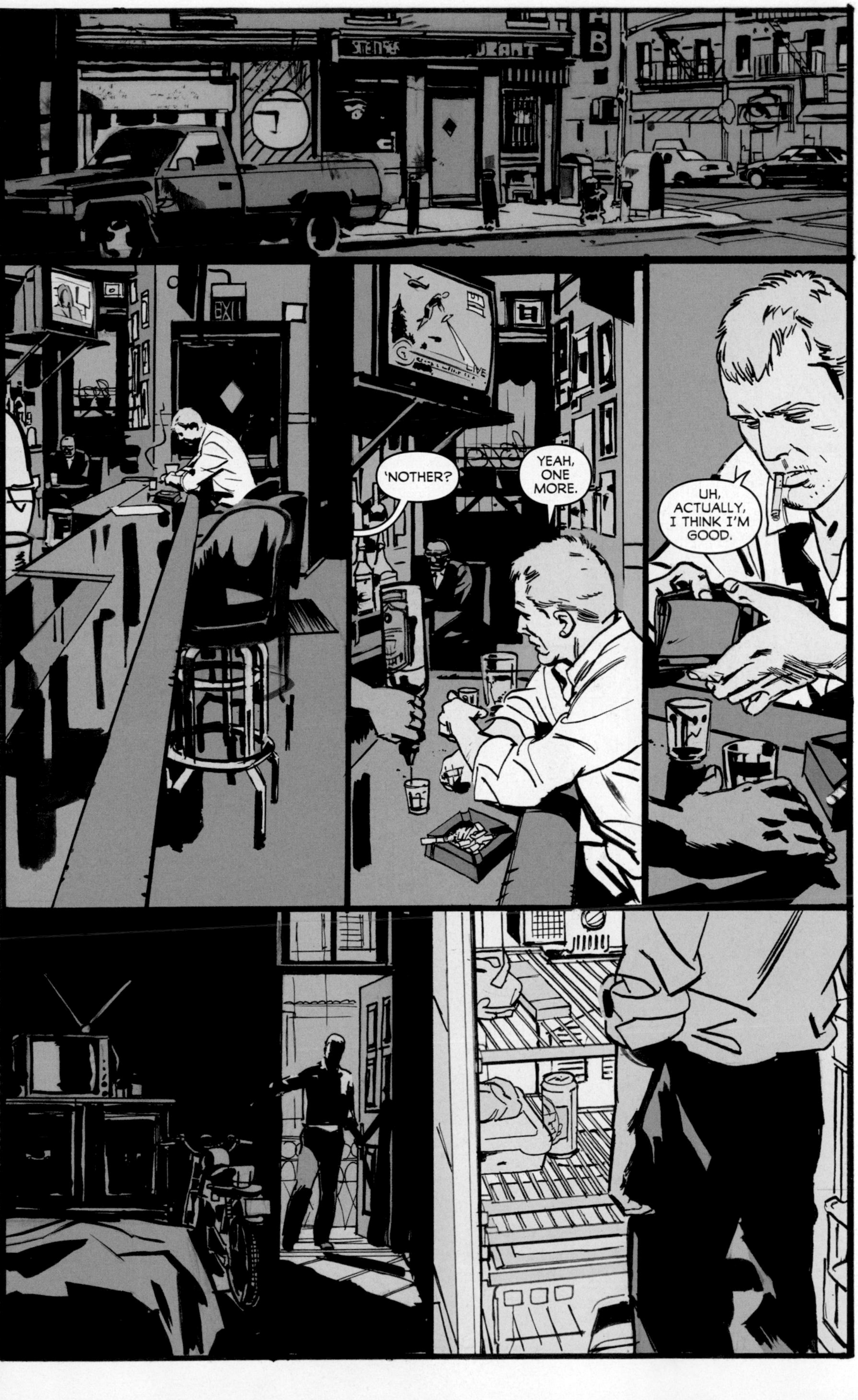
'NOTHER?
YEAH, ONE MORE.
UH, ACTUALLY, I THINK I'M GOOD.

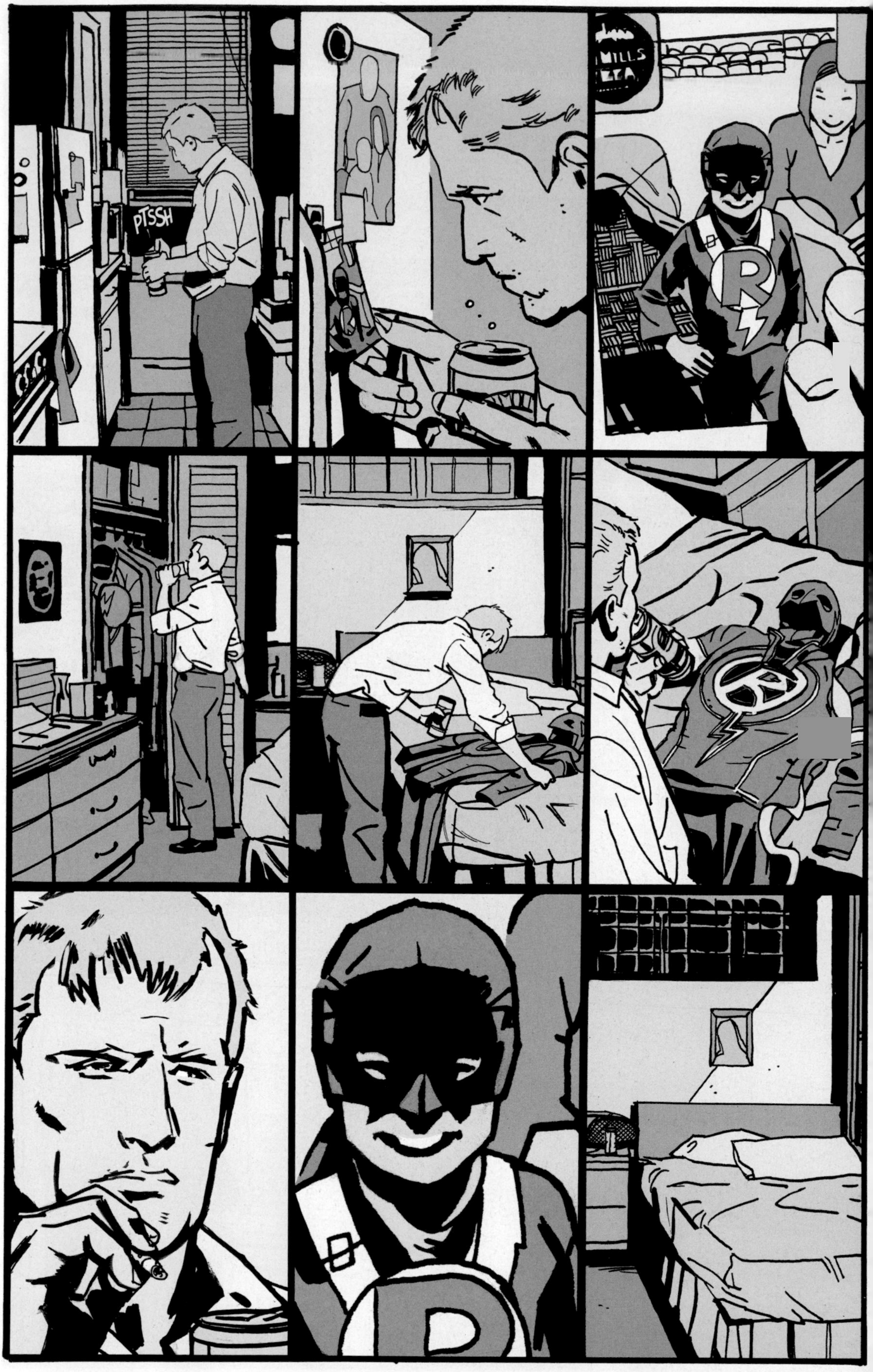
PTSSH
MILLS

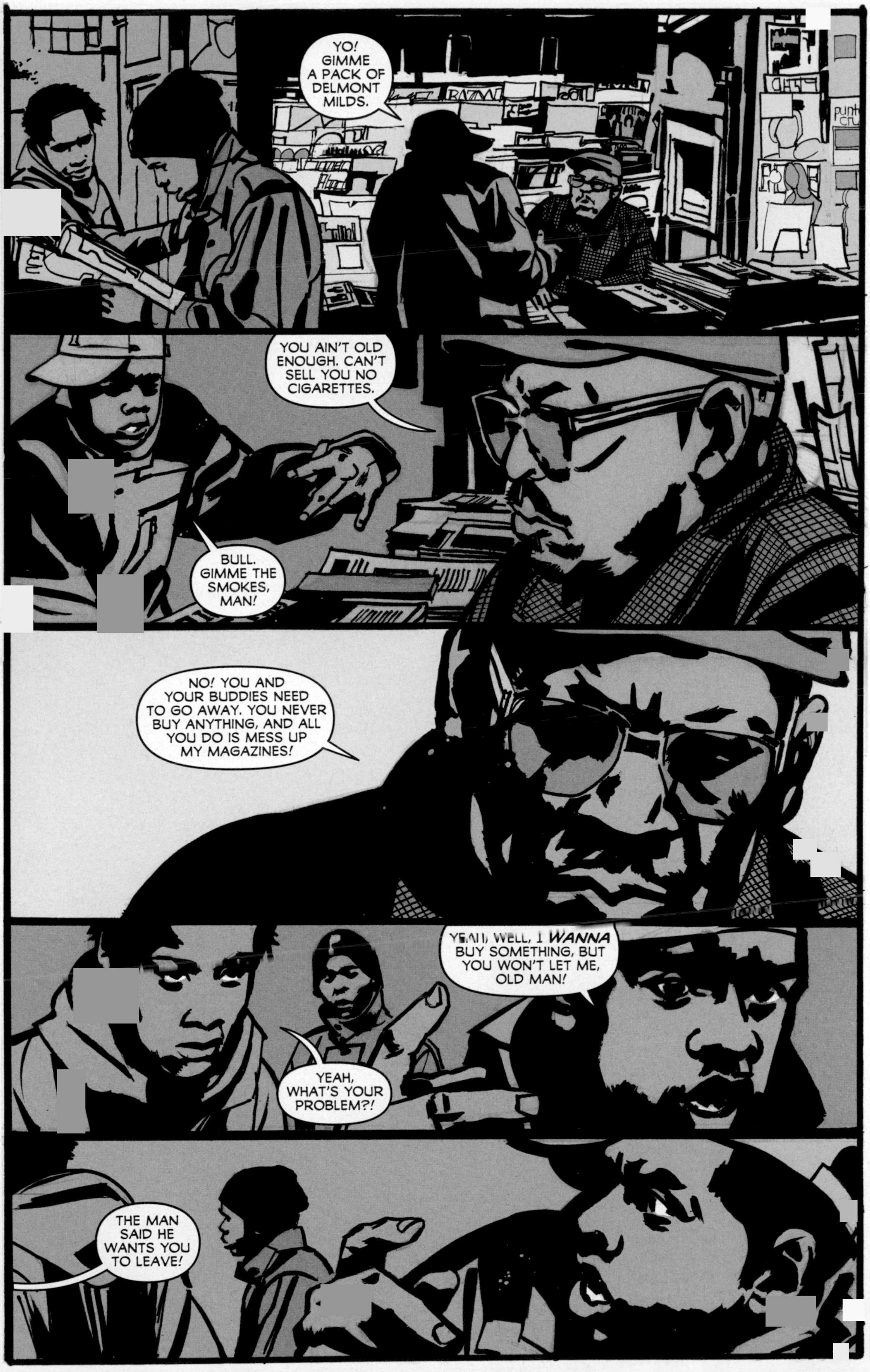
YO! GIMME A PACK OF DELMONT MILDS.
YOU AIN'T OLD ENOUGH. CAN'T SELL YOU NO CIGARETTES.
BULL. GIMME THE SMOKES, MAN!
NO! YOU AND YOUR BUDDIES NEED TO GO AWAY. YOU NEVER BUY ANYTHING, AND ALL YOU DO IS MESS UP MY MAGAZINES!
YEAH, WELL, I WANNA BUY SOMETHING, BUT YOU WON'T LET ME, OLD MAN!
YEAH, WHAT'S YOUR PROBLEM?!
THE MAN SAID HE WANTS YOU TO LEAVE!

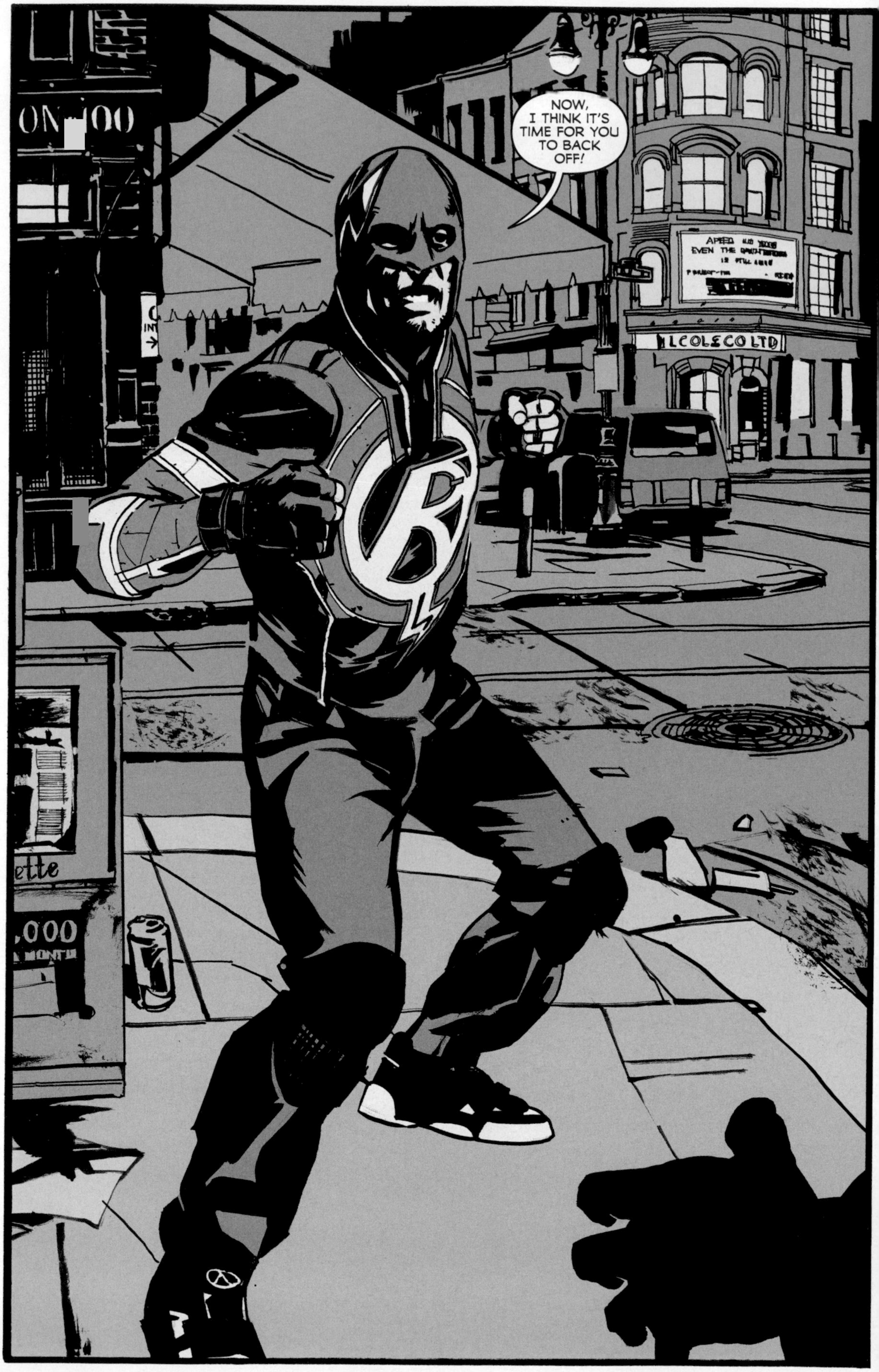
NOW, I THINK IT'S TIME FOR YOU TO BACK OFF!

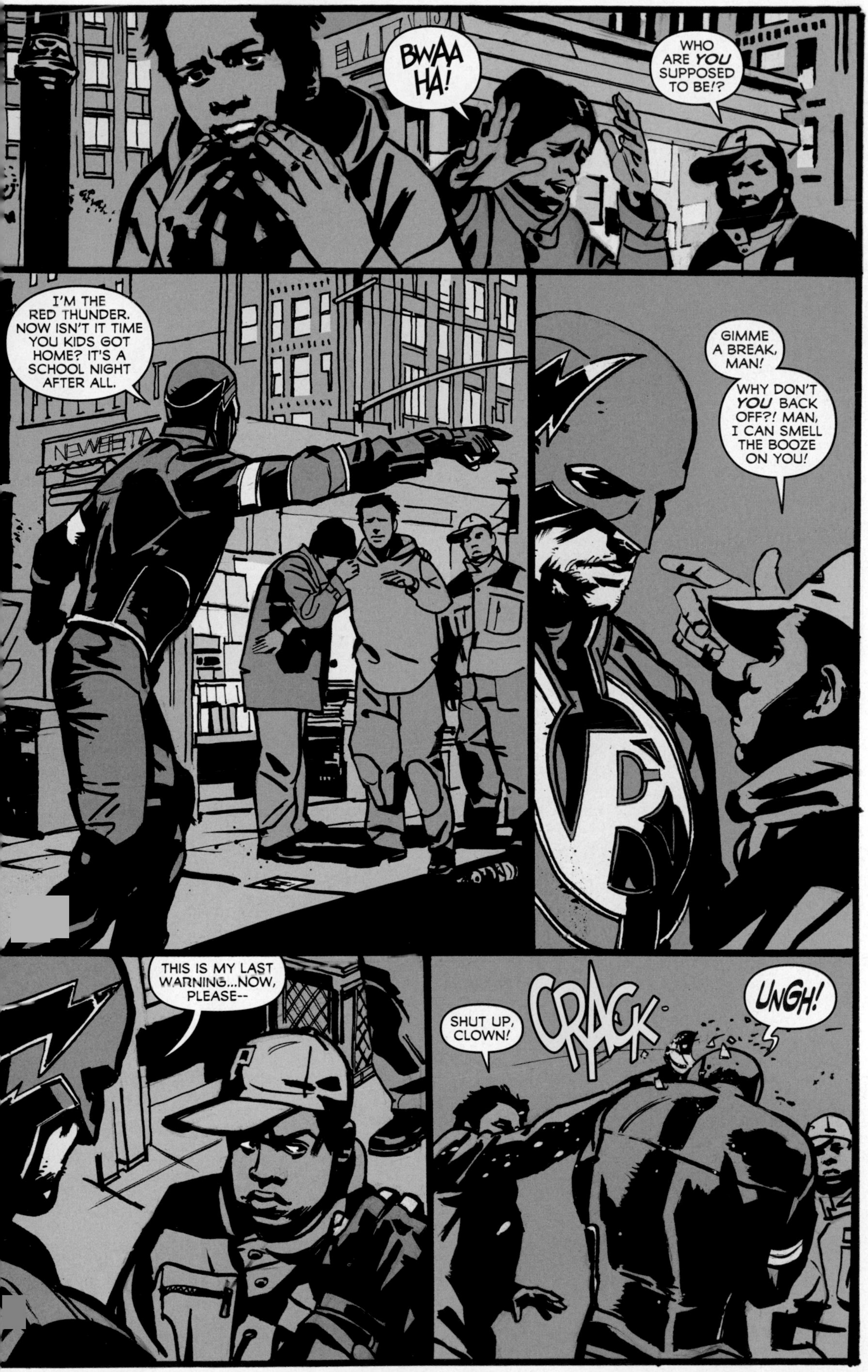
BWAA HA!
WHO ARE YOU SUPPOSED TO BE!?
I'M THE RED THUNDER. NOW ISN'T IT TIME YOU KIDS GOT HOME? IT'S A SCHOOL NIGHT AFTER ALL.
GIMME A BREAK, MAN!
WHY DON'T YOU BACK OFF?! MAN, I CAN SMELL THE BOOZE ON YOU!
THIS IS MY LAST WARNING...NOW, PLEASE--
SHUT UP, CLOWN!
CRACK
UNGH!

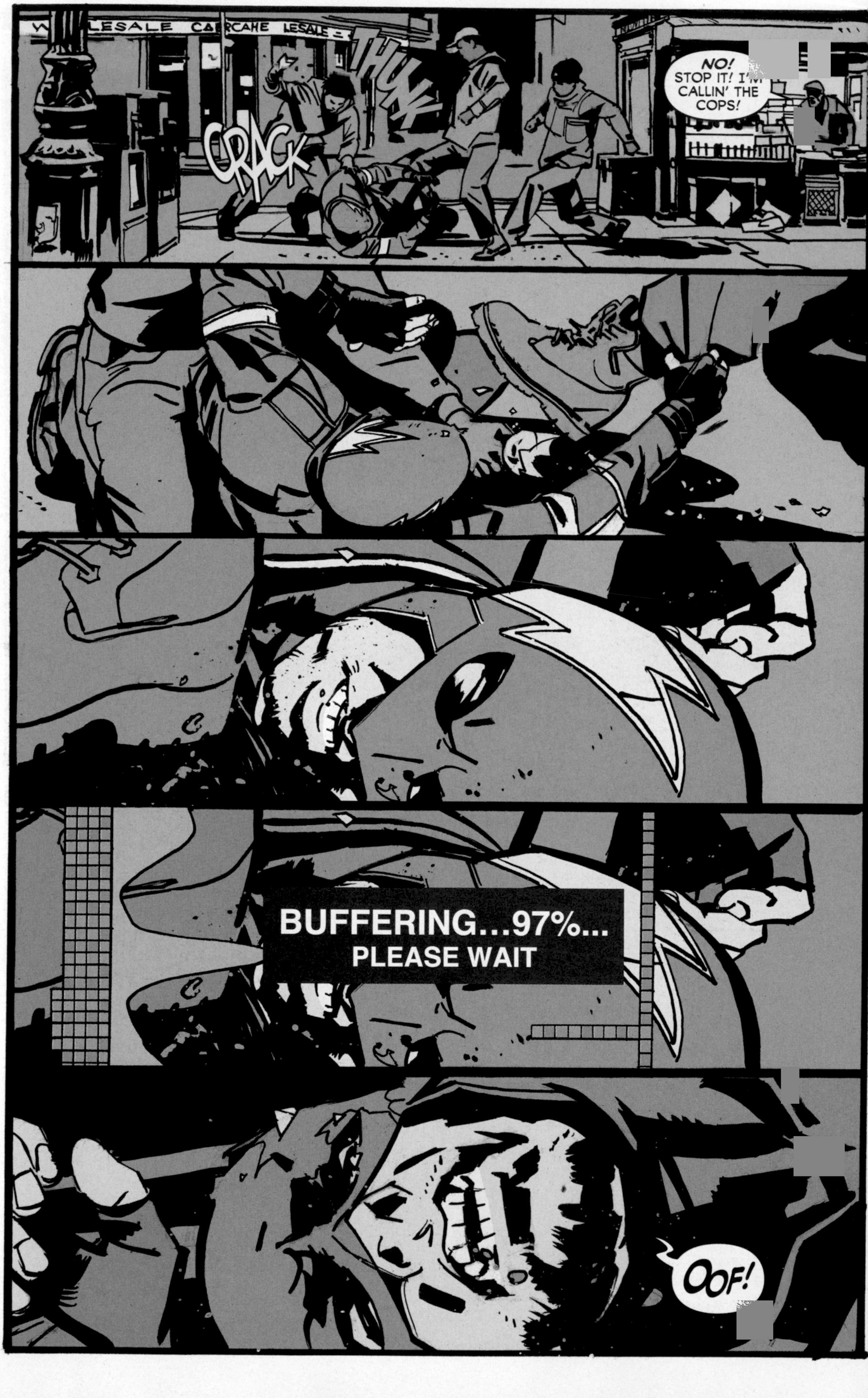
CRACK
THUNK
NO! STOP IT! I'M CALLIN' THE COPS!
BUFFERING...97%...
PLEASE WAIT
OOF!

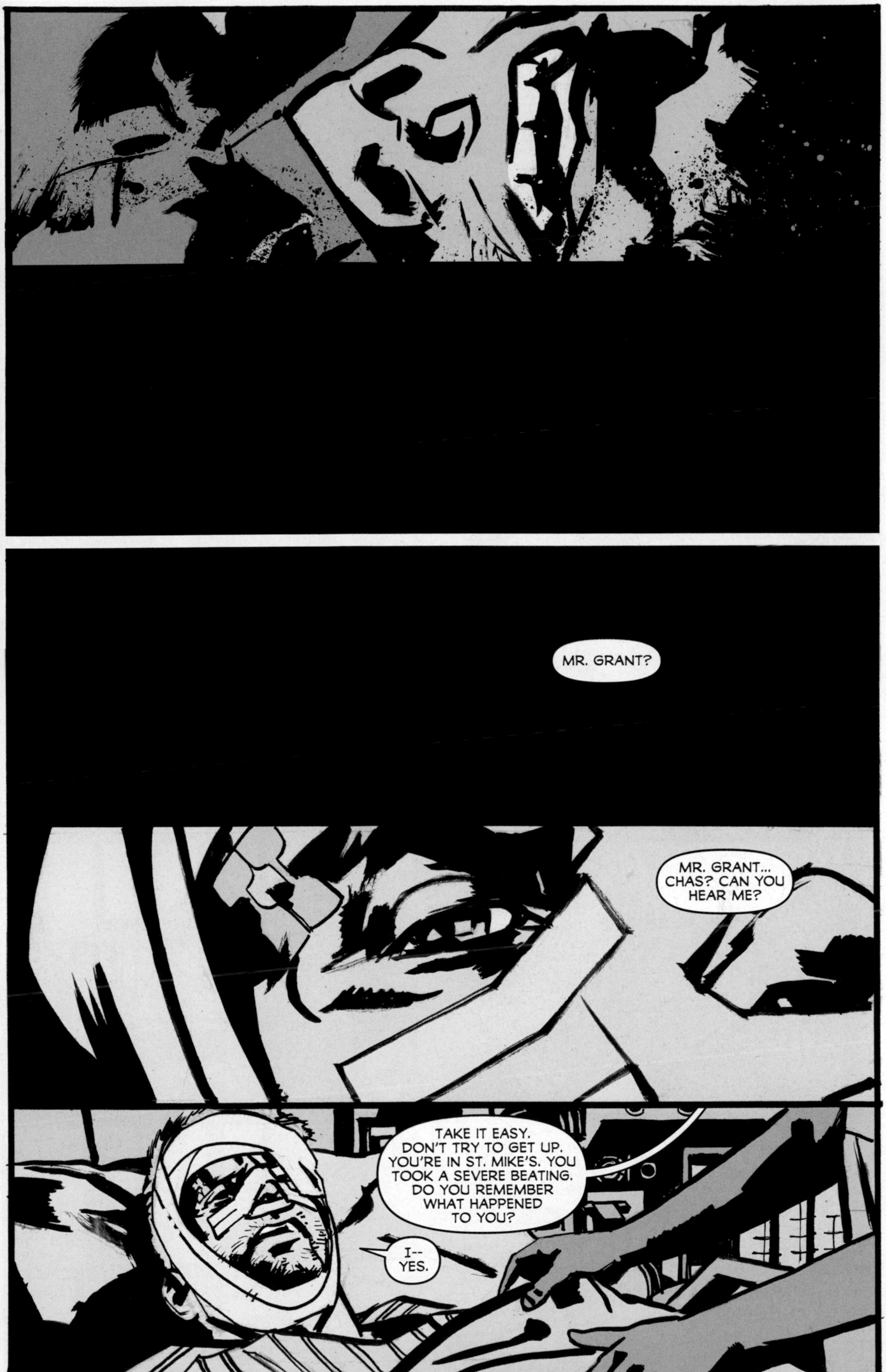
MR. GRANT?
MR. GRANT... CHAS? CAN YOU HEAR ME?
TAKE IT EASY. DON'T TRY TO GET UP. YOU'RE IN ST. MIKE'S. YOU TOOK A SEVERE BEATING. DO YOU REMEMBER WHAT HAPPENED TO YOU?
I-- YES.

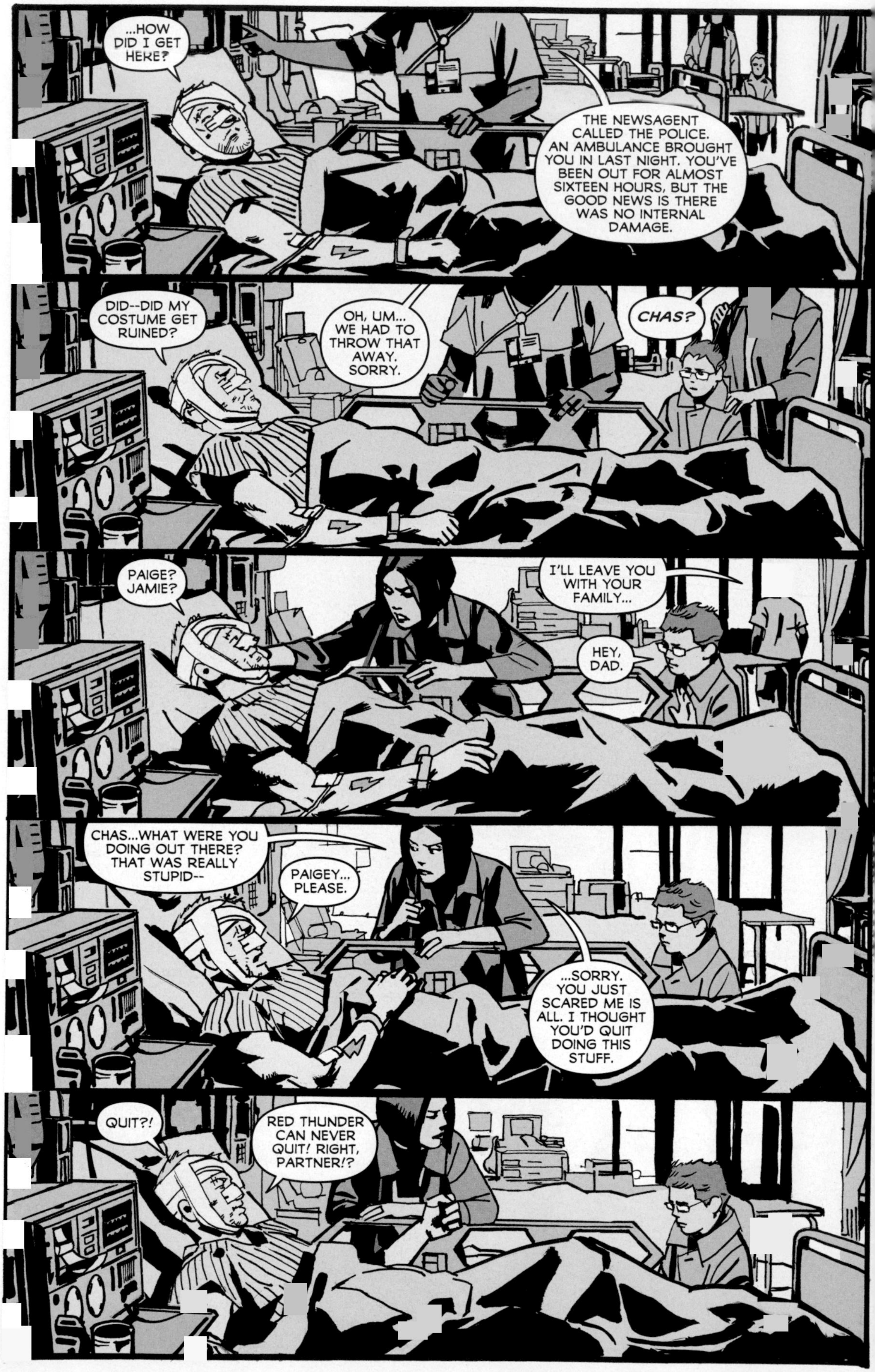
...HOW DID I GET HERE?
THE NEWSAGENT CALLED THE POLICE. AN AMBULANCE BROUGHT YOU IN LAST NIGHT. YOU'VE BEEN OUT FOR ALMOST SIXTEEN HOURS, BUT THE GOOD NEWS IS THERE WAS NO INTERNAL DAMAGE.
DID--DID MY COSTUME GET RUINED?
OH, UM... WE HAD TO THROW THAT AWAY. SORRY.
CHAS?
PAIGE? JAMIE?
I'LL LEAVE YOU WITH YOUR FAMILY...
HEY, DAD.
CHAS...WHAT WERE YOU DOING OUT THERE? THAT WAS REALLY STUPID--
PAIGEY... PLEASE.
...SORRY. YOU JUST SCARED ME IS ALL. I THOUGHT YOU'D QUIT DOING THIS STUFF.
QUIT?!
RED THUNDER CAN NEVER QUIT! RIGHT, PARTNER!?

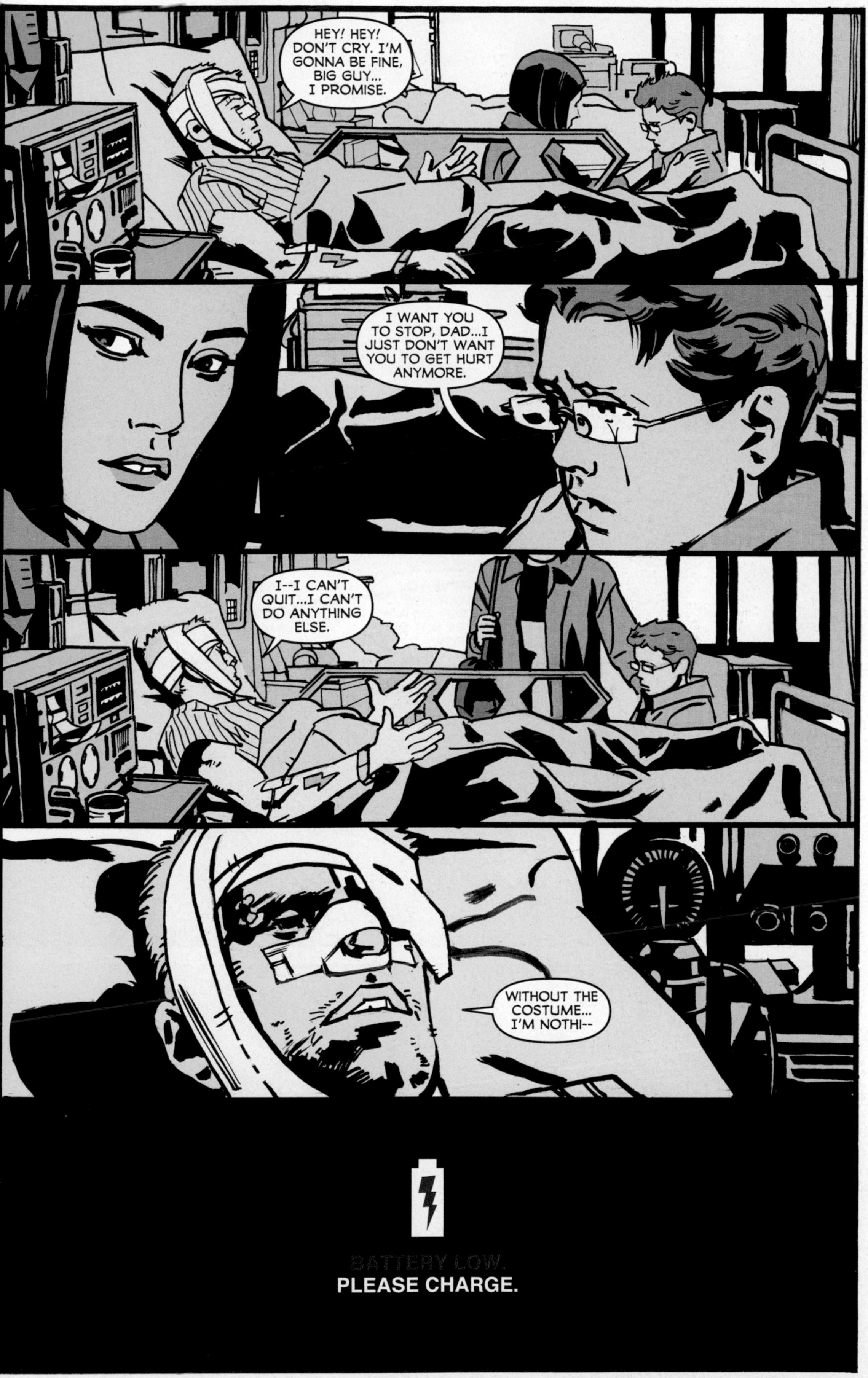
HEY! HEY! DON'T CRY. I'M GONNA BE FINE, BIG GUY... I PROMISE.
I WANT YOU TO STOP, DAD...I JUST DON'T WANT YOU TO GET HURT ANYMORE.
I--I CAN'T QUIT...I CAN'T DO ANYTHING ELSE.
WITHOUT THE COSTUME... I'M NOTHI--
BATTERY LOW.
PLEASE CHARGE.

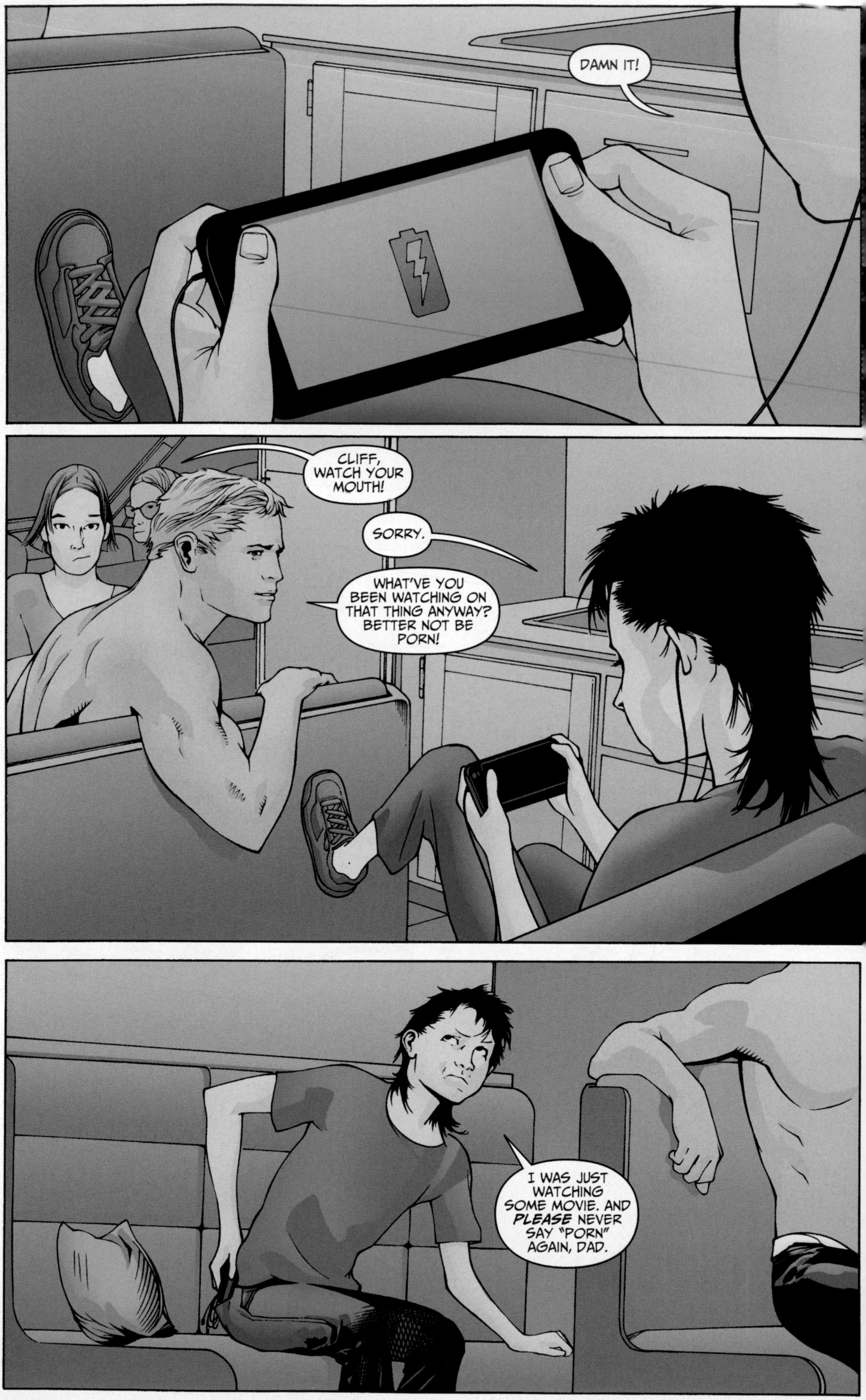
DAMN IT!
CLIFF, WATCH YOUR MOUTH!
SORRY.
WHAT'VE YOU BEEN WATCHING ON THAT THING ANYWAY? BETTER NOT BE PORN!
I WAS JUST WATCHING SOME MOVIE. AND *PLEASE* NEVER SAY "PORN" AGAIN, DAD.

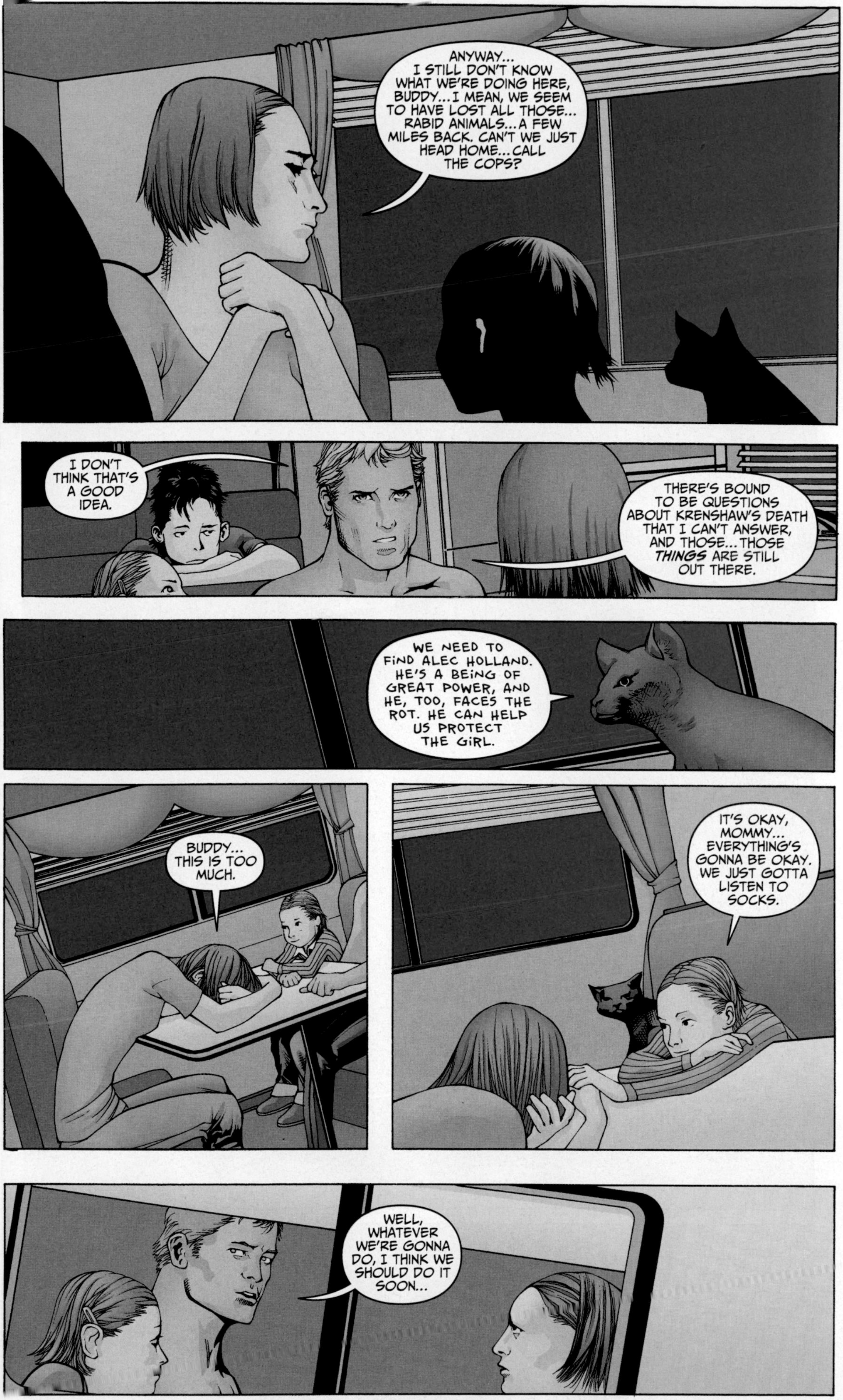
ANYWAY... I STILL DON'T KNOW WHAT WE'RE DOING HERE, BUDDY... I MEAN, WE SEEM TO HAVE LOST ALL THOSE... RABID ANIMALS... A FEW MILES BACK. CAN'T WE JUST HEAD HOME... CALL THE COPS?
I DON'T THINK THAT'S A GOOD IDEA.
THERE'S BOUND TO BE QUESTIONS ABOUT KRENSHAW'S DEATH THAT I CAN'T ANSWER, AND THOSE... THOSE *THINGS* ARE STILL OUT THERE.
WE NEED TO FIND ALEC HOLLAND. HE'S A BEING OF GREAT POWER, AND HE, TOO, FACES THE ROT. HE CAN HELP US PROTECT THE GIRL.
BUDDY... THIS IS TOO MUCH.
IT'S OKAY, MOMMY... EVERYTHING'S GONNA BE OKAY. WE JUST GOTTA LISTEN TO SOCKS.
WELL, WHATEVER WE'RE GONNA DO, I THINK WE SHOULD DO IT SOON...

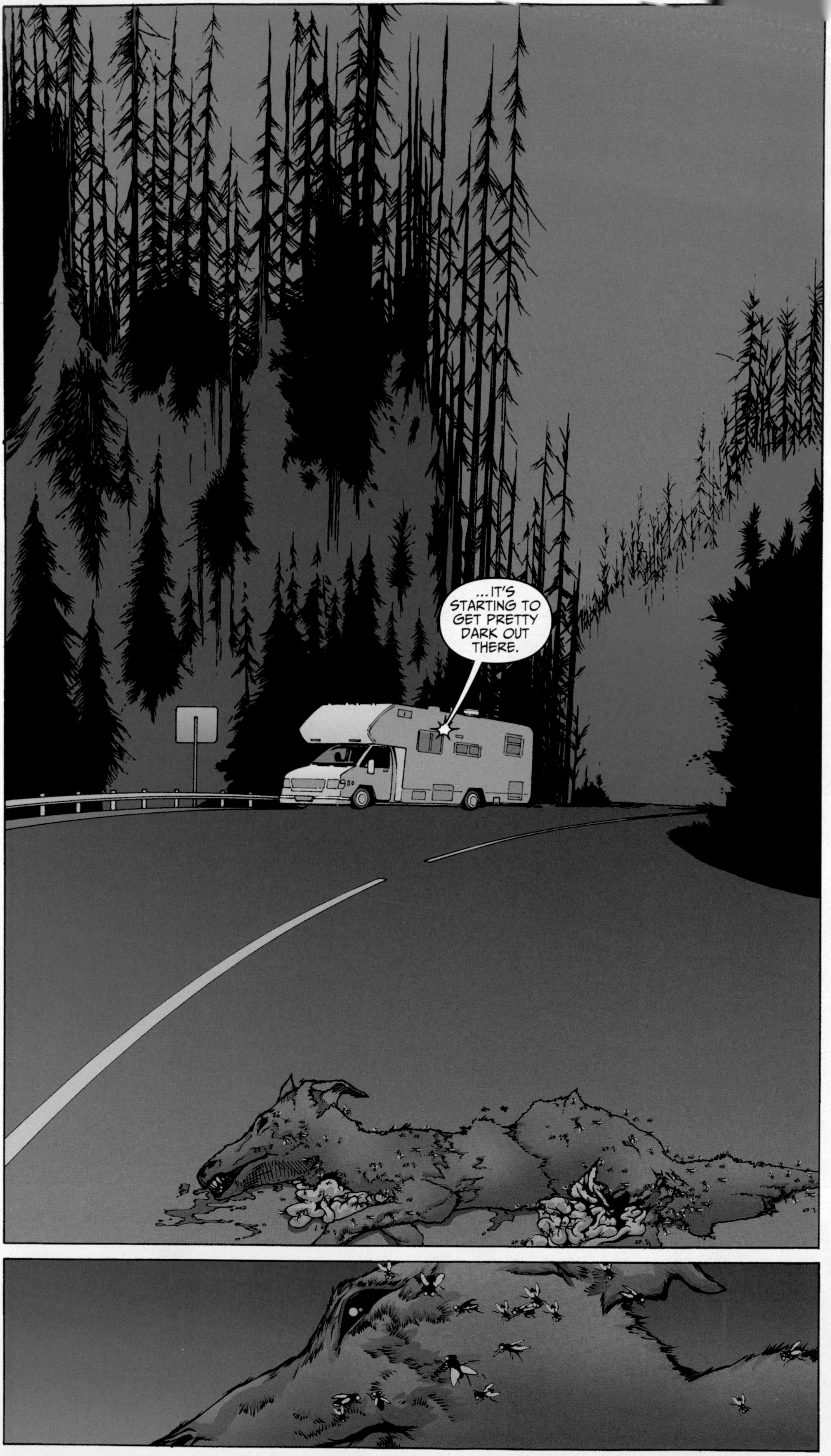
...IT'S STARTING TO GET PRETTY DARK OUT THERE.

ANIMAL MAN
SKETCHES AND DESIGNS BY TRAVEL FOREMAN

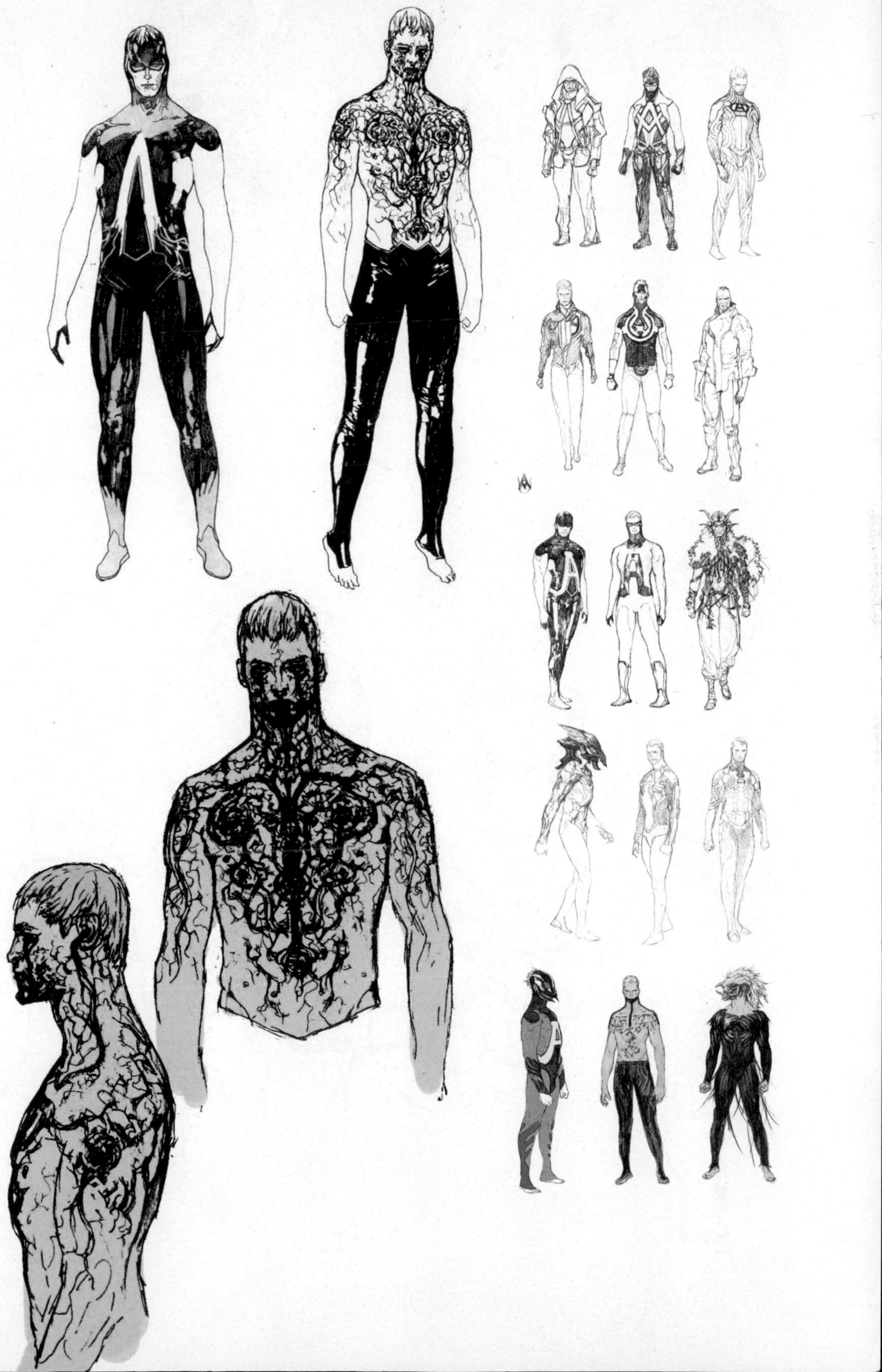

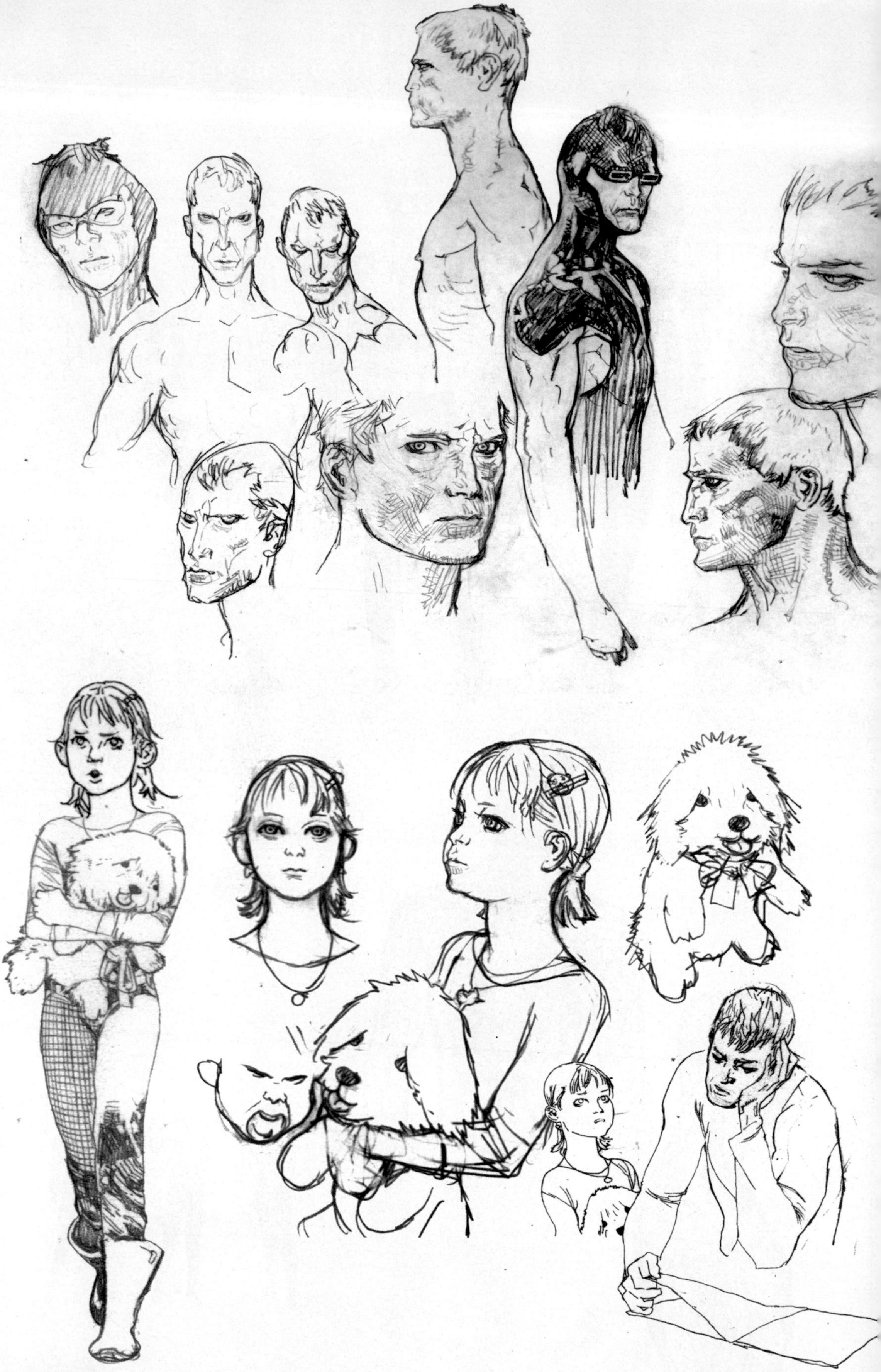

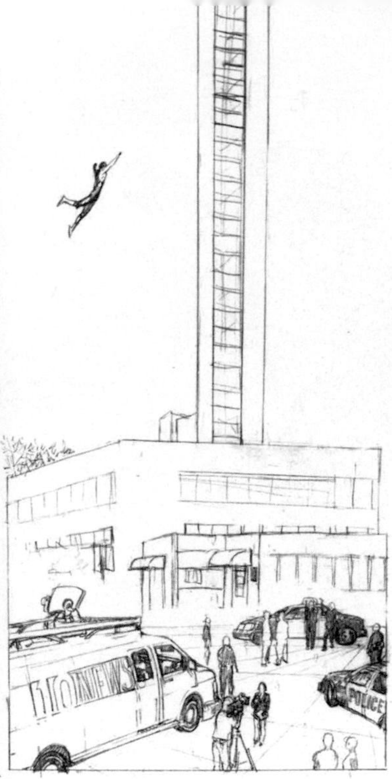
POLICE

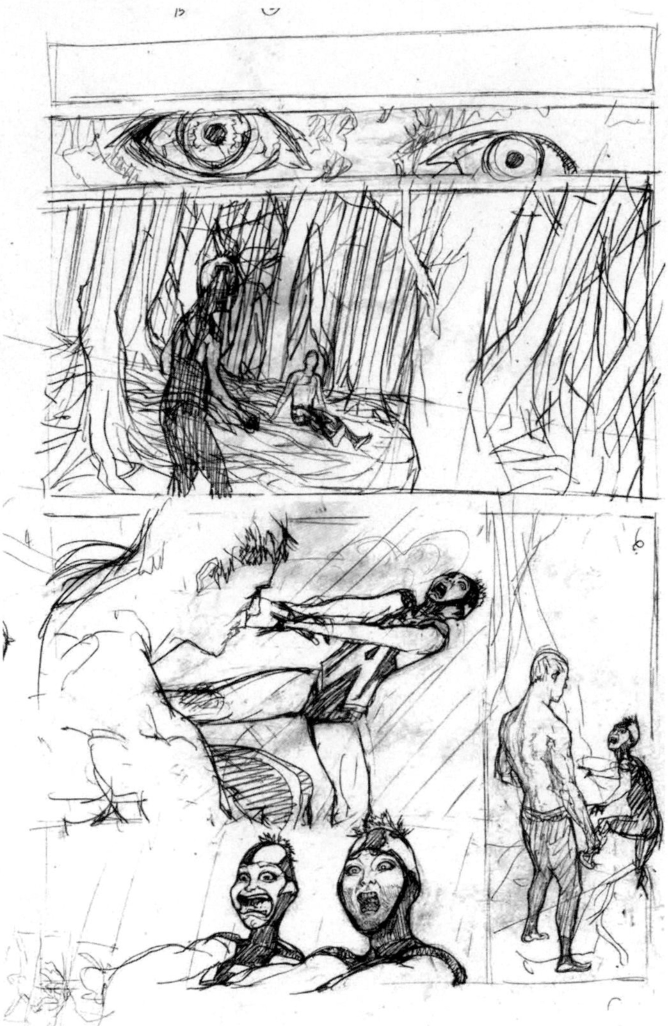

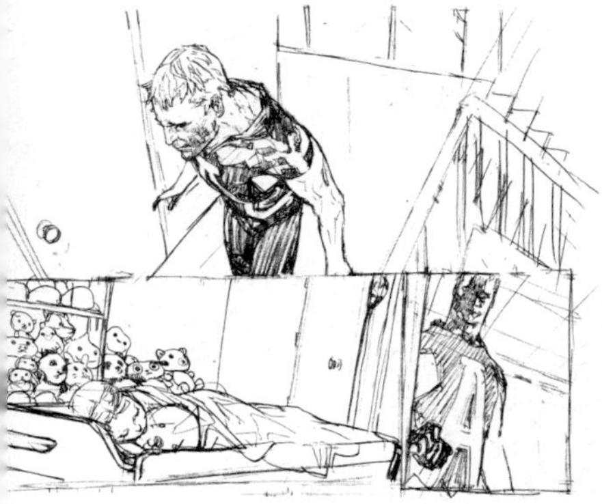

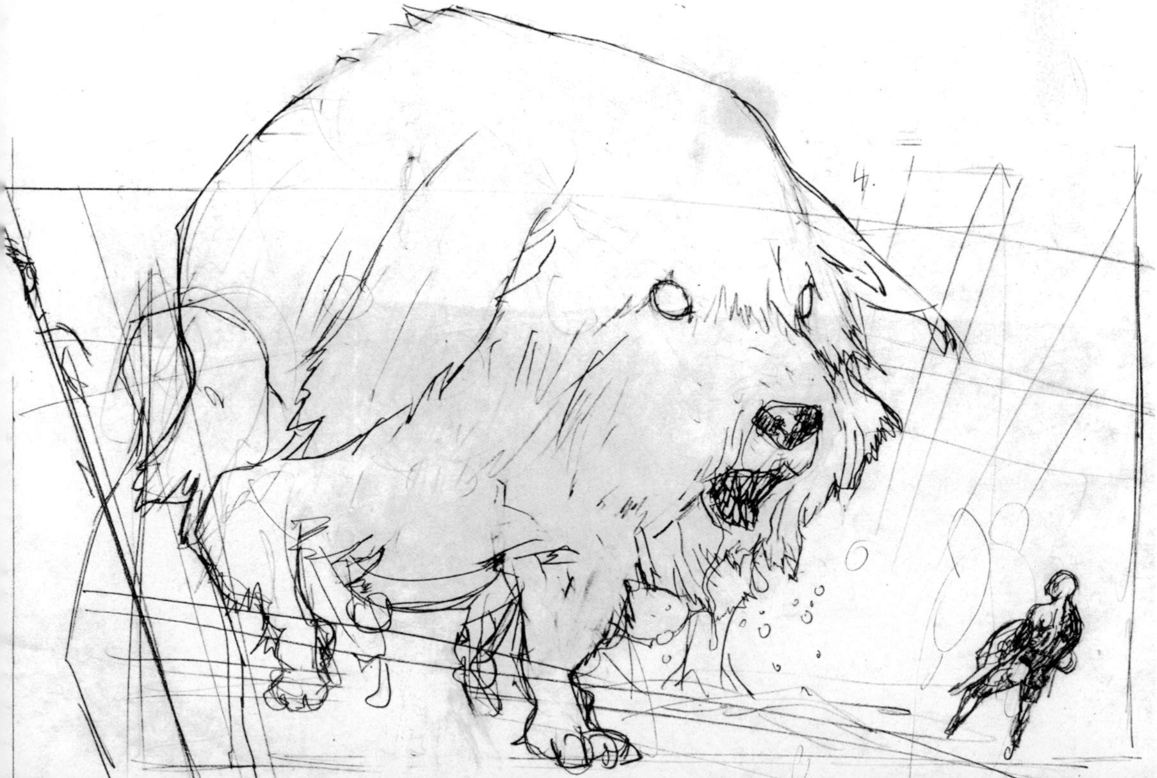

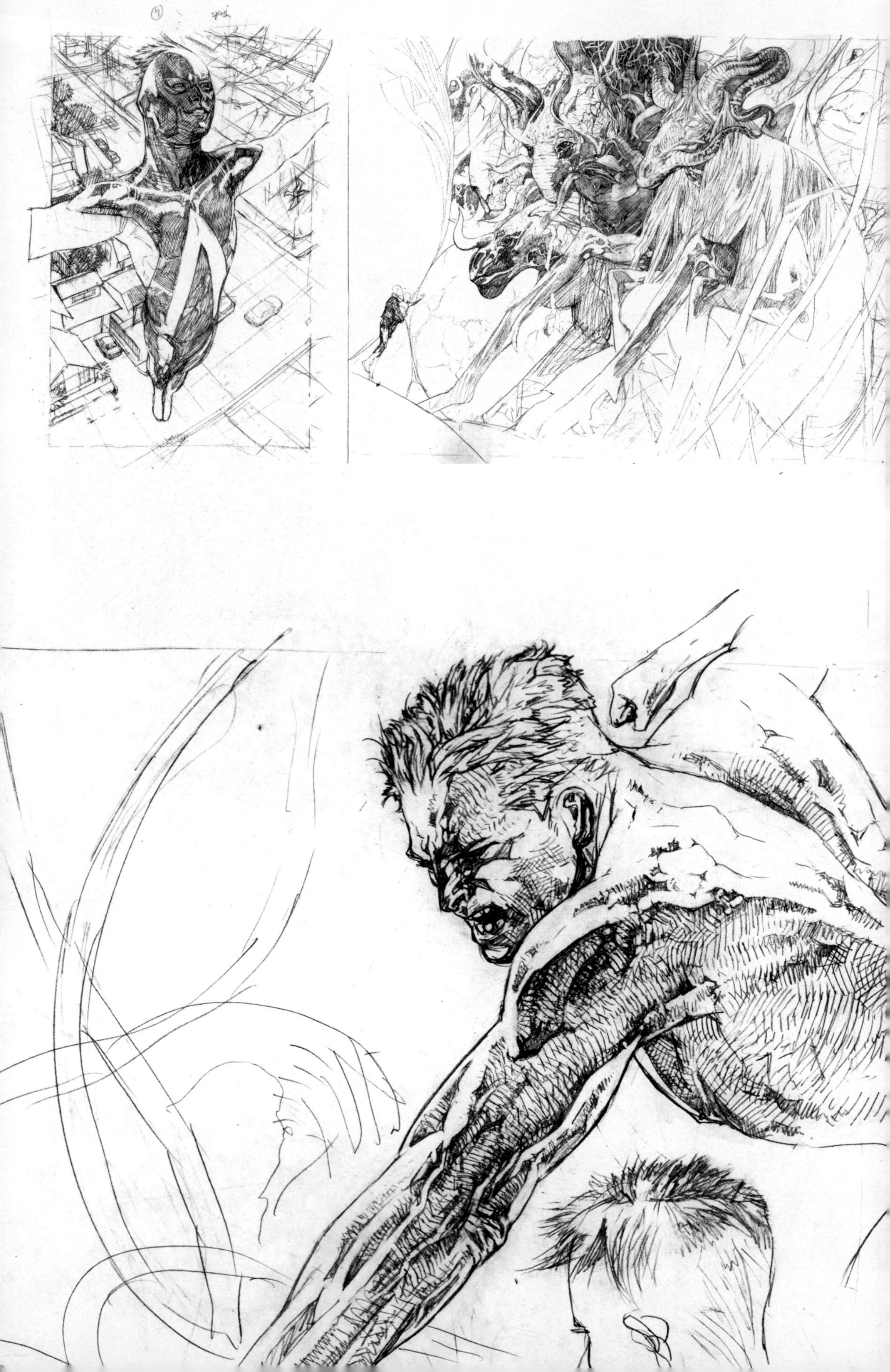

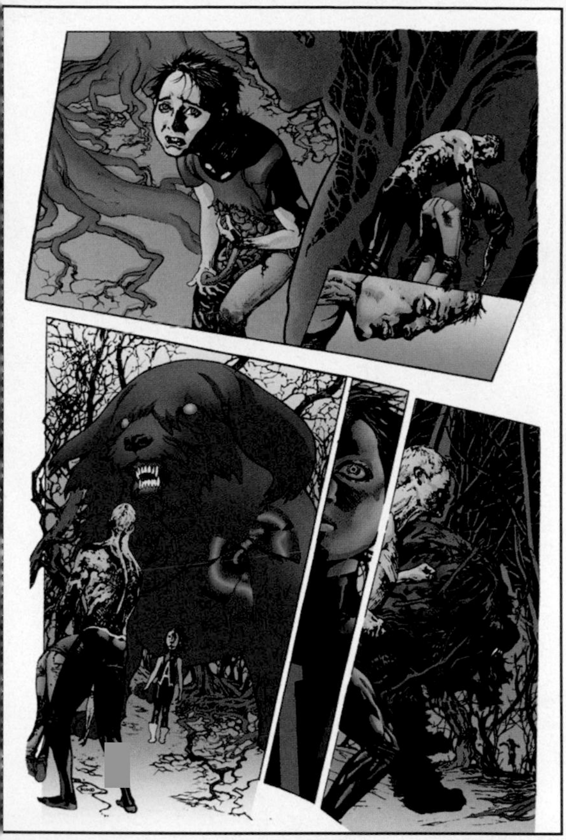

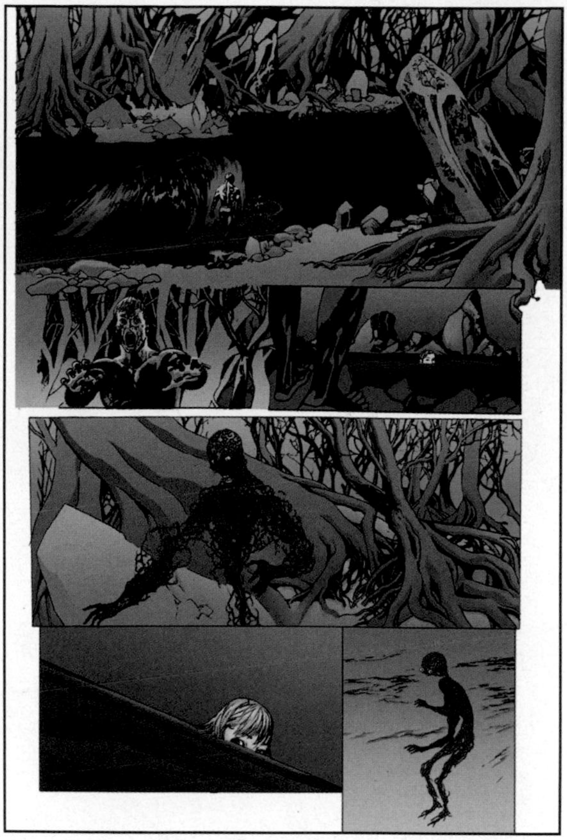

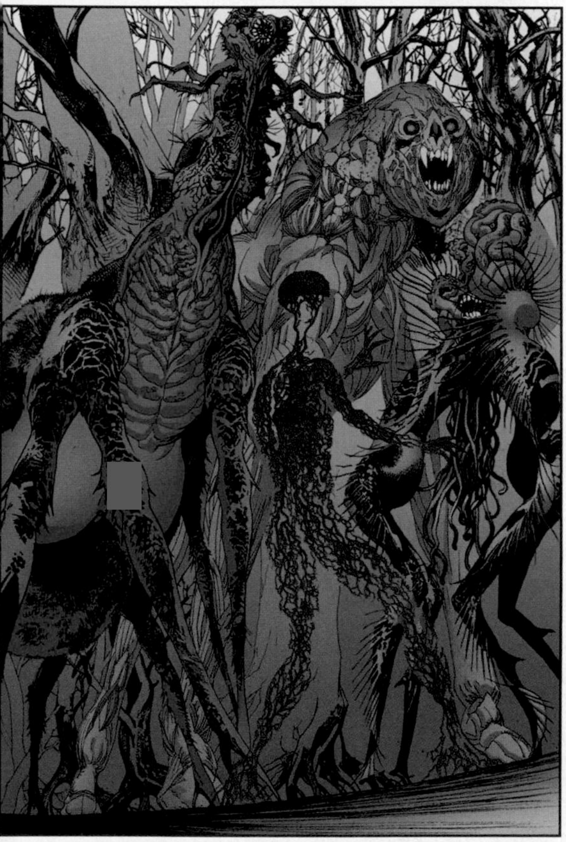

Unused full-color art of Buddy's dream sequence in issue #1, which would later be changed to black and white with red spot color. Art by Travel Foreman, colors by Lovern Kindzierski.

ANIMAL MAN
COVER SKETCHES BY TRAVEL FOREMAN

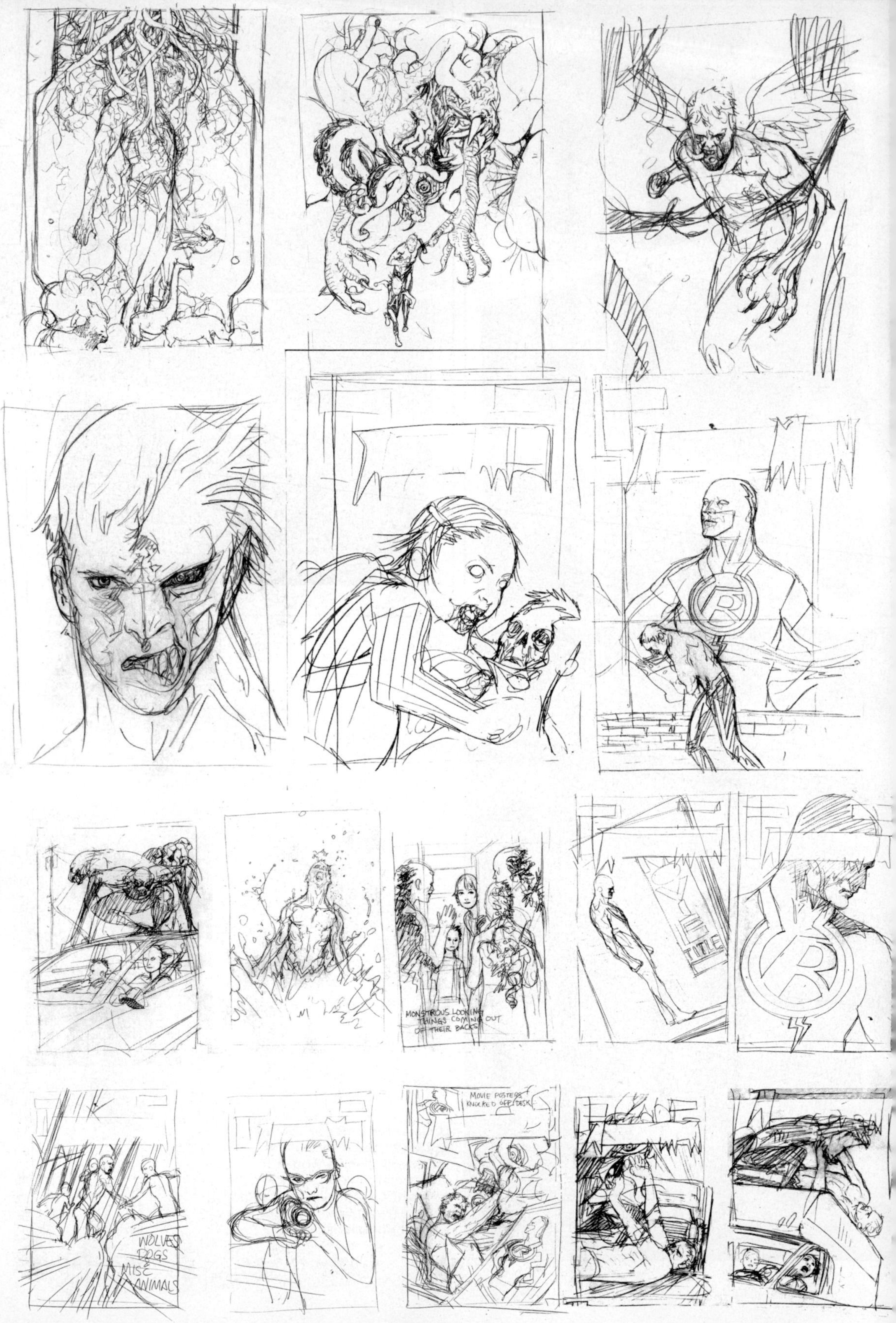
MONSTROUS LOOKING THINGS COMING OUT OF THEIR BACKS
TITLE
WOLVES DOGS & MISC ANIMALS
MOVIE POSTERS + KNOCKED OFF DESK

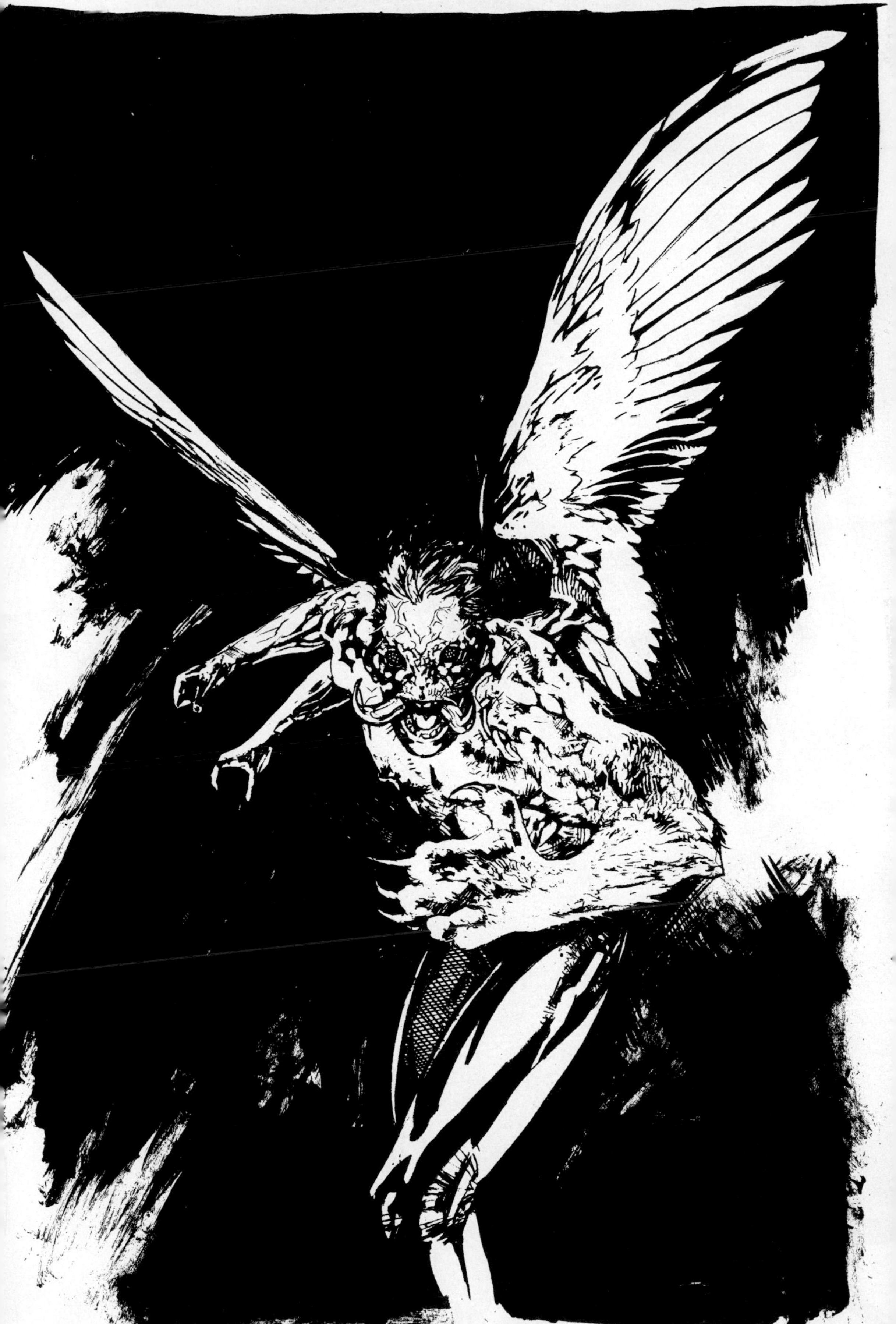

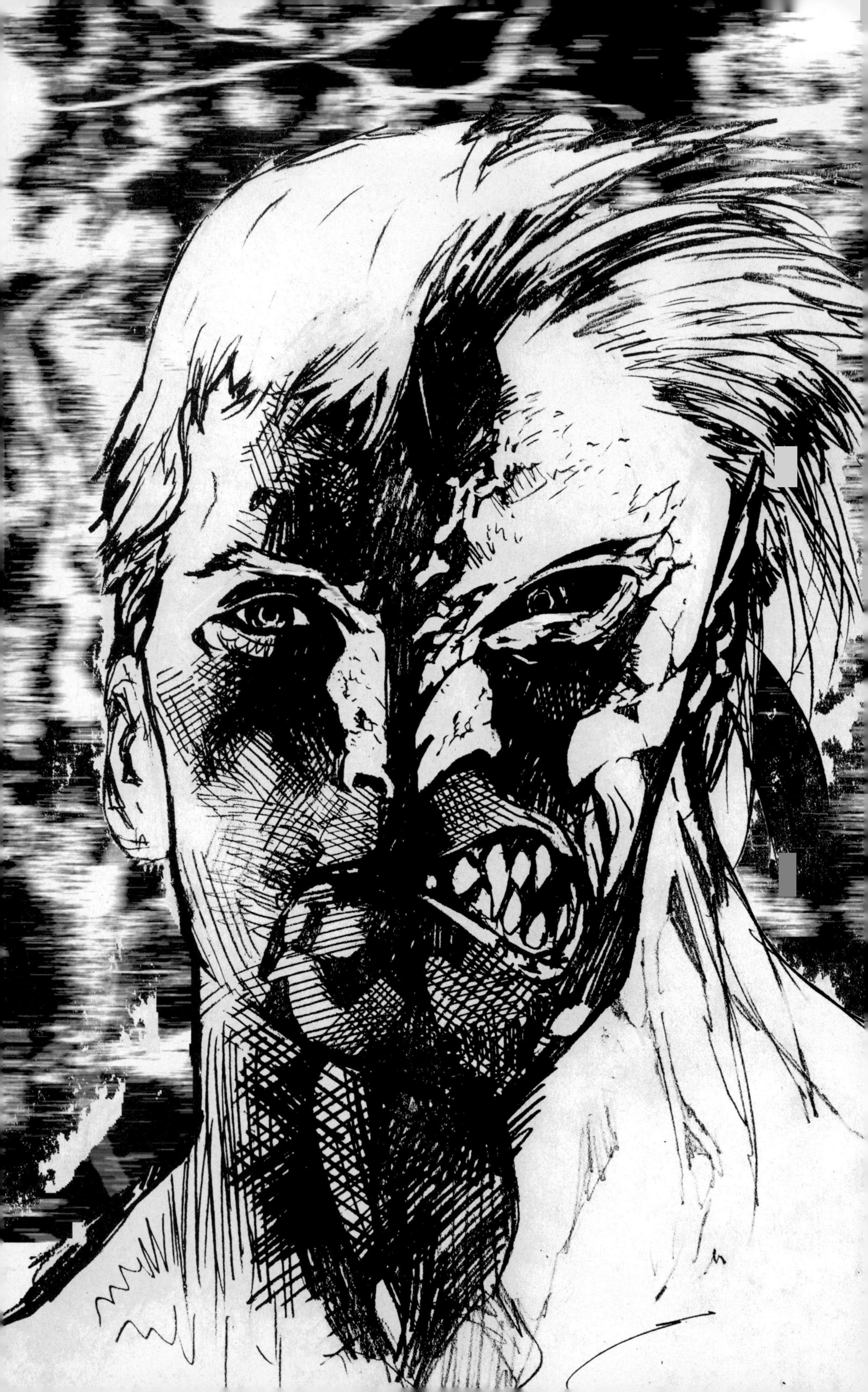